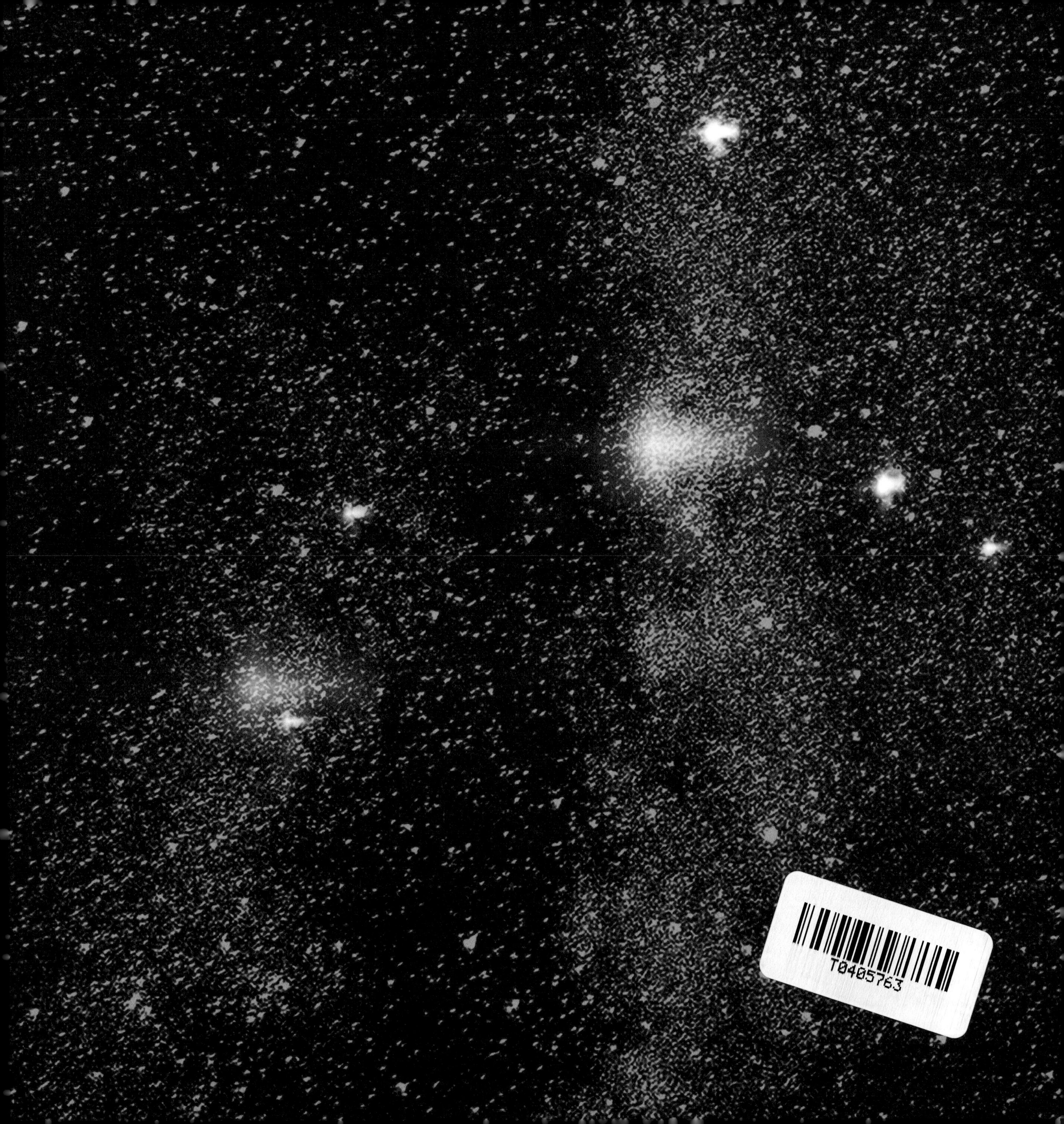

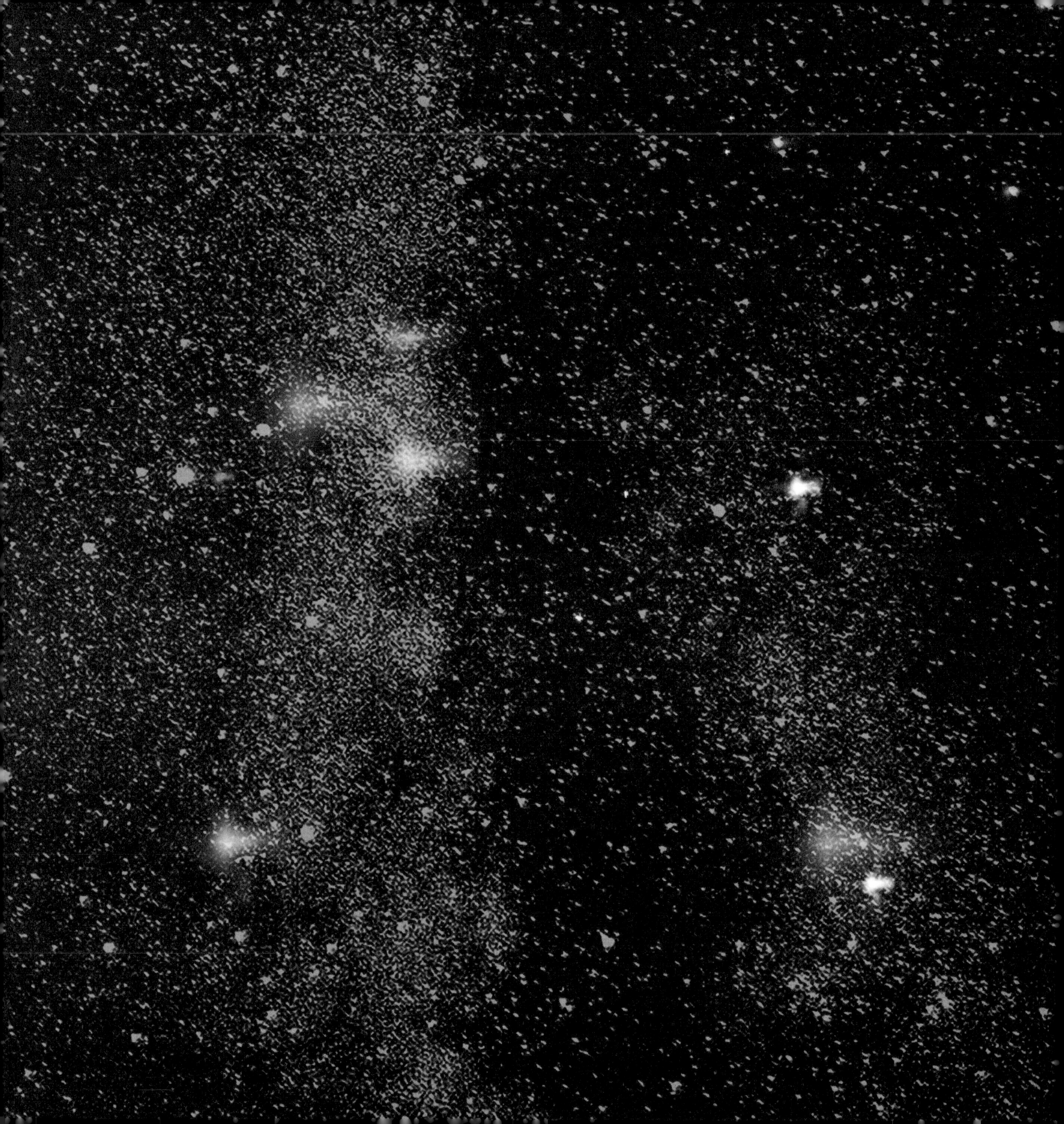

KISS THE SKY

JIMI HENDRIX 1942-1970

J. M. DUPONT   MEZZO

Translated by Ivanka Hahnenberger

For Félix, Joseph, and Pierre

KISS THE SKY: JIMI HENDRIX 1942-1970
Authors: Jean-Michel Dupont and Mezzo

© Editions Glénat 2022 by Dupont & Mezzo

All Rights reserved. No part of this book may be reproduced in any form, or by any electronic or mechanical means, including information storage and retrieval systems, without permission in writing from the publisher, except by reviewers, who may quote brief passages in a review.

Black Panel Press
St. John's, NL
Canada

www.blackpanelpress.com

First Edition
Printed in China

ISBN: 978-1-990521-27-0 (Hardcover)
ISBN: 978-1-990521-31-7 (E-book)

PREFACE

I get the distinct sense that Jimi Hendrix — were he still alive — would have been moved in all the right ways to see the advent of this book. Like Elvis Presley, Hendrix, as a child, grew up transfixed by comic books, and both fantasized endlessly about becoming the superheroes they worshipped on the printed page. Hendrix even carried his taste for the genre into adulthood. In the mid-60s, when everyone attempting to be 'hip' was devouring Kerouac's On the Road and mighty tomes about Eastern mysticism, the Seattle-born guitarist apparently preferred to pour over a literary mélange of obscure science-fiction paperbacks and his usual array of D.C. and Marvel comics. In later interviews, he'd sometimes allude to their influence on his lyrics.

So, to have a burning childhood ambition so spectacularly realized would have thrilled him to his core. And he would almost certainly have been dazzled by the artistry and the overall vision this book's two creators, scenarist Jean-Michel Dupont and dessinateur Mezzo, have brought to his life story.

It's a tale so rife with note-worthy incidents that even though Hendrix died at the ridiculously young age of 27, it makes sense to split the saga into two parts. A second volume will focus on Hendrix's glory years, starting in late '66 with his arrival in London and ending almost four years later with his untimely and somewhat suspicious demise in the same city.

Kiss the Sky Vol 1 focuses instead on Hendrix's work-in-progress period — the 24-year-long odyssey that immediately predates the formation of the Jimi Hendrix Experience in London and the whirlwind global success that followed so soon afterward. The story this book tells is fraught with sadness: a doomed alcoholic mother, a father hopelessly out of his depth as a parent and family provider, ongoing child abuse and neglect over a period of years, hard luck, meanness, humiliation, and poverty at every turn. It's a wonder that Hendrix didn't grow up to become a raging sociopath instead of arguably the greatest musical virtuoso (barring Miles and Coltrane) of the late 20th century and a devout purveyor of the message of love.

I've read many Hendrix biographies, and all refer to his pre-Experience early scuffling years, the plethora of side-man gigs with the likes of Little Richard and the Isley Bros, etc., but no one has captured that period for me in text with the detail and sheer impact that this recounting of those same times does. There's a tired old myth that Hendrix became an outstanding guitarist due to some 'deal' with the devil but the skills he developed painstakingly came from years of endless playing and hardscrabble gigging in very precarious places. It's like watching a really gripping Hendrix biopic. There are no moving pictures or audio but the effect is as vivid and plausible. It dares to take chances and, in the process, extends the medium itself, not unlike the way Hendrix himself shook up the sonic evolution of music in the late 60s.

Jimi Hendrix would be 80 this year, and I couldn't think of a better birthday present for the man. What a life he led, what Icarus-like heights he sealed. But as Kiss the Sky Vol.1 brilliantly depicts, in order to become a god, Hendrix first had to live the blues up close and personal in a word that cast him as a misfit and a laughing stock.

Nick KENT
July, 2022

Nick Kent, a British rock journalism legend, became one of the most celebrated writers at the New Musical Express during the 1970s. He rubbed shoulders with many icons such as the Rolling Stones, Led Zeppelin, David Bowie, Iggy Pop, and the Sex Pistols, adopting their legendary lifestyles, which inevitably left marks on his own life. Kent shared his wild adventures in two books that have been published in around ten countries, including France: «The Dark Stuff – The Flip Side of Rock» (Naïve, 2007) and «Apathy for the Devil – A Seventies Journey Through the Dark Side» (Payot & Rivages, 2012). Recently, he's made waves with his first novel, «The Unstable Boys,» which has garnered critical acclaim (Sonatine).

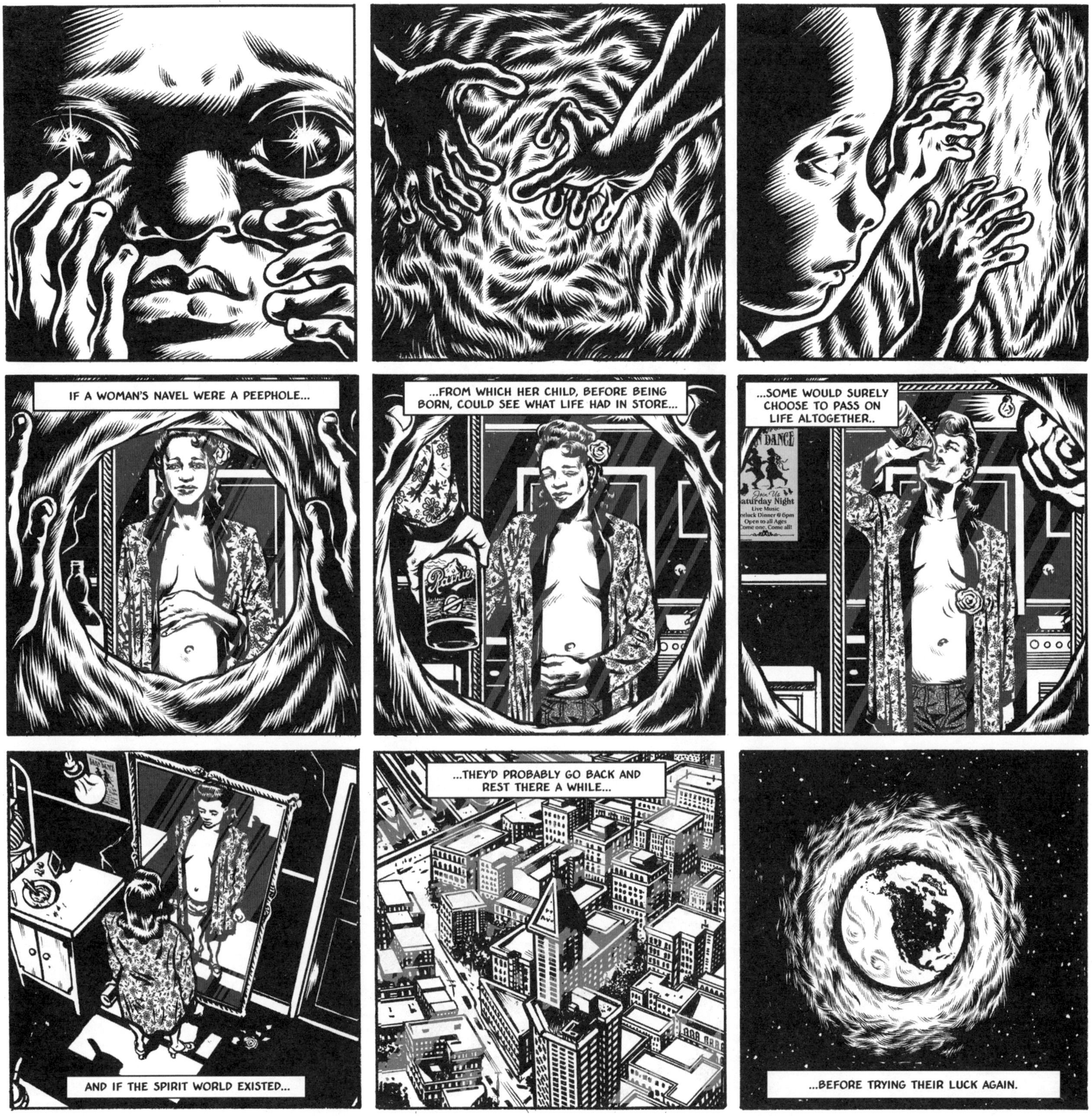
IF A WOMAN'S NAVEL WERE A PEEPHOLE...
...FROM WHICH HER CHILD, BEFORE BEING BORN, COULD SEE WHAT LIFE HAD IN STORE...
...SOME WOULD SURELY CHOOSE TO PASS ON LIFE ALTOGETHER..
AND IF THE SPIRIT WORLD EXISTED...
...THEY'D PROBABLY GO BACK AND REST THERE A WHILE...
...BEFORE TRYING THEIR LUCK AGAIN.

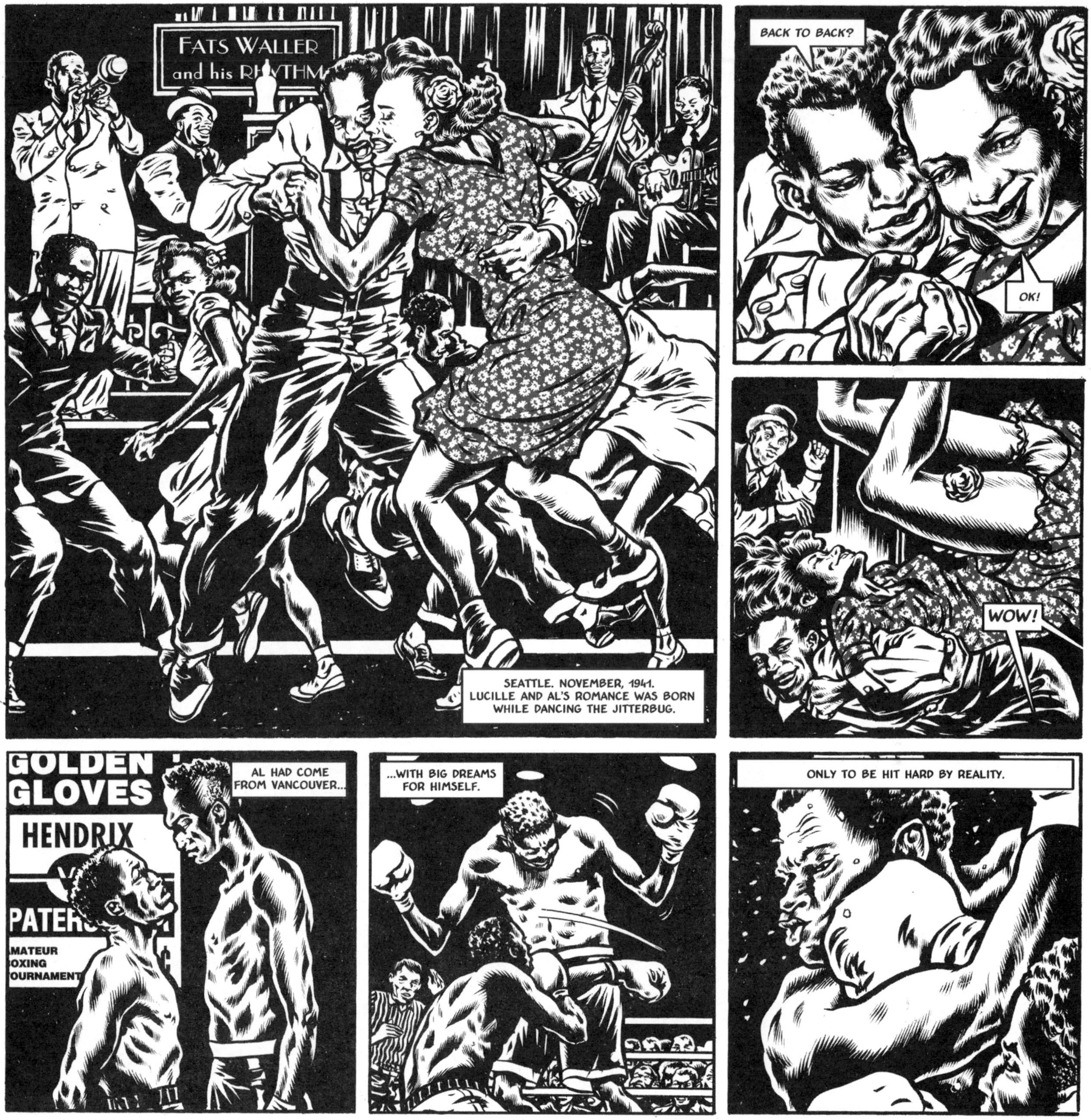
FATS WALLER
and his RHYTHM
SEATTLE. NOVEMBER, 1941.
LUCILLE AND AL'S ROMANCE WAS BORN
WHILE DANCING THE JITTERBUG.
BACK TO BACK?
OK!
WOW!
GOLDEN
GLOVES
HENDRIX
PATERS
MATEUR
OXING
OURNAMENT
AL HAD COME
FROM VANCOUVER...
...WITH BIG DREAMS
FOR HIMSELF.
ONLY TO BE HIT HARD BY REALITY.

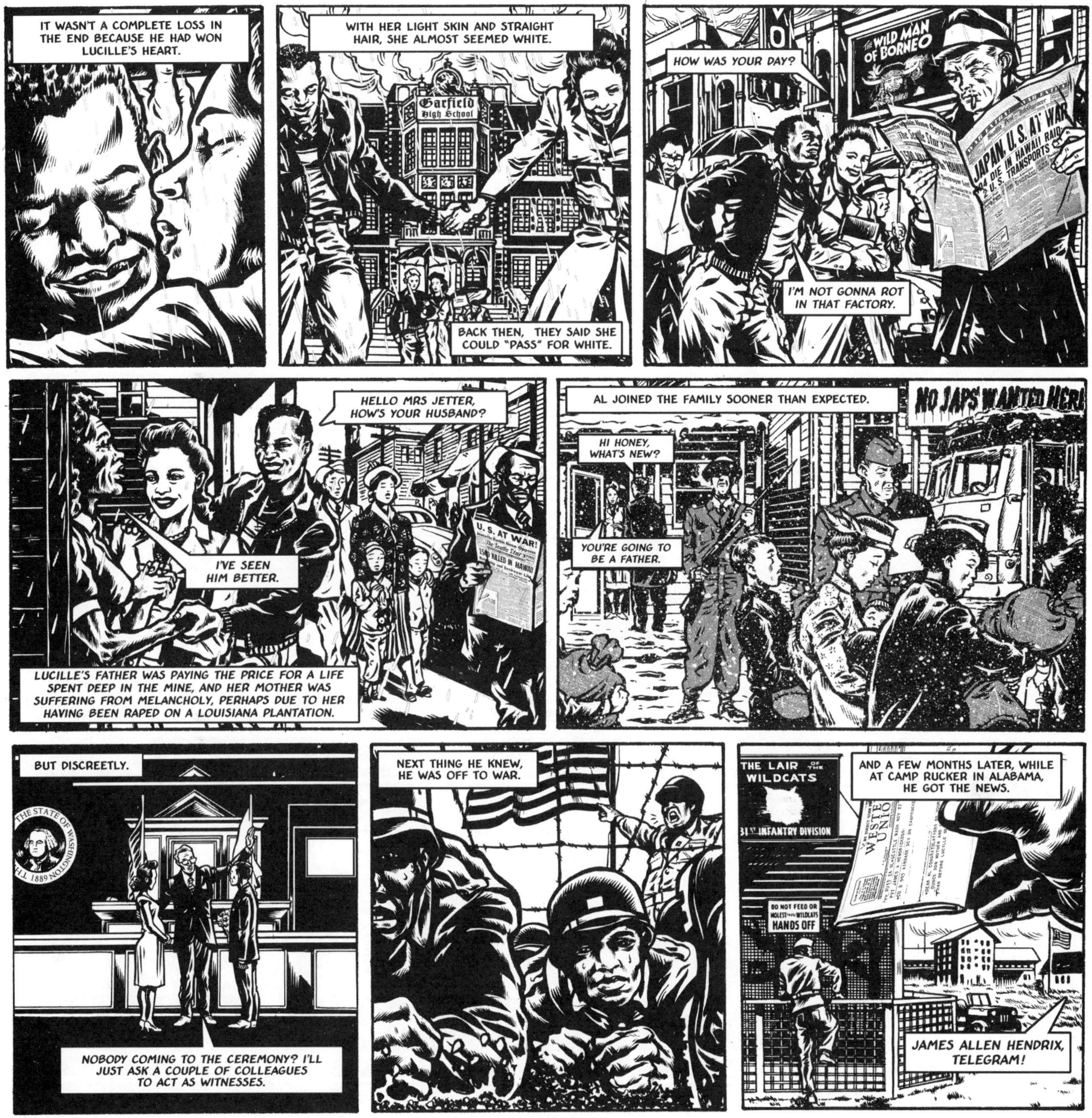
IT WASN'T A COMPLETE LOSS IN THE END BECAUSE HE HAD WON LUCILLE'S HEART.
WITH HER LIGHT SKIN AND STRAIGHT HAIR, SHE ALMOST SEEMED WHITE.
Garfield High School
BACK THEN, THEY SAID SHE COULD "PASS" FOR WHITE.
THE WILD MAN OF BORNEO
HOW WAS YOUR DAY?
JAPAN, U.S. AT WAR
I'M NOT GONNA ROT IN THAT FACTORY.
HELLO MRS JETTER, HOW'S YOUR HUSBAND?
I'VE SEEN HIM BETTER.
U.S. AT WAR!
LUCILLE'S FATHER WAS PAYING THE PRICE FOR A LIFE SPENT DEEP IN THE MINE, AND HER MOTHER WAS SUFFERING FROM MELANCHOLY, PERHAPS DUE TO HER HAVING BEEN RAPED ON A LOUISIANA PLANTATION.
AL JOINED THE FAMILY SOONER THAN EXPECTED.
NO JAPS WANTED HER
HI HONEY, WHAT'S NEW?
YOU'RE GOING TO BE A FATHER.
BUT DISCREETLY.
THE STATE OF WASHINGTON 1889
NOBODY COMING TO THE CEREMONY? I'LL JUST ASK A COUPLE OF COLLEAGUES TO ACT AS WITNESSES.
NEXT THING HE KNEW, HE WAS OFF TO WAR.
AND A FEW MONTHS LATER, WHILE AT CAMP RUCKER IN ALABAMA, HE GOT THE NEWS.
THE LAIR OF THE WILDCATS
31ST INFANTRY DIVISION
DO NOT FEED OR MOLEST THE WILDCATS
HANDS OFF
JAMES ALLEN HENDRIX, TELEGRAM!

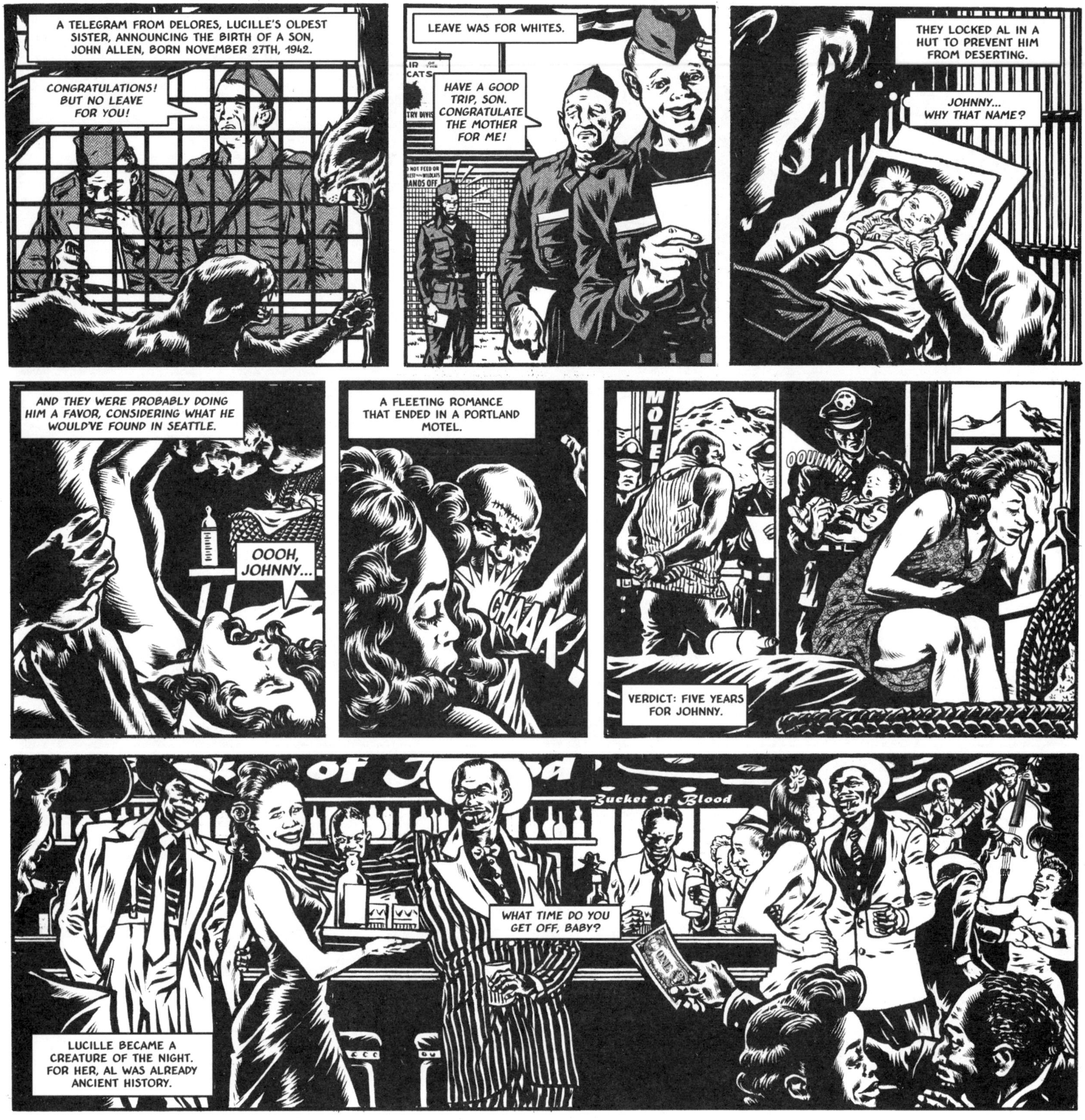

A TELEGRAM FROM DELORES, LUCILLE'S OLDEST SISTER, ANNOUNCING THE BIRTH OF A SON, JOHN ALLEN, BORN NOVEMBER 27TH, 1942.
CONGRATULATIONS! BUT NO LEAVE FOR YOU!
LEAVE WAS FOR WHITES.
HAVE A GOOD TRIP, SON. CONGRATULATE THE MOTHER FOR ME!
THEY LOCKED AL IN A HUT TO PREVENT HIM FROM DESERTING.
JOHNNY... WHY THAT NAME?
AND THEY WERE PROBABLY DOING HIM A FAVOR, CONSIDERING WHAT HE WOULD'VE FOUND IN SEATTLE.
OOOH, JOHNNY...
A FLEETING ROMANCE THAT ENDED IN A PORTLAND MOTEL.
CHAAK
MOTEL
OOUIINN!!
VERDICT: FIVE YEARS FOR JOHNNY.
Bucket of Blood
LUCILLE BECAME A CREATURE OF THE NIGHT. FOR HER, AL WAS ALREADY ANCIENT HISTORY.
WHAT TIME DO YOU GET OFF, BABY?

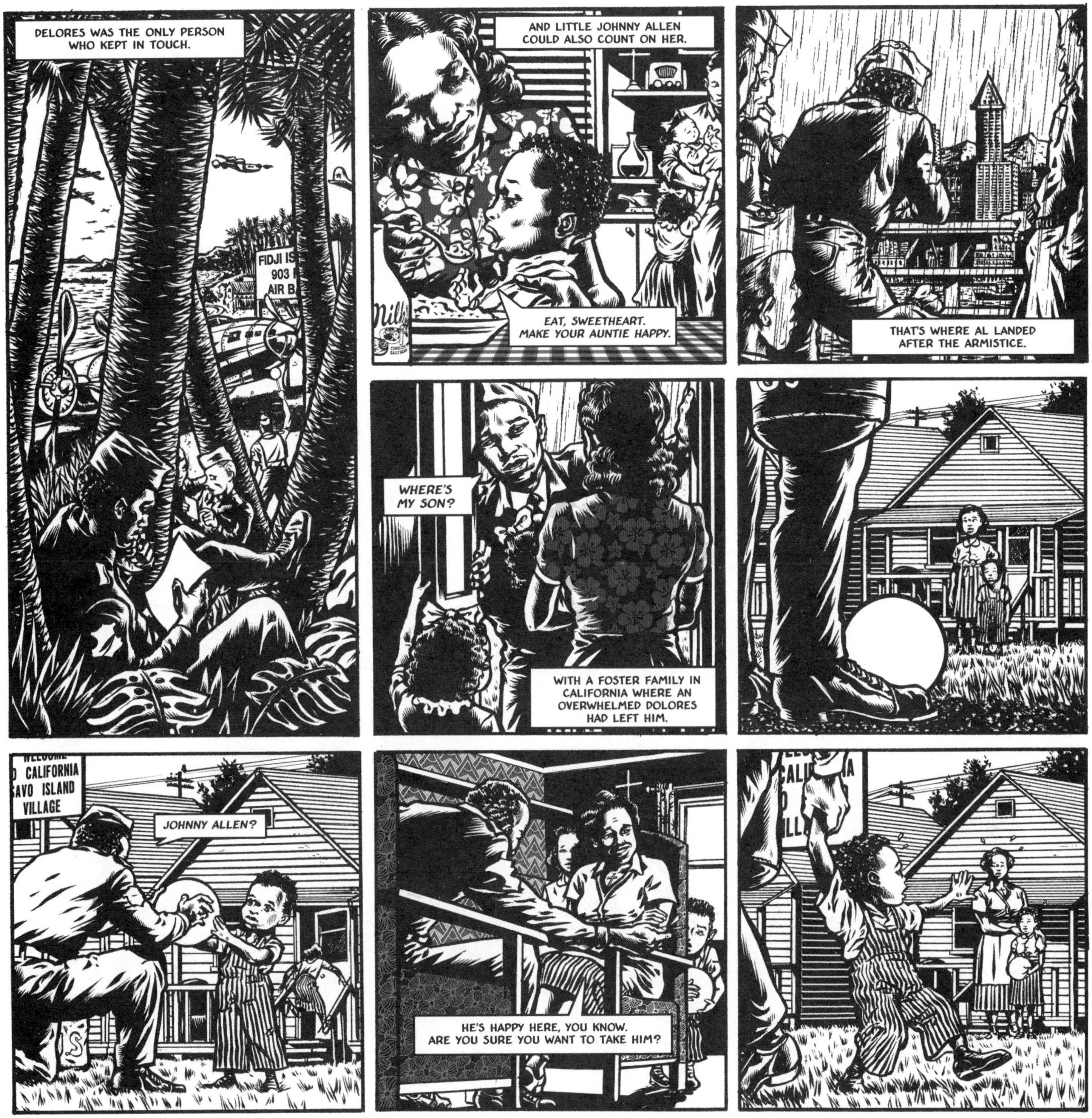
DELORES WAS THE ONLY PERSON WHO KEPT IN TOUCH.
AND LITTLE JOHNNY ALLEN COULD ALSO COUNT ON HER.
EAT, SWEETHEART. MAKE YOUR AUNTIE HAPPY.
THAT'S WHERE AL LANDED AFTER THE ARMISTICE.
WHERE'S MY SON?
WITH A FOSTER FAMILY IN CALIFORNIA WHERE AN OVERWHELMED DOLORES HAD LEFT HIM.
JOHNNY ALLEN?
HE'S HAPPY HERE, YOU KNOW. ARE YOU SURE YOU WANT TO TAKE HIM?

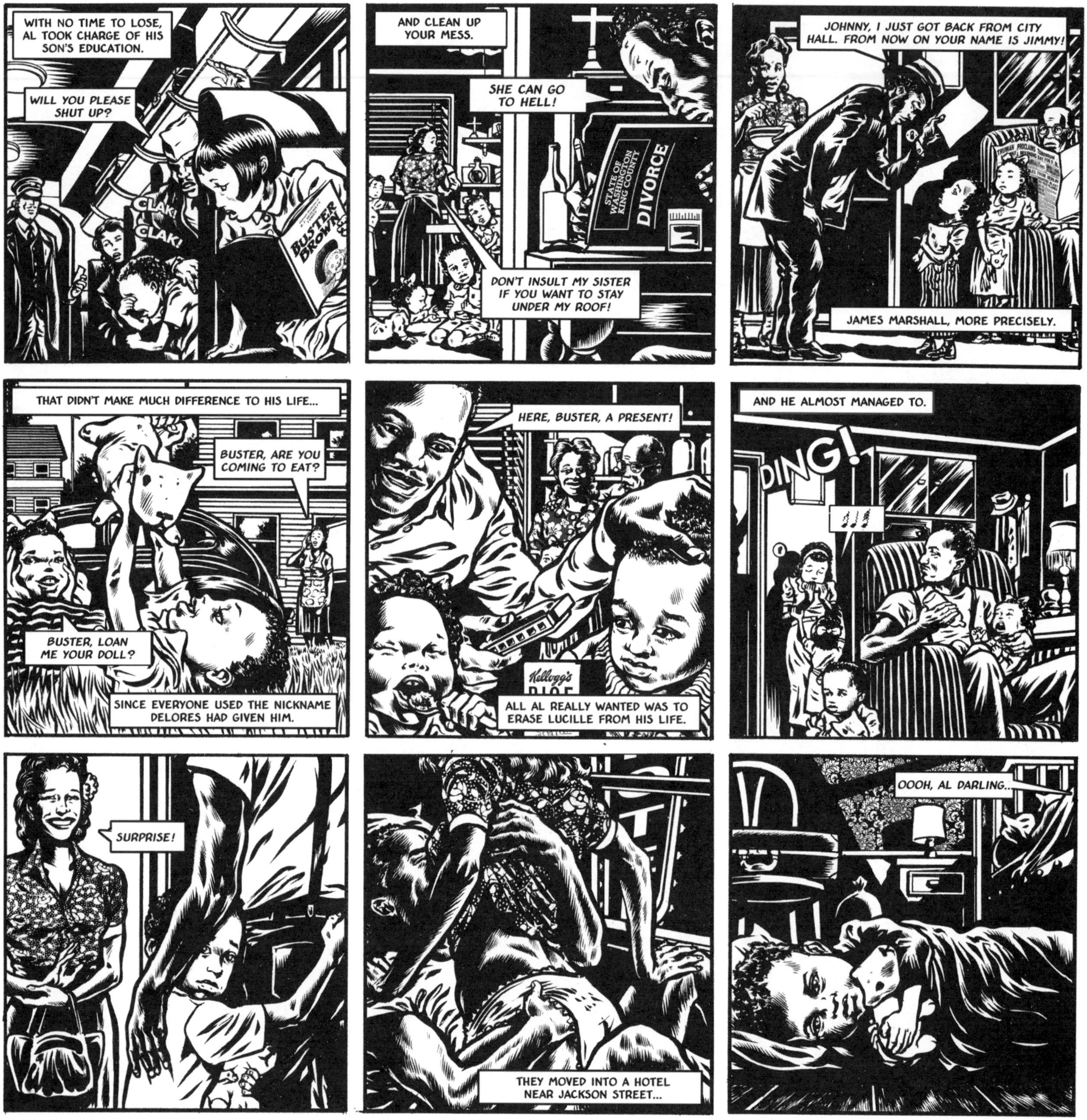
WITH NO TIME TO LOSE, AL TOOK CHARGE OF HIS SON'S EDUCATION.
WILL YOU PLEASE SHUT UP?
CLAK!
CLAK!
BUSTER BROWN
AND CLEAN UP YOUR MESS.
SHE CAN GO TO HELL!
STATE OF WASHINGTON KING COUNTY
DIVORCE
DON'T INSULT MY SISTER IF YOU WANT TO STAY UNDER MY ROOF!
JOHNNY, I JUST GOT BACK FROM CITY HALL. FROM NOW ON YOUR NAME IS JIMMY!
JAMES MARSHALL, MORE PRECISELY.
THAT DIDN'T MAKE MUCH DIFFERENCE TO HIS LIFE...
BUSTER, ARE YOU COMING TO EAT?
BUSTER, LOAN ME YOUR DOLL?
SINCE EVERYONE USED THE NICKNAME DELORES HAD GIVEN HIM.
HERE, BUSTER, A PRESENT!
Kellogg's
ALL AL REALLY WANTED WAS TO ERASE LUCILLE FROM HIS LIFE.
AND HE ALMOST MANAGED TO.
DING!
SURPRISE!
THEY MOVED INTO A HOTEL NEAR JACKSON STREET...
OOOH, AL DARLING...

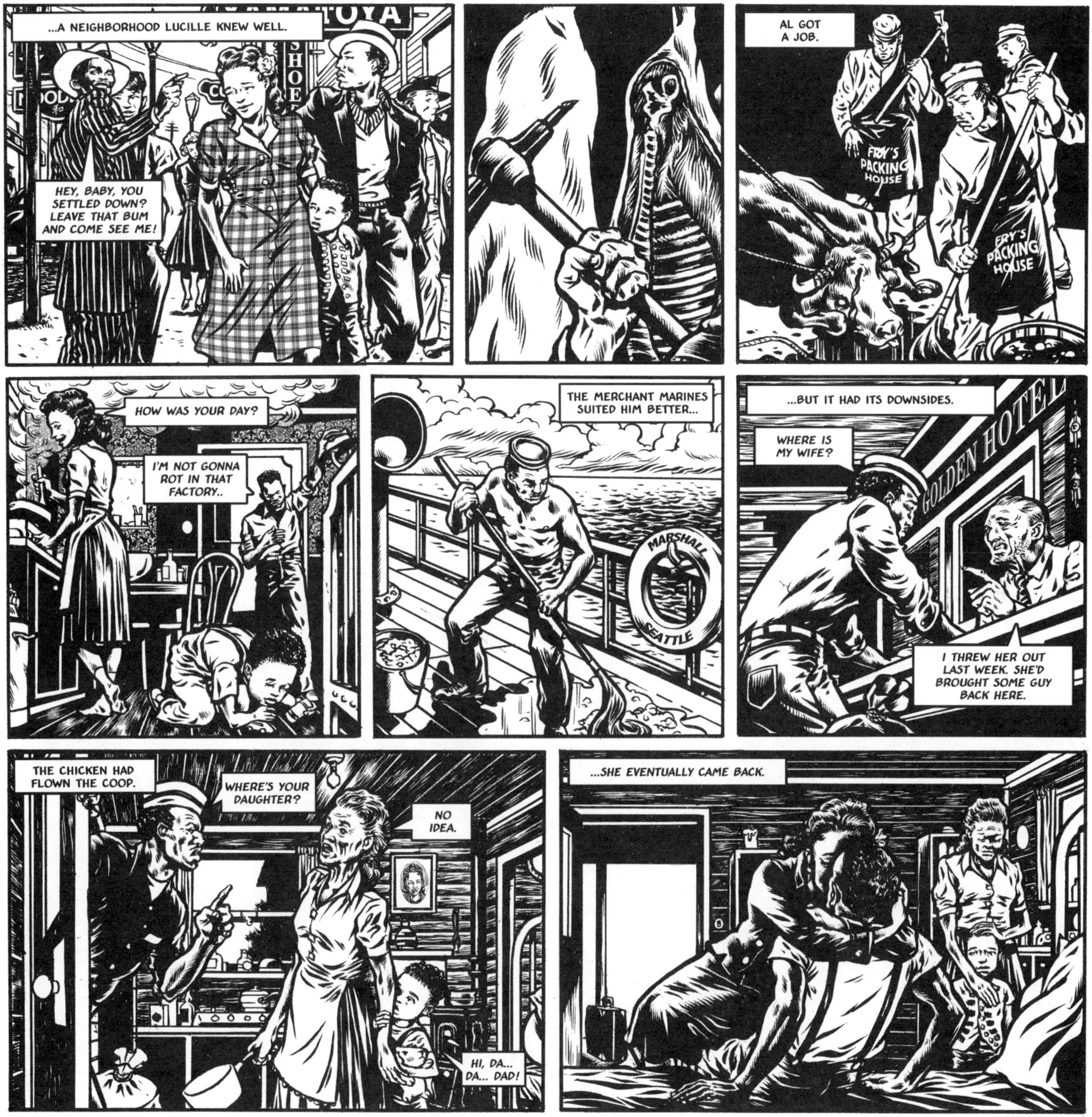
...A NEIGHBORHOOD LUCILLE KNEW WELL.
SHOE
HEY, BABY, YOU SETTLED DOWN? LEAVE THAT BUM AND COME SEE ME!
AL GOT A JOB.
FRY'S PACKING HOUSE
FRY'S PACKING HOUSE
HOW WAS YOUR DAY?
I'M NOT GONNA ROT IN THAT FACTORY..
THE MERCHANT MARINES SUITED HIM BETTER...
MARSHALL SEATTLE
...BUT IT HAD ITS DOWNSIDES.
GOLDEN HOTEL
WHERE IS MY WIFE?
I THREW HER OUT LAST WEEK. SHE'D BROUGHT SOME GUY BACK HERE.
THE CHICKEN HAD FLOWN THE COOP.
WHERE'S YOUR DAUGHTER?
NO IDEA.
HI, DA... DA... DAD!
...SHE EVENTUALLY CAME BACK.

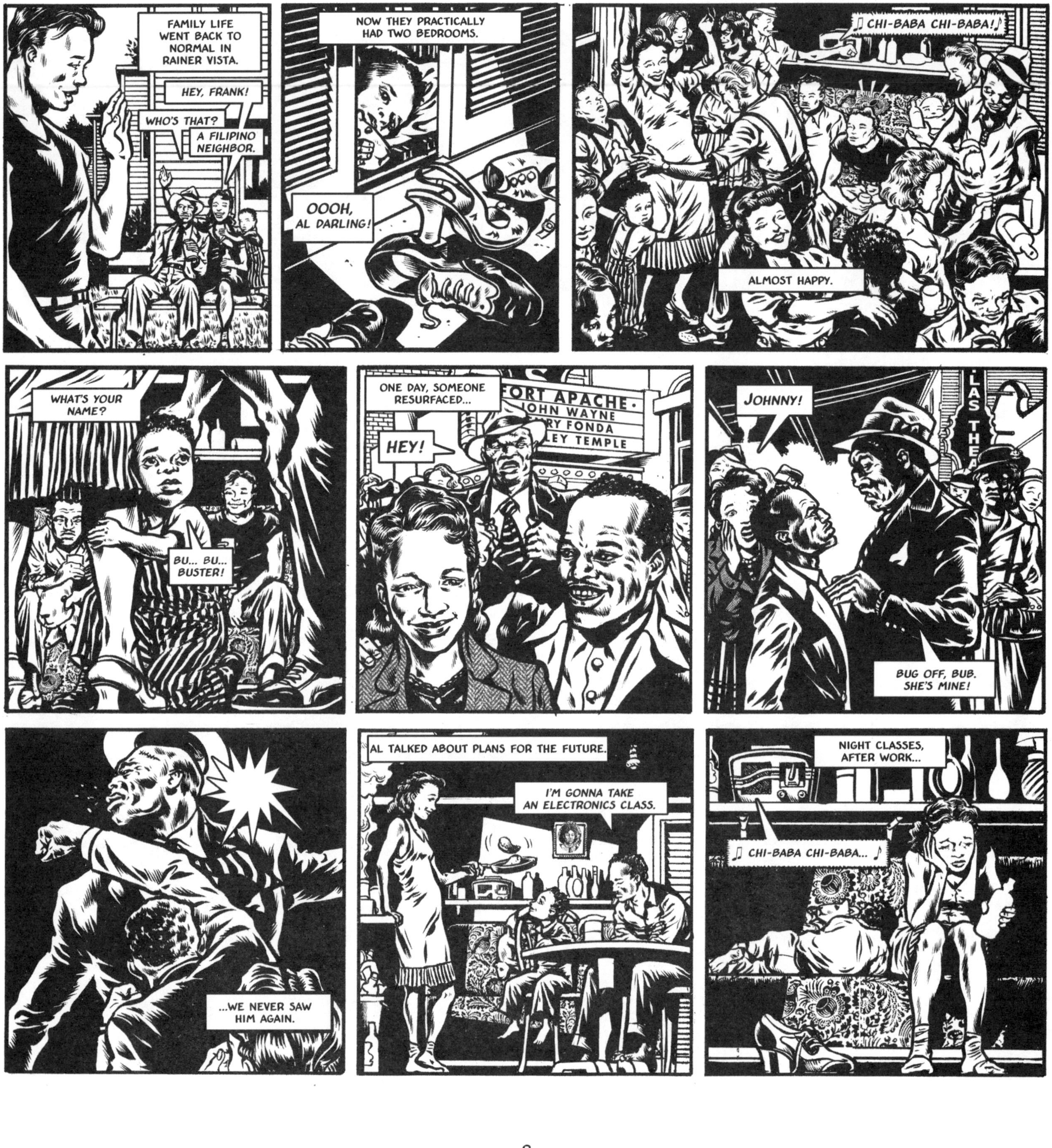
FAMILY LIFE WENT BACK TO NORMAL IN RAINER VISTA.
HEY, FRANK!
WHO'S THAT?
A FILIPINO NEIGHBOR.
NOW THEY PRACTICALLY HAD TWO BEDROOMS.
OOOH, AL DARLING!
♫ CHI-BABA CHI-BABA! ♪
ALMOST HAPPY.
WHAT'S YOUR NAME?
BU... BU... BUSTER!
ONE DAY, SOMEONE RESURFACED...
FORT APACHE
JOHN WAYNE
HEY!
JOHNNY!
BUG OFF, BUB. SHE'S MINE!
...WE NEVER SAW HIM AGAIN.
AL TALKED ABOUT PLANS FOR THE FUTURE.
I'M GONNA TAKE AN ELECTRONICS CLASS.
NIGHT CLASSES, AFTER WORK...
♫ CHI-BABA CHI-BABA... ♪

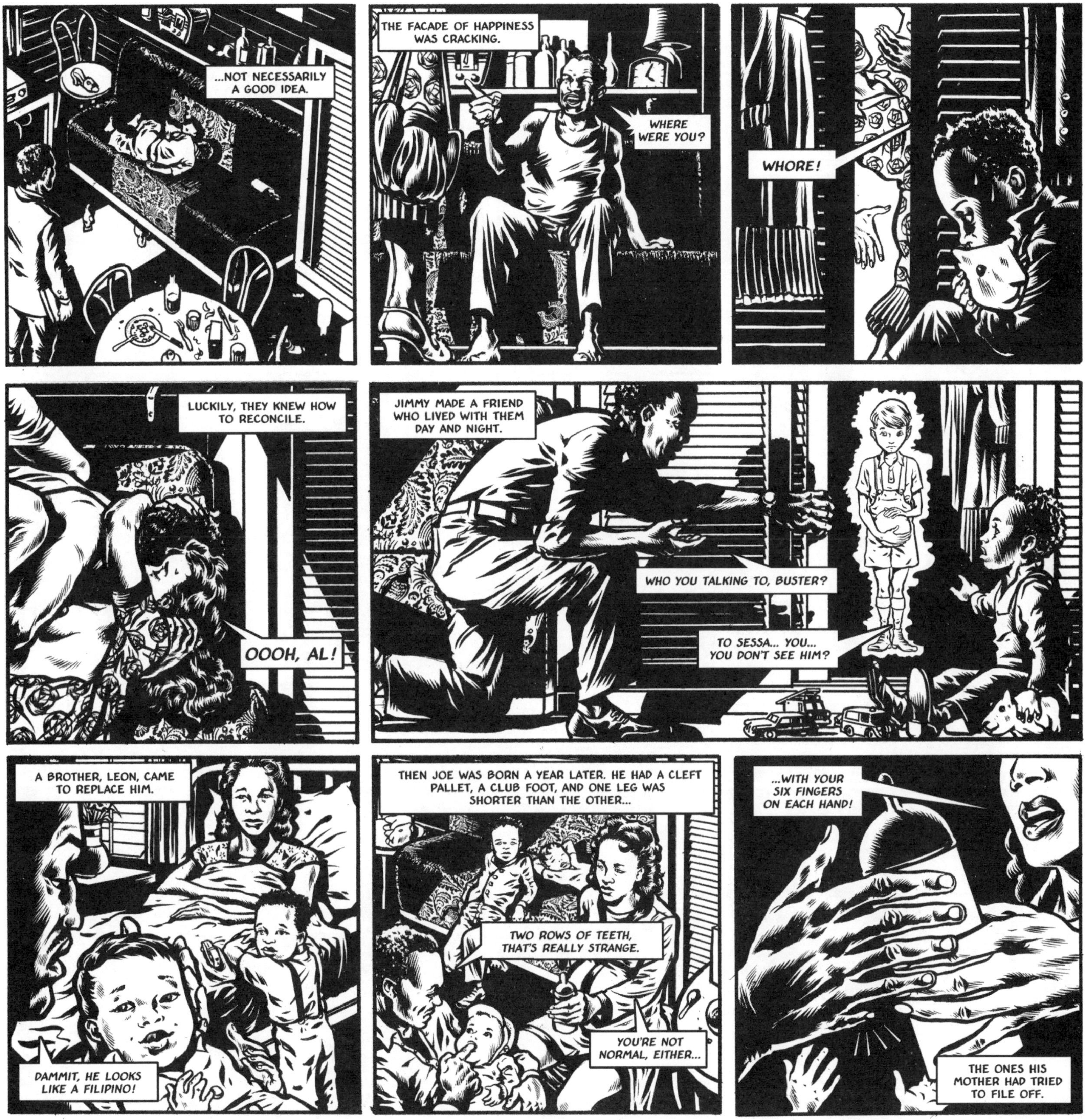
...NOT NECESSARILY A GOOD IDEA.
THE FACADE OF HAPPINESS WAS CRACKING.
WHERE WERE YOU?
WHORE!
LUCKILY, THEY KNEW HOW TO RECONCILE.
OOOH, AL!
JIMMY MADE A FRIEND WHO LIVED WITH THEM DAY AND NIGHT.
WHO YOU TALKING TO, BUSTER?
TO SESSA... YOU... YOU DON'T SEE HIM?
A BROTHER, LEON, CAME TO REPLACE HIM.
DAMMIT, HE LOOKS LIKE A FILIPINO!
THEN JOE WAS BORN A YEAR LATER. HE HAD A CLEFT PALLET, A CLUB FOOT, AND ONE LEG WAS SHORTER THAN THE OTHER...
TWO ROWS OF TEETH, THAT'S REALLY STRANGE.
YOU'RE NOT NORMAL, EITHER...
...WITH YOUR SIX FINGERS ON EACH HAND!
THE ONES HIS MOTHER HAD TRIED TO FILE OFF.

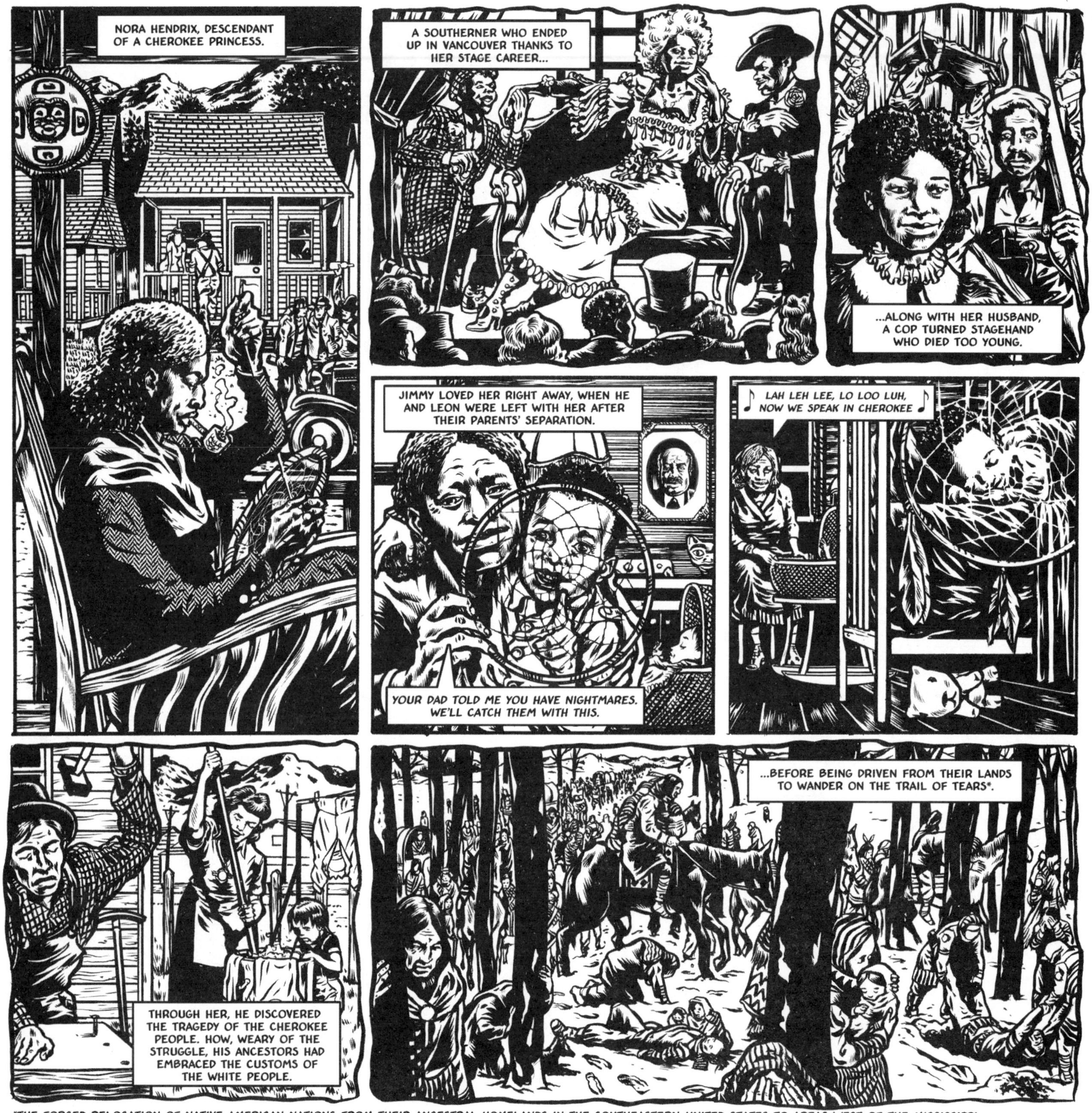
NORA HENDRIX, DESCENDANT OF A CHEROKEE PRINCESS.
A SOUTHERNER WHO ENDED UP IN VANCOUVER THANKS TO HER STAGE CAREER...
...ALONG WITH HER HUSBAND, A COP TURNED STAGEHAND WHO DIED TOO YOUNG.
JIMMY LOVED HER RIGHT AWAY, WHEN HE AND LEON WERE LEFT WITH HER AFTER THEIR PARENTS' SEPARATION.
YOUR DAD TOLD ME YOU HAVE NIGHTMARES. WE'LL CATCH THEM WITH THIS.
♪ LAH LEH LEE, LO LOO LUH, NOW WE SPEAK IN CHEROKEE ♪
THROUGH HER, HE DISCOVERED THE TRAGEDY OF THE CHEROKEE PEOPLE. HOW, WEARY OF THE STRUGGLE, HIS ANCESTORS HAD EMBRACED THE CUSTOMS OF THE WHITE PEOPLE.
...BEFORE BEING DRIVEN FROM THEIR LANDS TO WANDER ON THE TRAIL OF TEARS*.

*THE FORCED RELOCATION OF NATIVE AMERICAN NATIONS FROM THEIR ANCESTRAL HOMELANDS IN THE SOUTHEASTERN UNITED STATES TO AREAS WEST OF THE MISSISSIPPI RIVER DESIGNATED AS INDIAN TERRITORY.

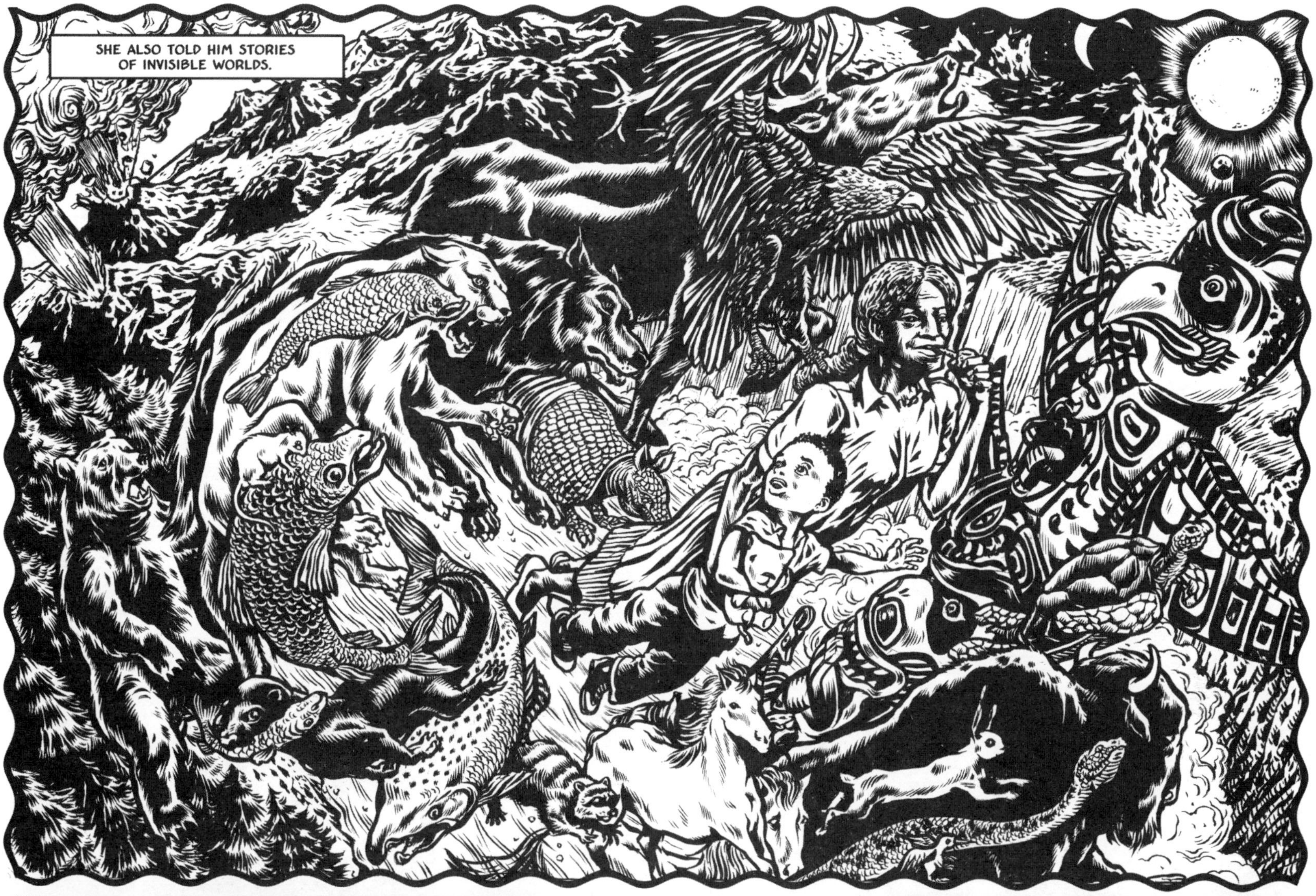
SHE ALSO TOLD HIM STORIES OF INVISIBLE WORLDS.

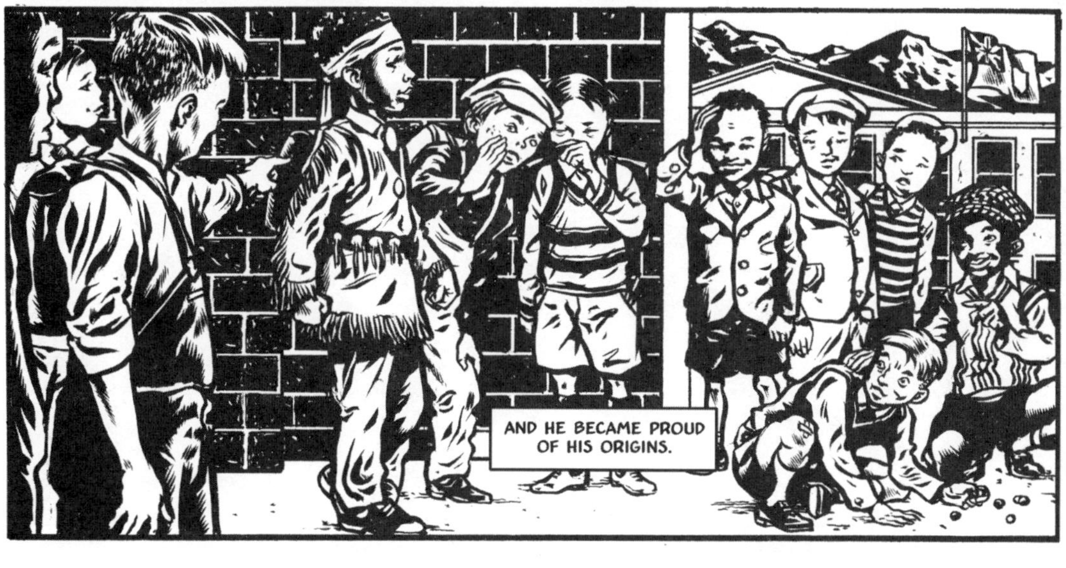
AND HE BECAME PROUD OF HIS ORIGINS.

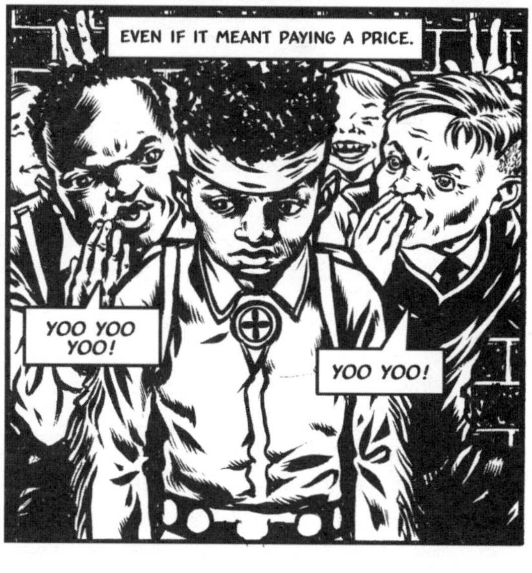
EVEN IF IT MEANT PAYING A PRICE.
YOO YOO YOO!
YOO YOO!

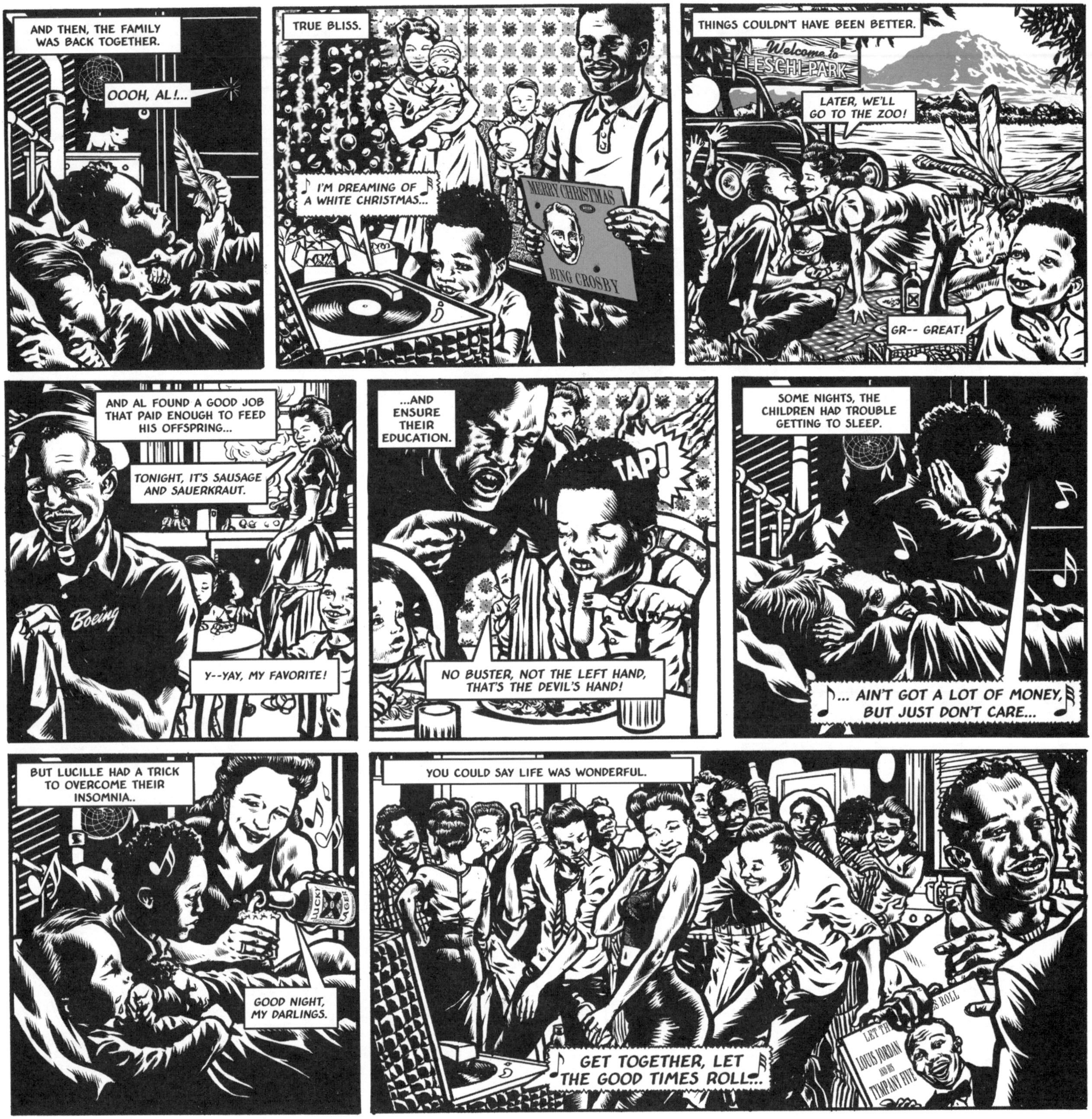
AND THEN, THE FAMILY WAS BACK TOGETHER.
OOOH, AL!...
TRUE BLISS.
I'M DREAMING OF A WHITE CHRISTMAS...
MERRY CHRISTMAS
BING CROSBY
THINGS COULDN'T HAVE BEEN BETTER.
Welcome to LESCHI PARK
LATER, WE'LL GO TO THE ZOO!
GR-- GREAT!
AND AL FOUND A GOOD JOB THAT PAID ENOUGH TO FEED HIS OFFSPRING...
TONIGHT, IT'S SAUSAGE AND SAUERKRAUT.
Boeing
Y--YAY, MY FAVORITE!
...AND ENSURE THEIR EDUCATION.
TAP!
NO BUSTER, NOT THE LEFT HAND, THAT'S THE DEVIL'S HAND!
SOME NIGHTS, THE CHILDREN HAD TROUBLE GETTING TO SLEEP.
... AIN'T GOT A LOT OF MONEY, BUT JUST DON'T CARE...
BUT LUCILLE HAD A TRICK TO OVERCOME THEIR INSOMNIA..
GOOD NIGHT, MY DARLINGS.
YOU COULD SAY LIFE WAS WONDERFUL.
GET TOGETHER, LET THE GOOD TIMES ROLL!...
LOUIS JORDAN AND HIS TYMPANY FIVE

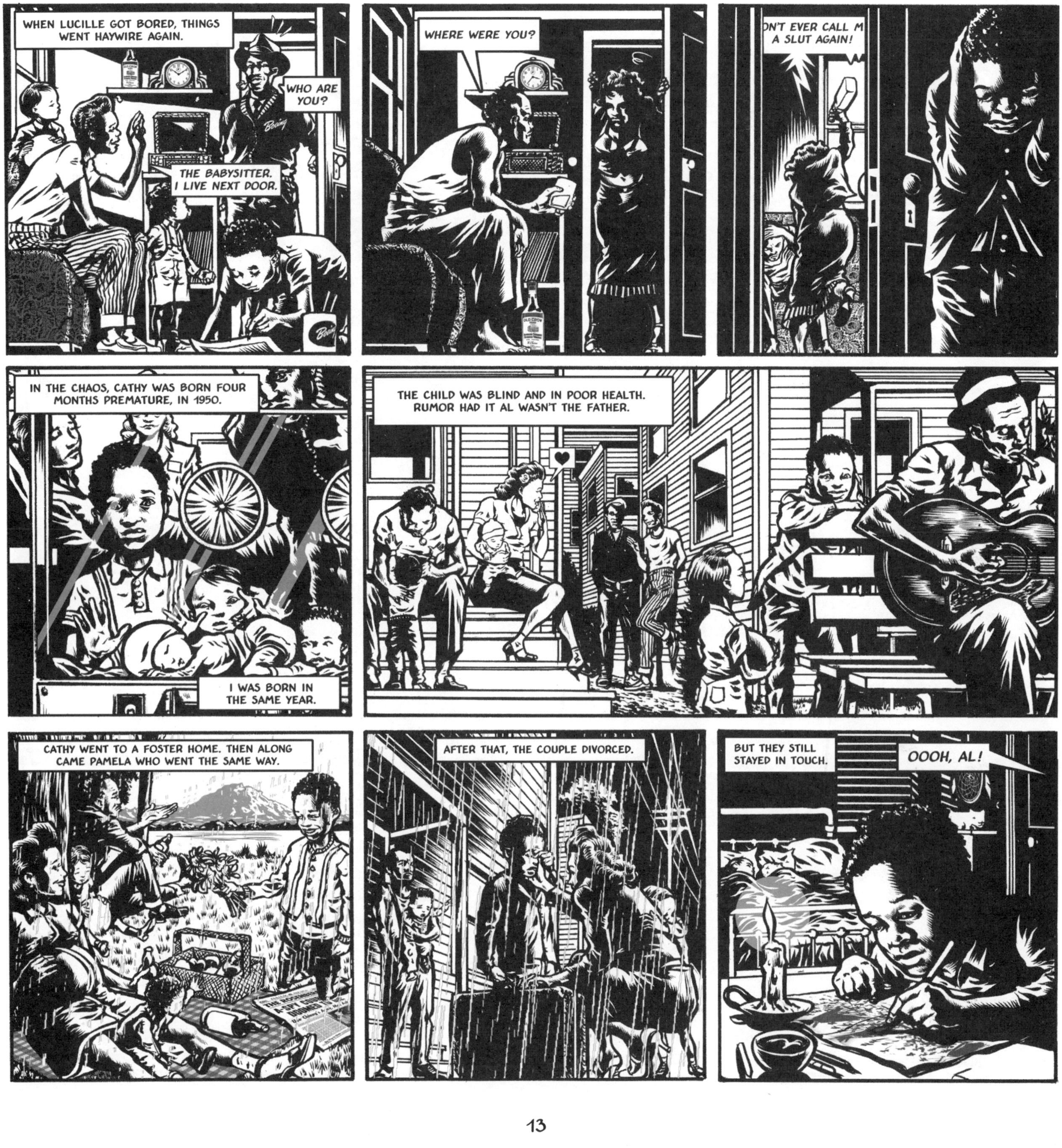
WHEN LUCILLE GOT BORED, THINGS WENT HAYWIRE AGAIN.
WHO ARE YOU?
THE BABYSITTER. I LIVE NEXT DOOR.
WHERE WERE YOU?
ON'T EVER CALL M A SLUT AGAIN!
IN THE CHAOS, CATHY WAS BORN FOUR MONTHS PREMATURE, IN 1950.
I WAS BORN IN THE SAME YEAR.
THE CHILD WAS BLIND AND IN POOR HEALTH. RUMOR HAD IT AL WASN'T THE FATHER.
CATHY WENT TO A FOSTER HOME. THEN ALONG CAME PAMELA WHO WENT THE SAME WAY.
AFTER THAT, THE COUPLE DIVORCED.
BUT THEY STILL STAYED IN TOUCH.
OOOH, AL!

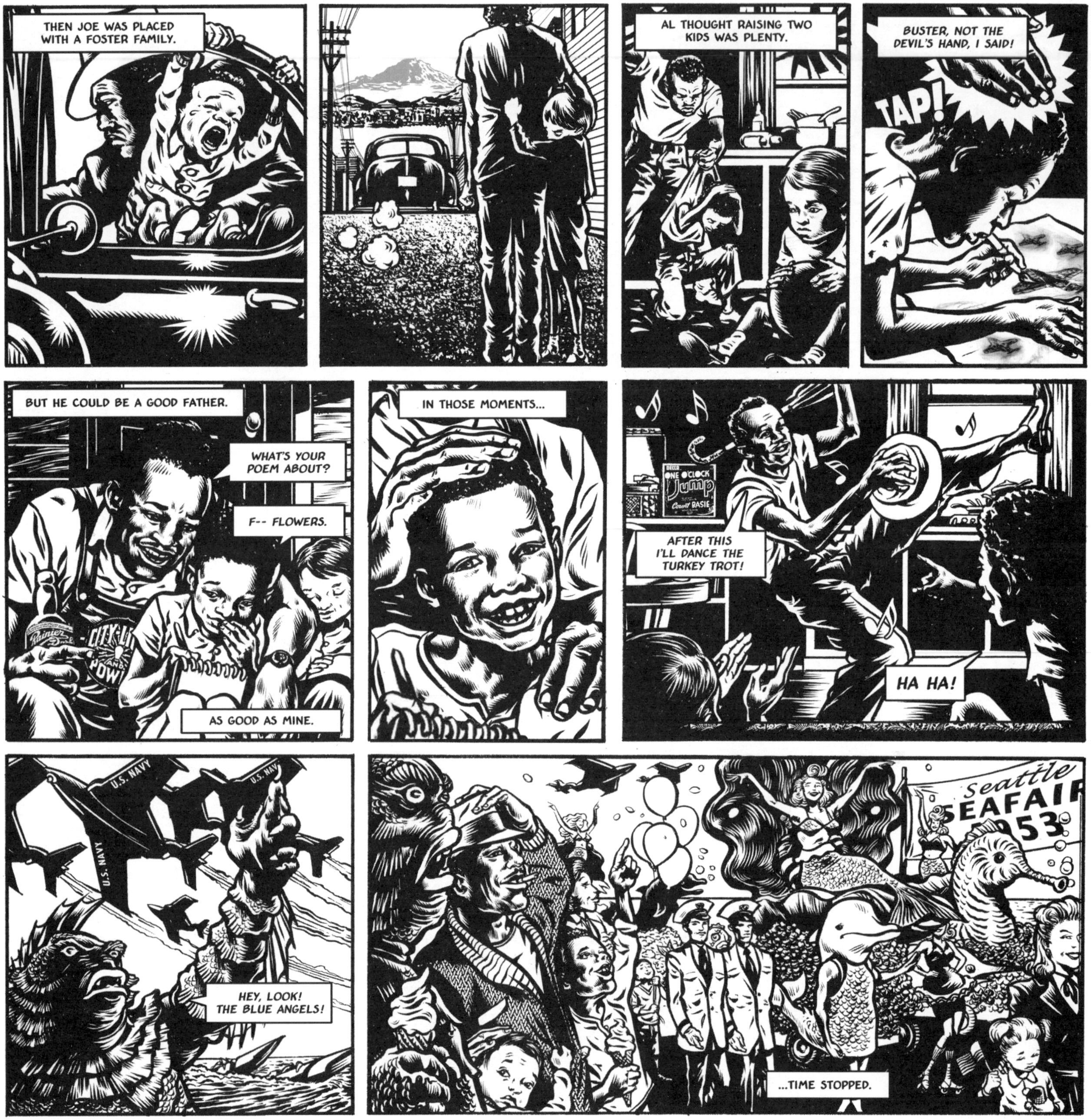
THEN JOE WAS PLACED WITH A FOSTER FAMILY.
AL THOUGHT RAISING TWO KIDS WAS PLENTY.
BUSTER, NOT THE DEVIL'S HAND, I SAID!
TAP!
BUT HE COULD BE A GOOD FATHER.
WHAT'S YOUR POEM ABOUT?
F-- FLOWERS.
AS GOOD AS MINE.
IN THOSE MOMENTS...
ONE O'CLOCK Jump
AFTER THIS I'LL DANCE THE TURKEY TROT!
HA HA!
U.S. NAVY
HEY, LOOK! THE BLUE ANGELS!
Seattle
...TIME STOPPED.

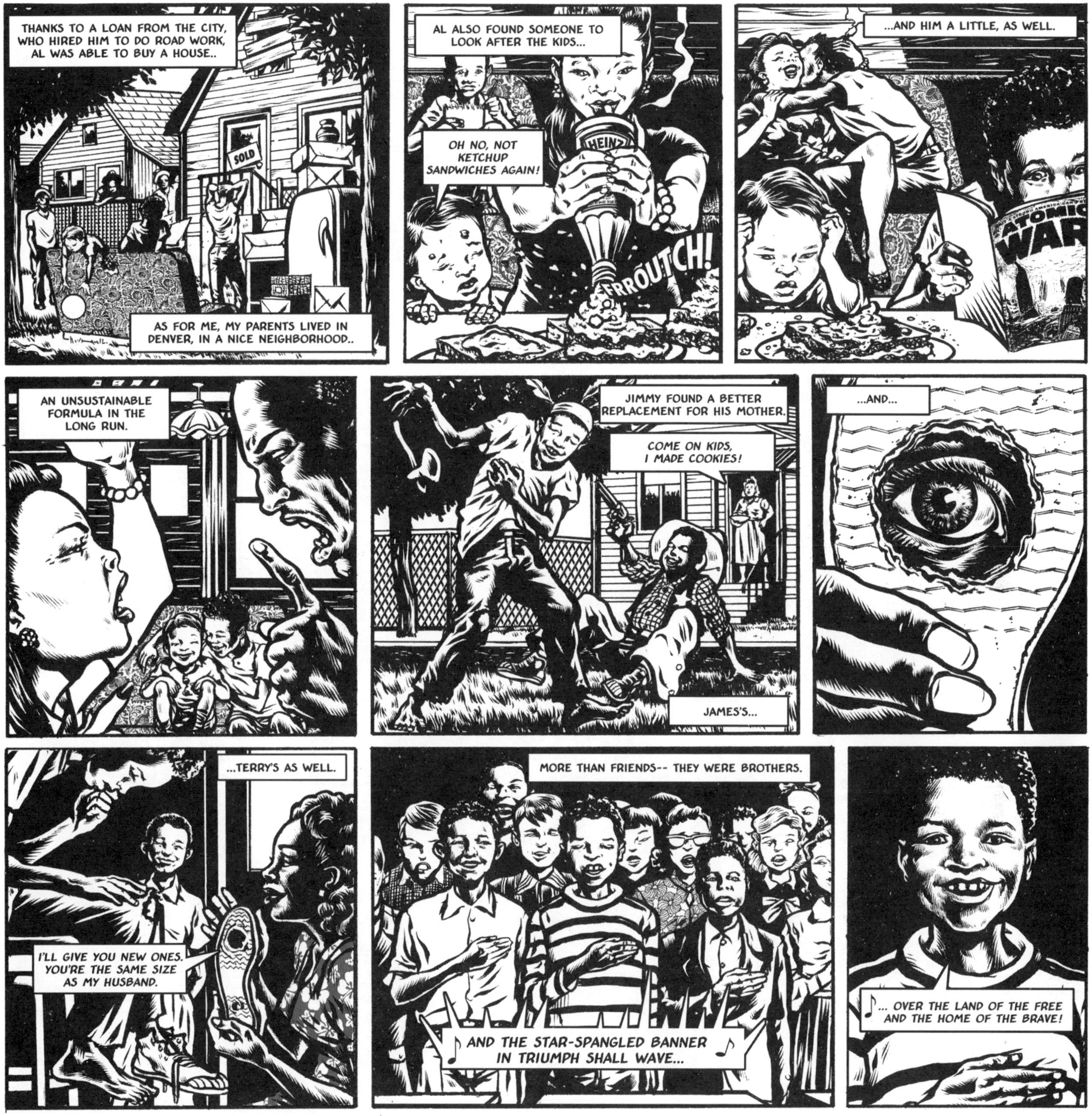
THANKS TO A LOAN FROM THE CITY, WHO HIRED HIM TO DO ROAD WORK, AL WAS ABLE TO BUY A HOUSE..
SOLD
AS FOR ME, MY PARENTS LIVED IN DENVER, IN A NICE NEIGHBORHOOD..
AL ALSO FOUND SOMEONE TO LOOK AFTER THE KIDS...
OH NO, NOT KETCHUP SANDWICHES AGAIN!
HEINZ
FRROUTCH!
...AND HIM A LITTLE, AS WELL.
ATOMIC WAR
AN UNSUSTAINABLE FORMULA IN THE LONG RUN.
JIMMY FOUND A BETTER REPLACEMENT FOR HIS MOTHER.
COME ON KIDS, I MADE COOKIES!
JAMES'S...
...AND...
...TERRY'S AS WELL.
I'LL GIVE YOU NEW ONES. YOU'RE THE SAME SIZE AS MY HUSBAND.
MORE THAN FRIENDS-- THEY WERE BROTHERS.
♪ AND THE STAR-SPANGLED BANNER IN TRIUMPH SHALL WAVE... ♪
♪... OVER THE LAND OF THE FREE AND THE HOME OF THE BRAVE!

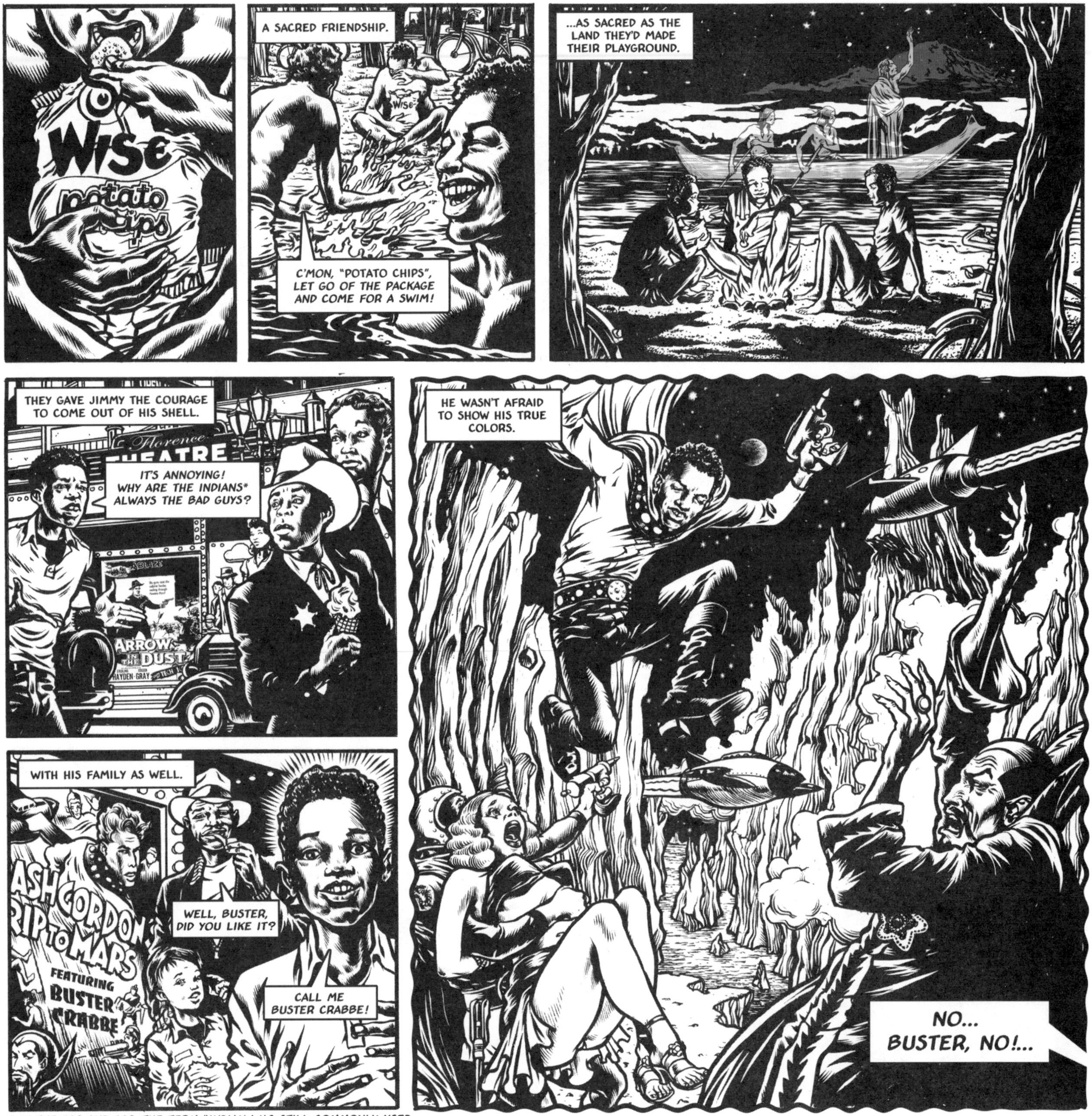
Wise
potato chips
A SACRED FRIENDSHIP.
C'MON, "POTATO CHIPS", LET GO OF THE PACKAGE AND COME FOR A SWIM!
...AS SACRED AS THE LAND THEY'D MADE THEIR PLAYGROUND.
THEY GAVE JIMMY THE COURAGE TO COME OUT OF HIS SHELL.
Florence
THEATRE
IT'S ANNOYING! WHY ARE THE INDIANS* ALWAYS THE BAD GUYS?
ARROW IN THE DUST
HAYDEN GRAY
HE WASN'T AFRAID TO SHOW HIS TRUE COLORS.
WITH HIS FAMILY AS WELL.
ASH GORDON'S RIP TO MARS
FEATURING BUSTER CRABBE
WELL, BUSTER, DID YOU LIKE IT?
CALL ME BUSTER CRABBE!
NO... BUSTER, NO!...

* IN THE 50S AND 60S, THE TERM "INDIAN WAS STILL COMMONLY USED.

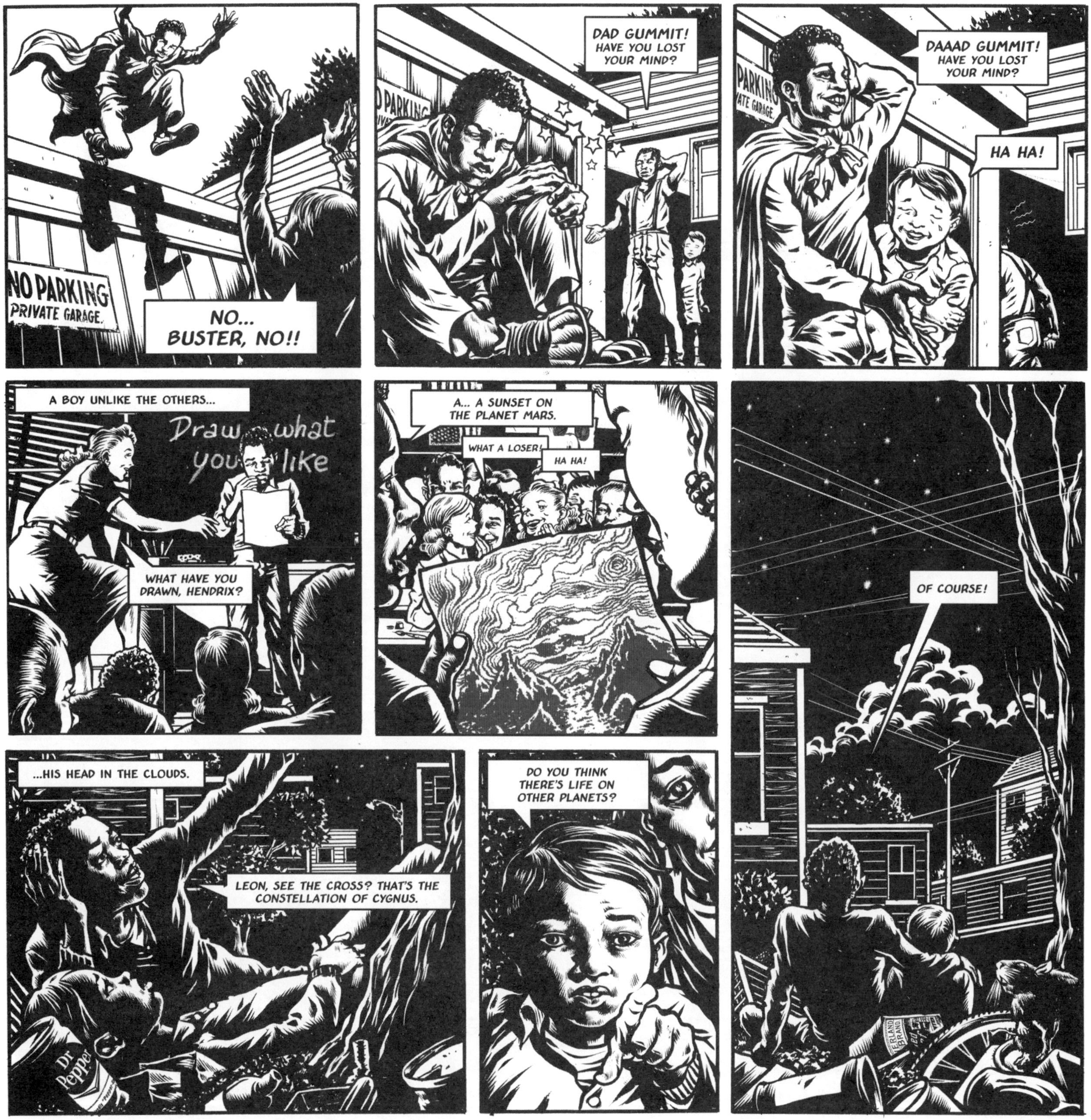
NO PARKING
PRIVATE GARAGE.
NO... BUSTER, NO!!
DAD GUMMIT! HAVE YOU LOST YOUR MIND?
DAAAD GUMMIT! HAVE YOU LOST YOUR MIND?
HA HA!
A BOY UNLIKE THE OTHERS...
Draw what you like
WHAT HAVE YOU DRAWN, HENDRIX?
A... A SUNSET ON THE PLANET MARS.
WHAT A LOSER!
HA HA!
...HIS HEAD IN THE CLOUDS.
LEON, SEE THE CROSS? THAT'S THE CONSTELLATION OF CYGNUS.
Dr Pepper
DO YOU THINK THERE'S LIFE ON OTHER PLANETS?
OF COURSE!

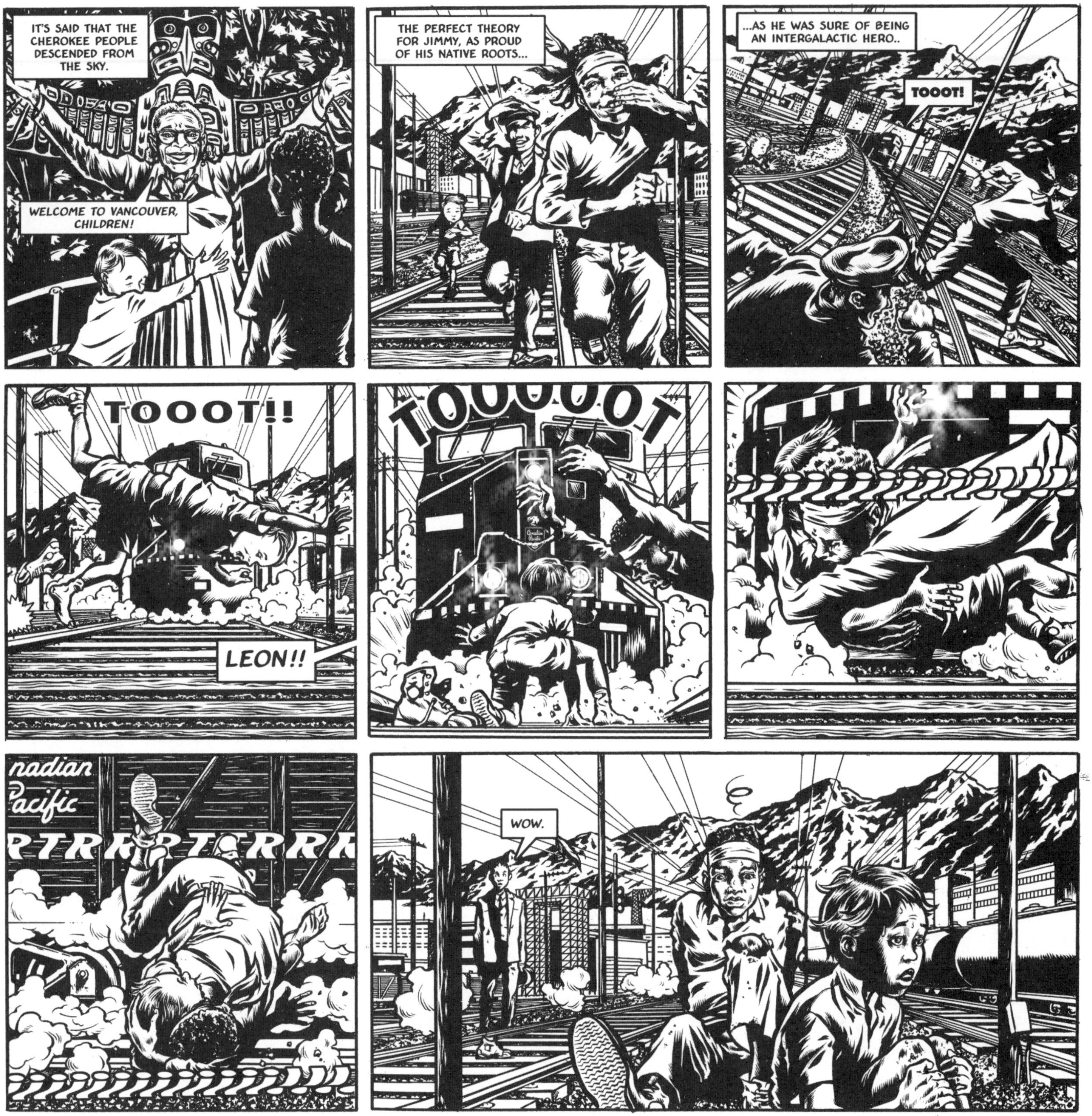
IT'S SAID THAT THE CHEROKEE PEOPLE DESCENDED FROM THE SKY.
WELCOME TO VANCOUVER, CHILDREN!
THE PERFECT THEORY FOR JIMMY, AS PROUD OF HIS NATIVE ROOTS...
...AS HE WAS SURE OF BEING AN INTERGALACTIC HERO..
TOOOT!
TOOOT!!
LEON!!
TOOOOOT
nadian
Pacific
WOW.

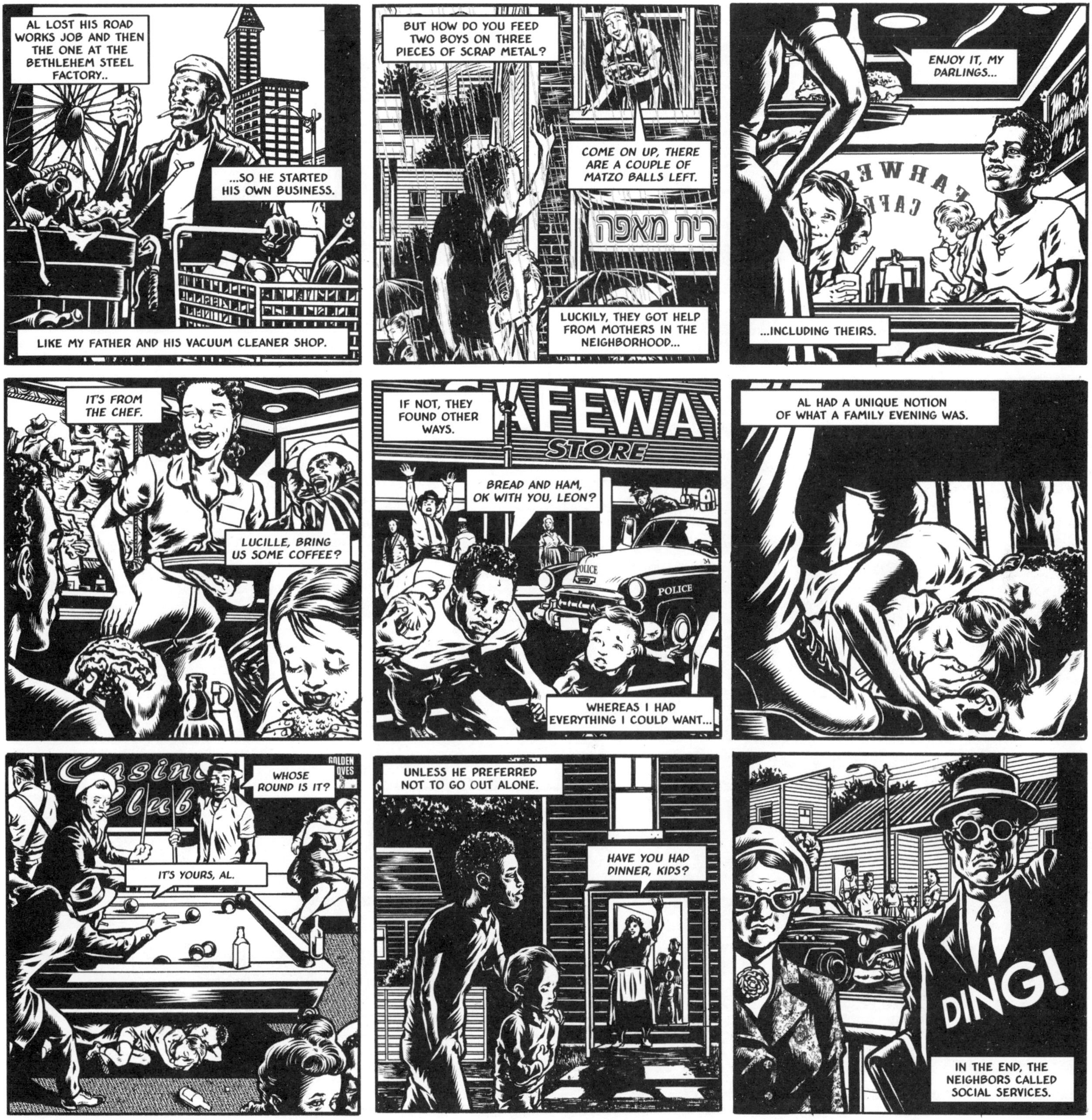
AL LOST HIS ROAD WORKS JOB AND THEN THE ONE AT THE BETHLEHEM STEEL FACTORY..
...SO HE STARTED HIS OWN BUSINESS.
LIKE MY FATHER AND HIS VACUUM CLEANER SHOP.
BUT HOW DO YOU FEED TWO BOYS ON THREE PIECES OF SCRAP METAL?
COME ON UP, THERE ARE A COUPLE OF MATZO BALLS LEFT.
בית מאפה
LUCKILY, THEY GOT HELP FROM MOTHERS IN THE NEIGHBORHOOD...
ENJOY IT, MY DARLINGS...
...INCLUDING THEIRS.
IT'S FROM THE CHEF.
LUCILLE, BRING US SOME COFFEE?
IF NOT, THEY FOUND OTHER WAYS.
STORE
BREAD AND HAM, OK WITH YOU, LEON?
POLICE
WHEREAS I HAD EVERYTHING I COULD WANT...
AL HAD A UNIQUE NOTION OF WHAT A FAMILY EVENING WAS.
Casin
Club
WHOSE ROUND IS IT?
IT'S YOURS, AL.
UNLESS HE PREFERRED NOT TO GO OUT ALONE.
HAVE YOU HAD DINNER, KIDS?
DING!
IN THE END, THE NEIGHBORS CALLED SOCIAL SERVICES.

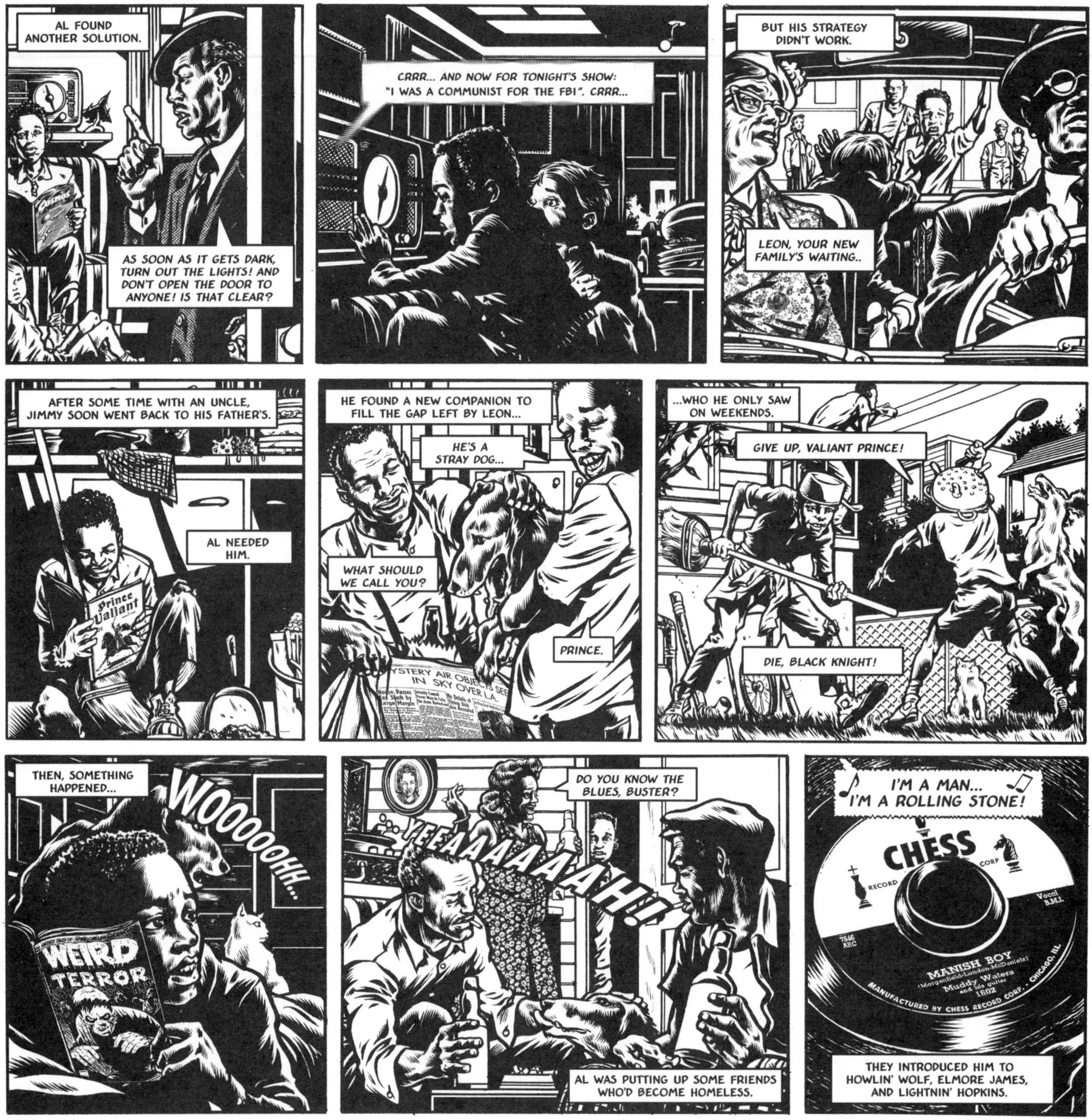

AL FOUND ANOTHER SOLUTION.
AS SOON AS IT GETS DARK, TURN OUT THE LIGHTS! AND DON'T OPEN THE DOOR TO ANYONE! IS THAT CLEAR?
CRRR... AND NOW FOR TONIGHT'S SHOW: "I WAS A COMMUNIST FOR THE FBI". CRRR...
BUT HIS STRATEGY DIDN'T WORK.
LEON, YOUR NEW FAMILY'S WAITING..
AFTER SOME TIME WITH AN UNCLE, JIMMY SOON WENT BACK TO HIS FATHER'S.
AL NEEDED HIM.
Prince Valiant
HE FOUND A NEW COMPANION TO FILL THE GAP LEFT BY LEON...
HE'S A STRAY DOG...
WHAT SHOULD WE CALL YOU?
PRINCE.
...WHO HE ONLY SAW ON WEEKENDS.
GIVE UP, VALIANT PRINCE!
DIE, BLACK KNIGHT!
THEN, SOMETHING HAPPENED...
WOOOOOOHH...
WEIRD TERROR
DO YOU KNOW THE BLUES, BUSTER?
YEEAAAAAAAAH!!
AL WAS PUTTING UP SOME FRIENDS WHO'D BECOME HOMELESS.
I'M A MAN... I'M A ROLLING STONE!
CHESS
RECORD CORP
MANISH BOY
Muddy Waters
1602
MANUFACTURED BY CHESS RECORD CORP. • CHICAGO, ILL.
THEY INTRODUCED HIM TO HOWLIN' WOLF, ELMORE JAMES, AND LIGHTNIN' HOPKINS.

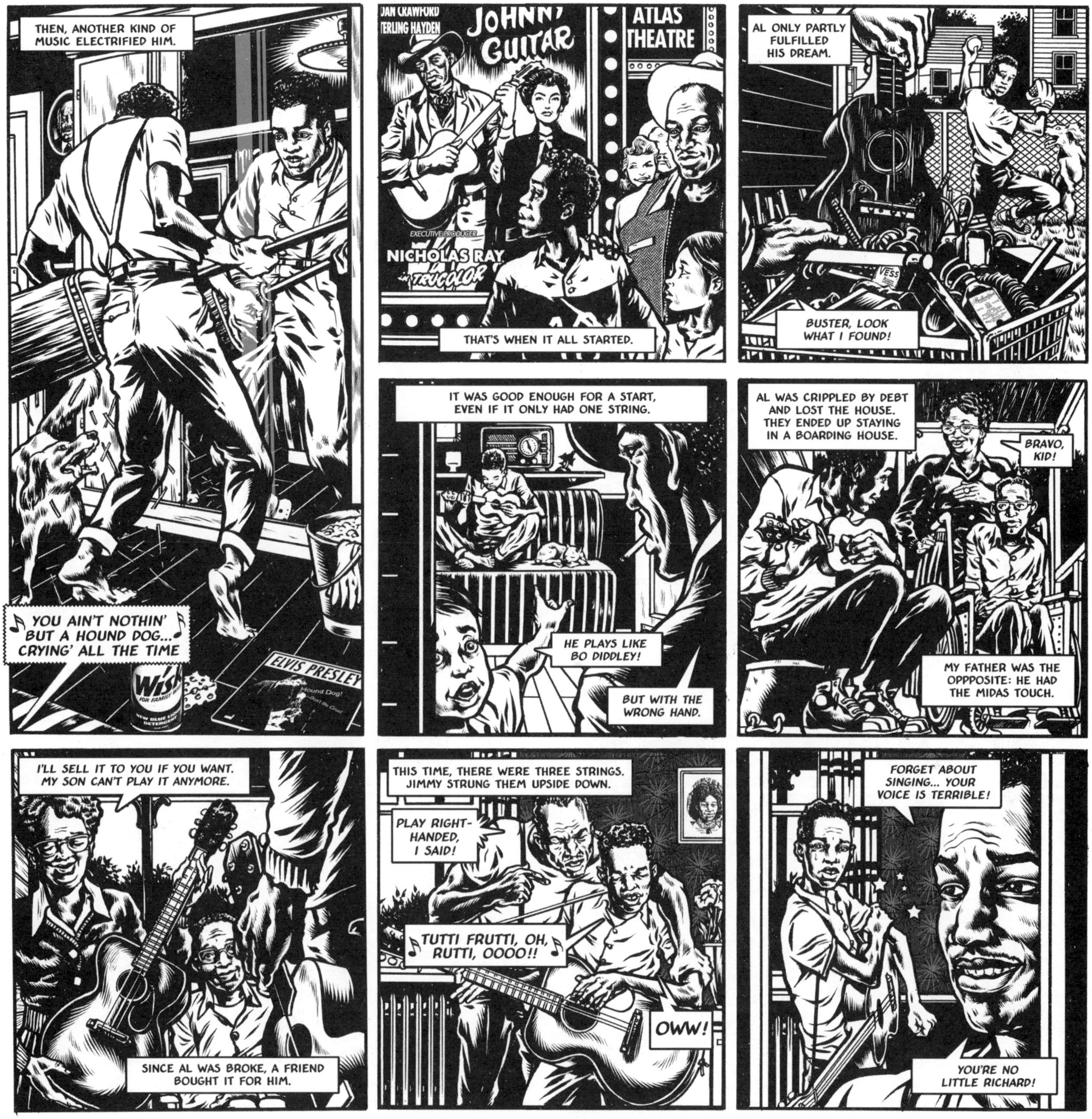
THEN, ANOTHER KIND OF MUSIC ELECTRIFIED HIM.
YOU AIN'T NOTHIN' BUT A HOUND DOG... CRYING' ALL THE TIME
ELVIS PRESLEY
Hound Dog!
WISK
JOHNNY GUITAR
ATLAS THEATRE
EXECUTIVE PRODUCER
NICHOLAS RAY
TRUCOLOR
THAT'S WHEN IT ALL STARTED.
AL ONLY PARTLY FULFILLED HIS DREAM.
BUSTER, LOOK WHAT I FOUND!
IT WAS GOOD ENOUGH FOR A START, EVEN IF IT ONLY HAD ONE STRING.
HE PLAYS LIKE BO DIDDLEY!
BUT WITH THE WRONG HAND.
AL WAS CRIPPLED BY DEBT AND LOST THE HOUSE. THEY ENDED UP STAYING IN A BOARDING HOUSE.
BRAVO, KID!
MY FATHER WAS THE OPPPOSITE: HE HAD THE MIDAS TOUCH.
I'LL SELL IT TO YOU IF YOU WANT. MY SON CAN'T PLAY IT ANYMORE.
SINCE AL WAS BROKE, A FRIEND BOUGHT IT FOR HIM.
THIS TIME, THERE WERE THREE STRINGS. JIMMY STRUNG THEM UPSIDE DOWN.
PLAY RIGHT-HANDED, I SAID!
TUTTI FRUTTI, OH, RUTTI, OOOO!!
OWW!
FORGET ABOUT SINGING... YOUR VOICE IS TERRIBLE!
YOU'RE NO LITTLE RICHARD!

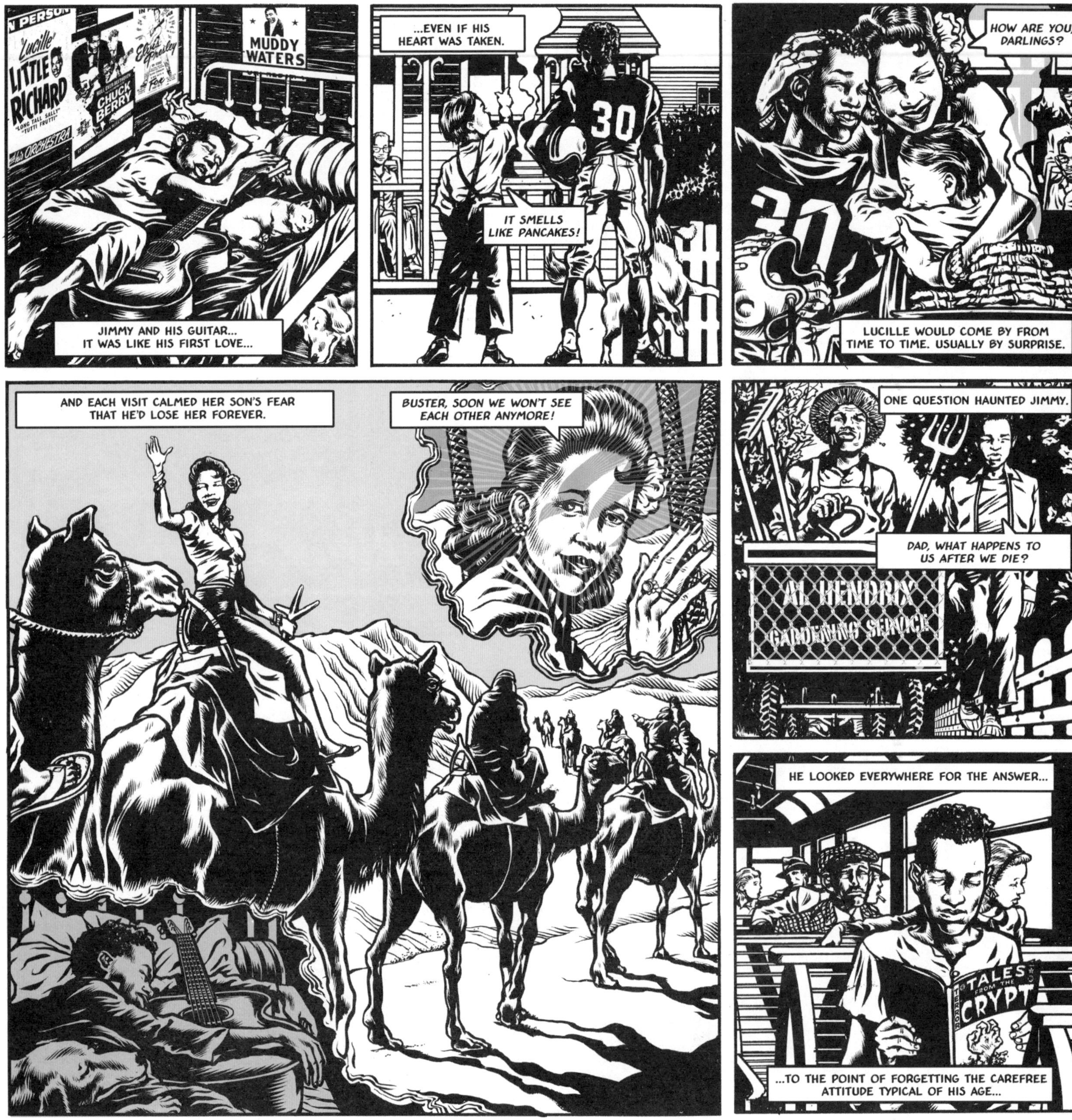

MUDDY WATERS
LITTLE RICHARD
CHUCK BERRY
JIMMY AND HIS GUITAR... IT WAS LIKE HIS FIRST LOVE...
...EVEN IF HIS HEART WAS TAKEN.
30
IT SMELLS LIKE PANCAKES!
HOW ARE YOU, DARLINGS?
LUCILLE WOULD COME BY FROM TIME TO TIME. USUALLY BY SURPRISE.
AND EACH VISIT CALMED HER SON'S FEAR THAT HE'D LOSE HER FOREVER.
BUSTER, SOON WE WON'T SEE EACH OTHER ANYMORE!
ONE QUESTION HAUNTED JIMMY.
DAD, WHAT HAPPENS TO US AFTER WE DIE?
AL HENDRIX GARDENING SERVICE
HE LOOKED EVERYWHERE FOR THE ANSWER...
TALES FROM THE CRYPT
...TO THE POINT OF FORGETTING THE CAREFREE ATTITUDE TYPICAL OF HIS AGE...

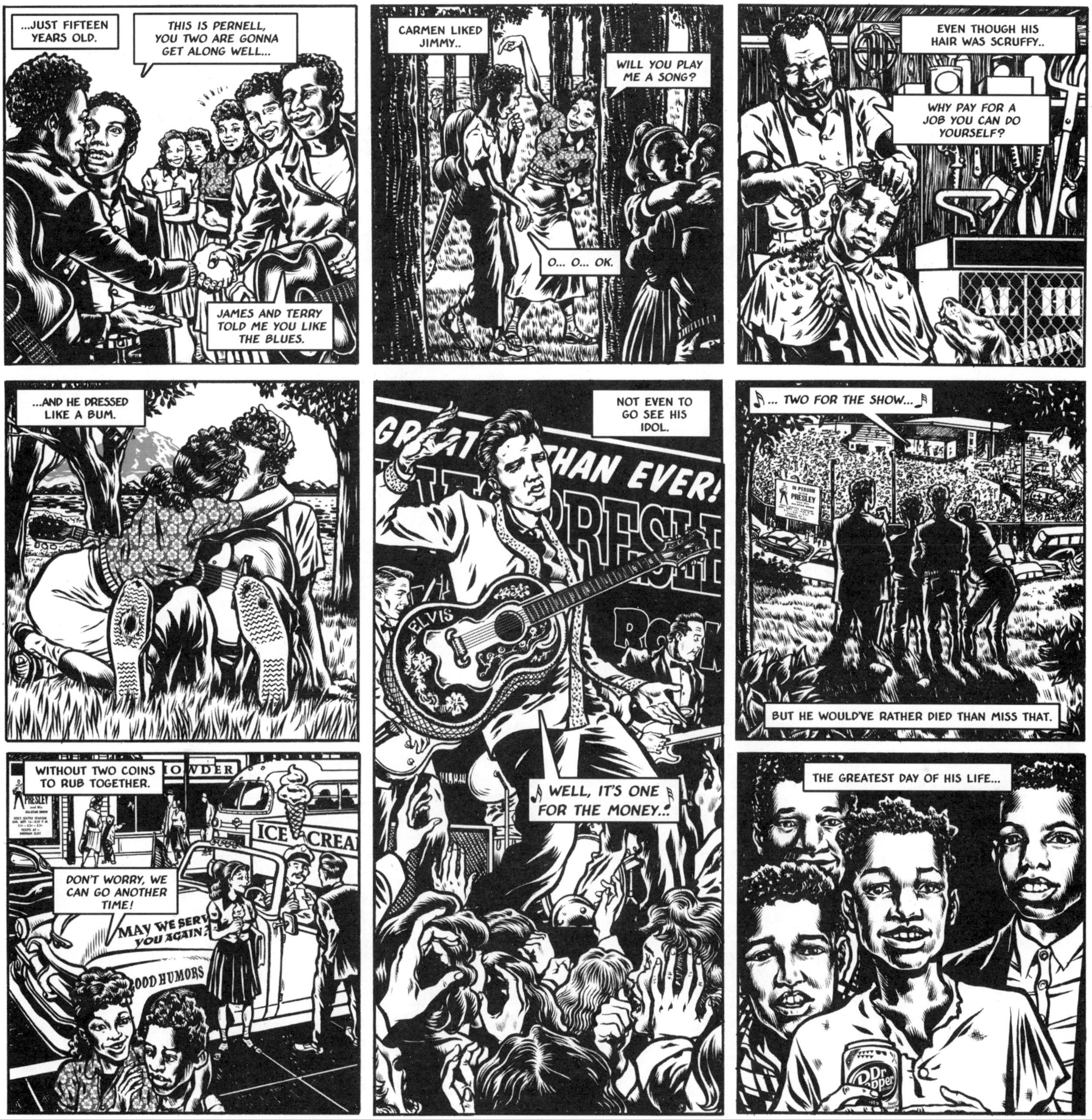
...JUST FIFTEEN YEARS OLD.
THIS IS PERNELL, YOU TWO ARE GONNA GET ALONG WELL...
JAMES AND TERRY TOLD ME YOU LIKE THE BLUES.
CARMEN LIKED JIMMY..
WILL YOU PLAY ME A SONG?
O... O... OK.
EVEN THOUGH HIS HAIR WAS SCRUFFY..
WHY PAY FOR A JOB YOU CAN DO YOURSELF?
...AND HE DRESSED LIKE A BUM.
WITHOUT TWO COINS TO RUB TOGETHER.
DON'T WORRY, WE CAN GO ANOTHER TIME!
NOT EVEN TO GO SEE HIS IDOL.
ELVIS
♪ WELL, IT'S ONE FOR THE MONEY.. ♪
♪... TWO FOR THE SHOW... ♪
BUT HE WOULD'VE RATHER DIED THAN MISS THAT.
THE GREATEST DAY OF HIS LIFE...

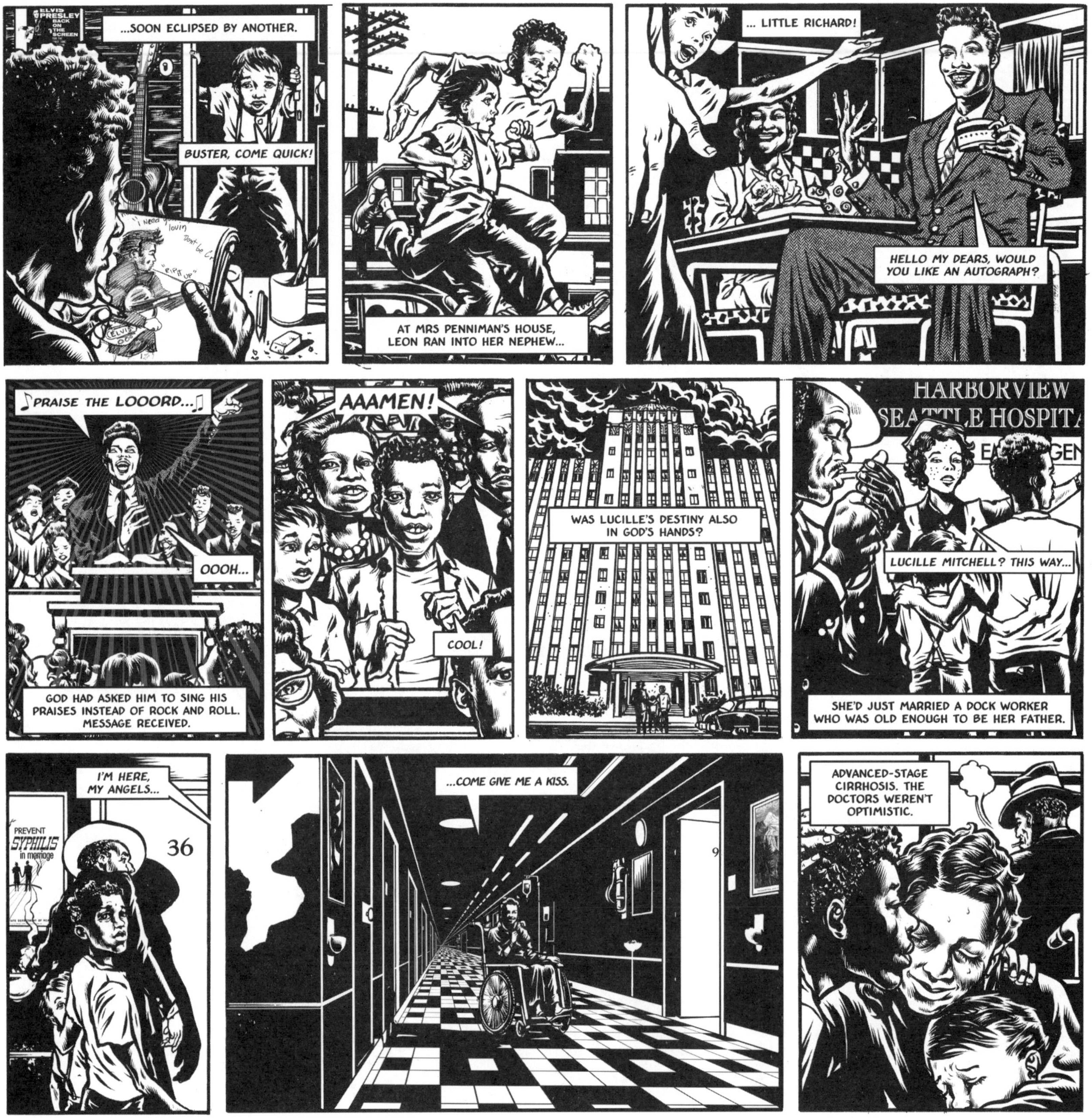
ELVIS PRESLEY
BACK ON THE SCREEN
...SOON ECLIPSED BY ANOTHER.
BUSTER, COME QUICK!
AT MRS PENNIMAN'S HOUSE, LEON RAN INTO HER NEPHEW...
... LITTLE RICHARD!
HELLO MY DEARS, WOULD YOU LIKE AN AUTOGRAPH?
PRAISE THE LOOORD...
OOOH...
GOD HAD ASKED HIM TO SING HIS PRAISES INSTEAD OF ROCK AND ROLL. MESSAGE RECEIVED.
AAAMEN!
COOL!
WAS LUCILLE'S DESTINY ALSO IN GOD'S HANDS?
HARBORVIEW
SEATTLE HOSPITA
LUCILLE MITCHELL? THIS WAY...
SHE'D JUST MARRIED A DOCK WORKER WHO WAS OLD ENOUGH TO BE HER FATHER.
I'M HERE, MY ANGELS...
PREVENT
SYPHILIS
in marriage
36
...COME GIVE ME A KISS.
ADVANCED-STAGE CIRRHOSIS. THE DOCTORS WEREN'T OPTIMISTIC.

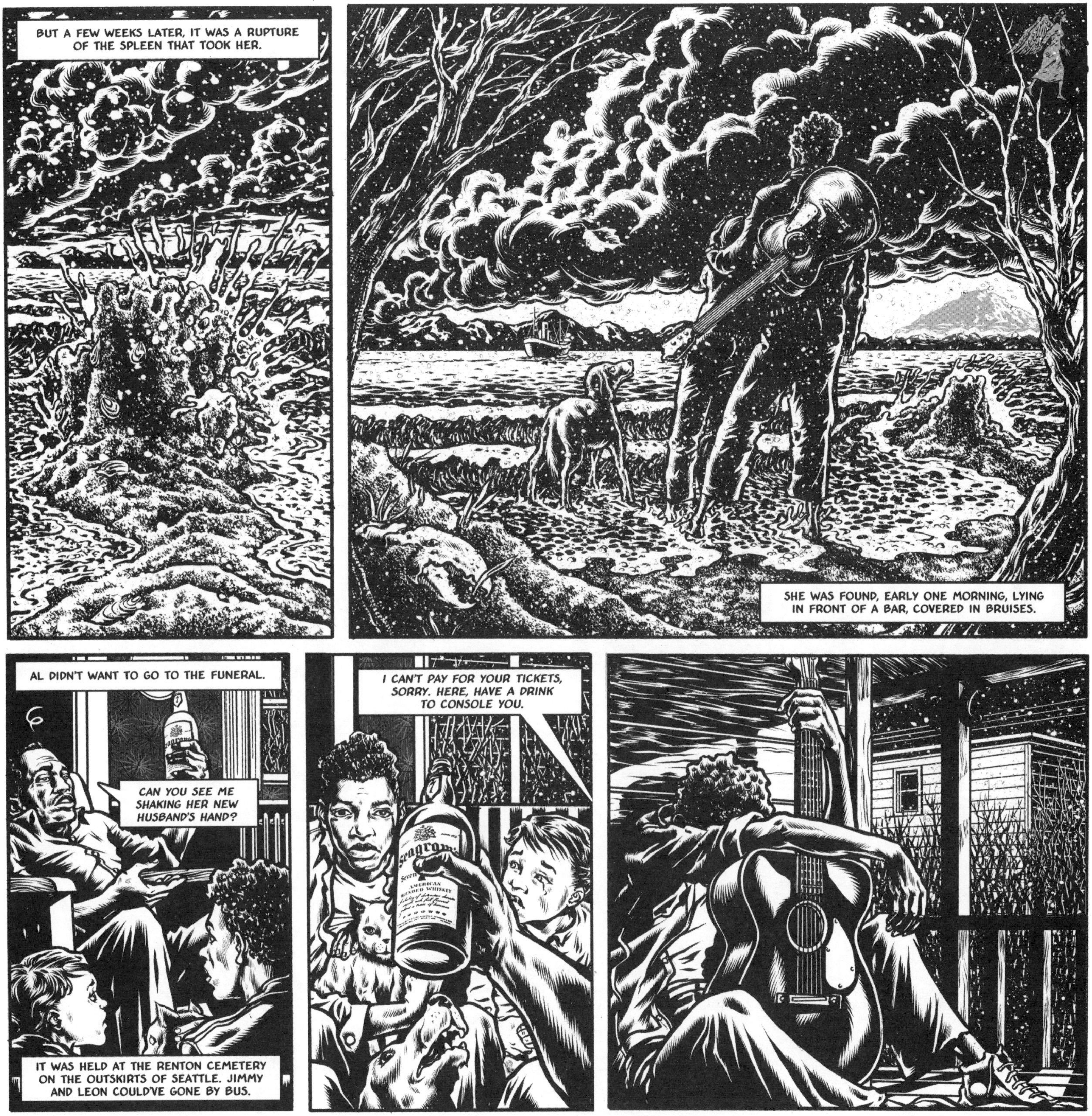
BUT A FEW WEEKS LATER, IT WAS A RUPTURE OF THE SPLEEN THAT TOOK HER.
SHE WAS FOUND, EARLY ONE MORNING, LYING IN FRONT OF A BAR, COVERED IN BRUISES.
AL DIDN'T WANT TO GO TO THE FUNERAL.
CAN YOU SEE ME SHAKING HER NEW HUSBAND'S HAND?
IT WAS HELD AT THE RENTON CEMETERY ON THE OUTSKIRTS OF SEATTLE. JIMMY AND LEON COULD'VE GONE BY BUS.
I CAN'T PAY FOR YOUR TICKETS, SORRY. HERE, HAVE A DRINK TO CONSOLE YOU.

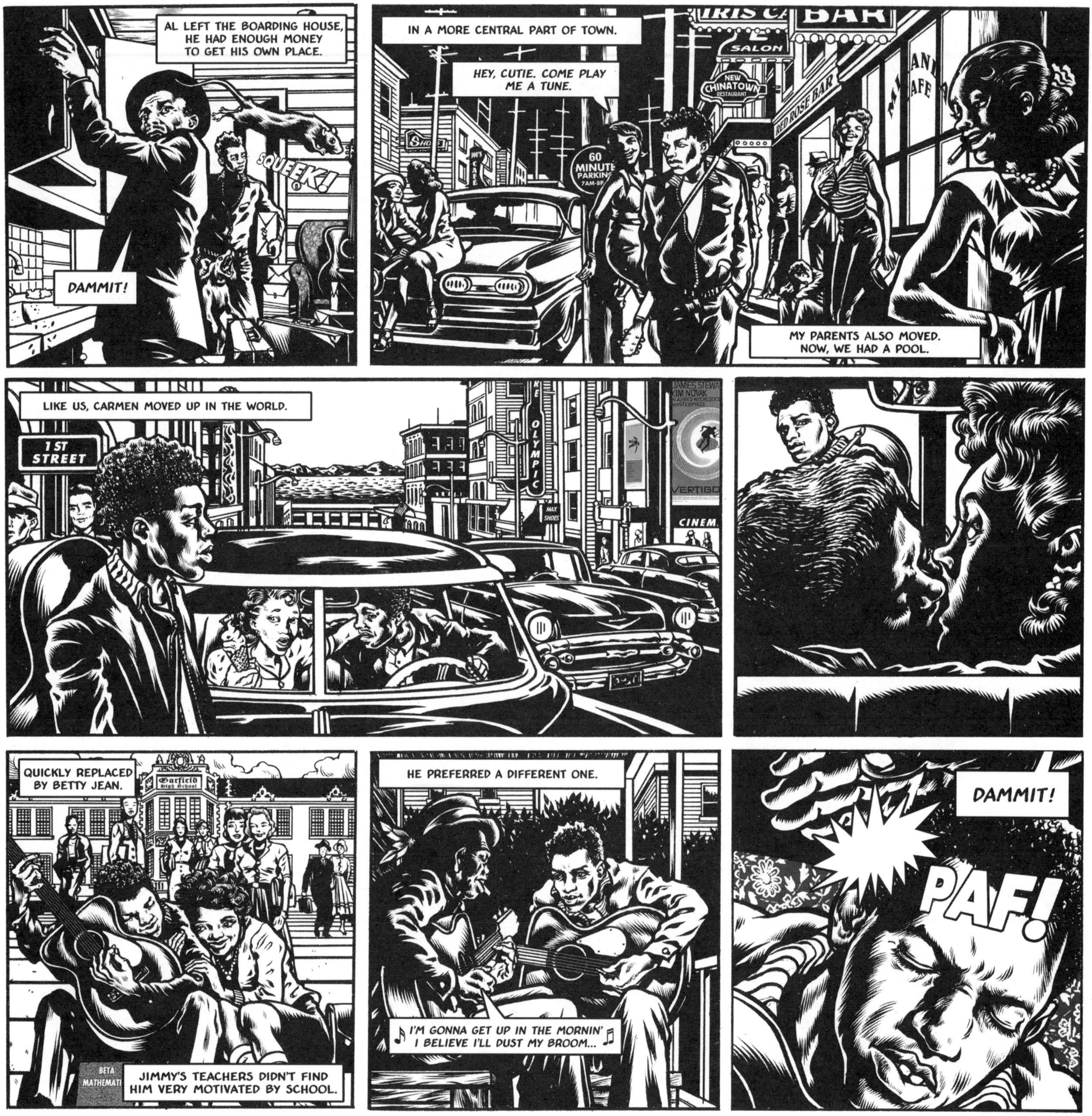
AL LEFT THE BOARDING HOUSE, HE HAD ENOUGH MONEY TO GET HIS OWN PLACE.
SQUEEK!
DAMMIT!
IN A MORE CENTRAL PART OF TOWN.
HEY, CUTIE. COME PLAY ME A TUNE.
60 MINUTE PARKING
SALON
NEW CHINATOWN RESTAURANT
BAR
RED ROSE BAR
MY PARENTS ALSO MOVED. NOW, WE HAD A POOL.
LIKE US, CARMEN MOVED UP IN THE WORLD.
1 ST STREET
OLYMPIC
MAX SHOES
VERTIGO
CINEM
QUICKLY REPLACED BY BETTY JEAN.
Garfield High School
JIMMY'S TEACHERS DIDN'T FIND HIM VERY MOTIVATED BY SCHOOL.
HE PREFERRED A DIFFERENT ONE.
♪ I'M GONNA GET UP IN THE MORNIN' I BELIEVE I'LL DUST MY BROOM... ♫
DAMMIT!
PAF!

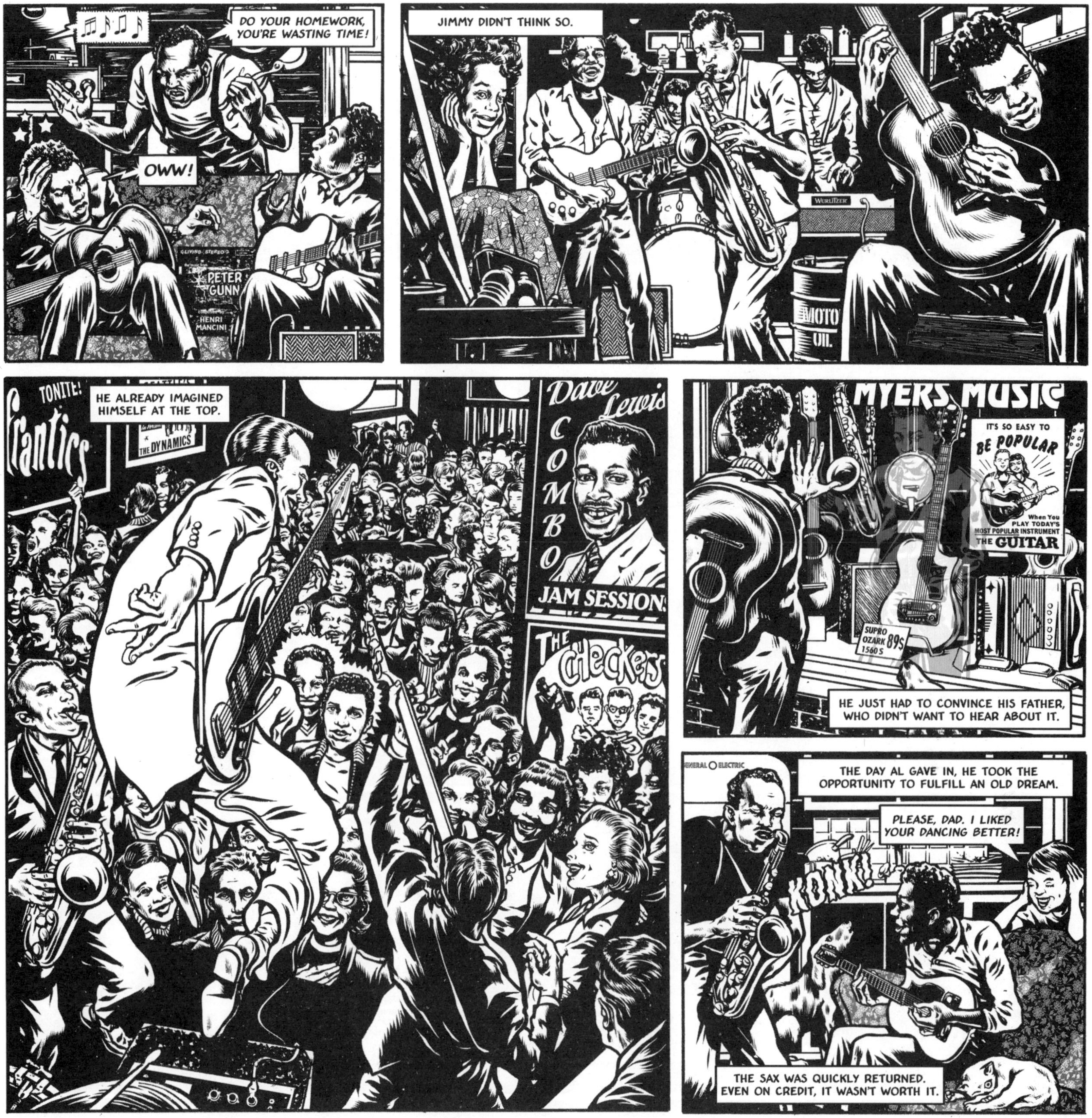

DO YOUR HOMEWORK, YOU'RE WASTING TIME!
OWW!
PETER GUNN
HENRI MANCINI
JIMMY DIDN'T THINK SO.
WURLITZER
TONITE!
frantics
THE DYNAMICS
HE ALREADY IMAGINED HIMSELF AT THE TOP.
Dave Lewis COMBO
JAM SESSIONS
The Checkers
MYERS MUSIC
IT'S SO EASY TO BE POPULAR
When You PLAY TODAY'S MOST POPULAR INSTRUMENT THE GUITAR
SUPRO OZARK 89$ 1560 S
HE JUST HAD TO CONVINCE HIS FATHER, WHO DIDN'T WANT TO HEAR ABOUT IT.
THE DAY AL GAVE IN, HE TOOK THE OPPORTUNITY TO FULFILL AN OLD DREAM.
PLEASE, DAD. I LIKED YOUR DANCING BETTER!
KONK!
THE SAX WAS QUICKLY RETURNED. EVEN ON CREDIT, IT WASN'T WORTH IT.

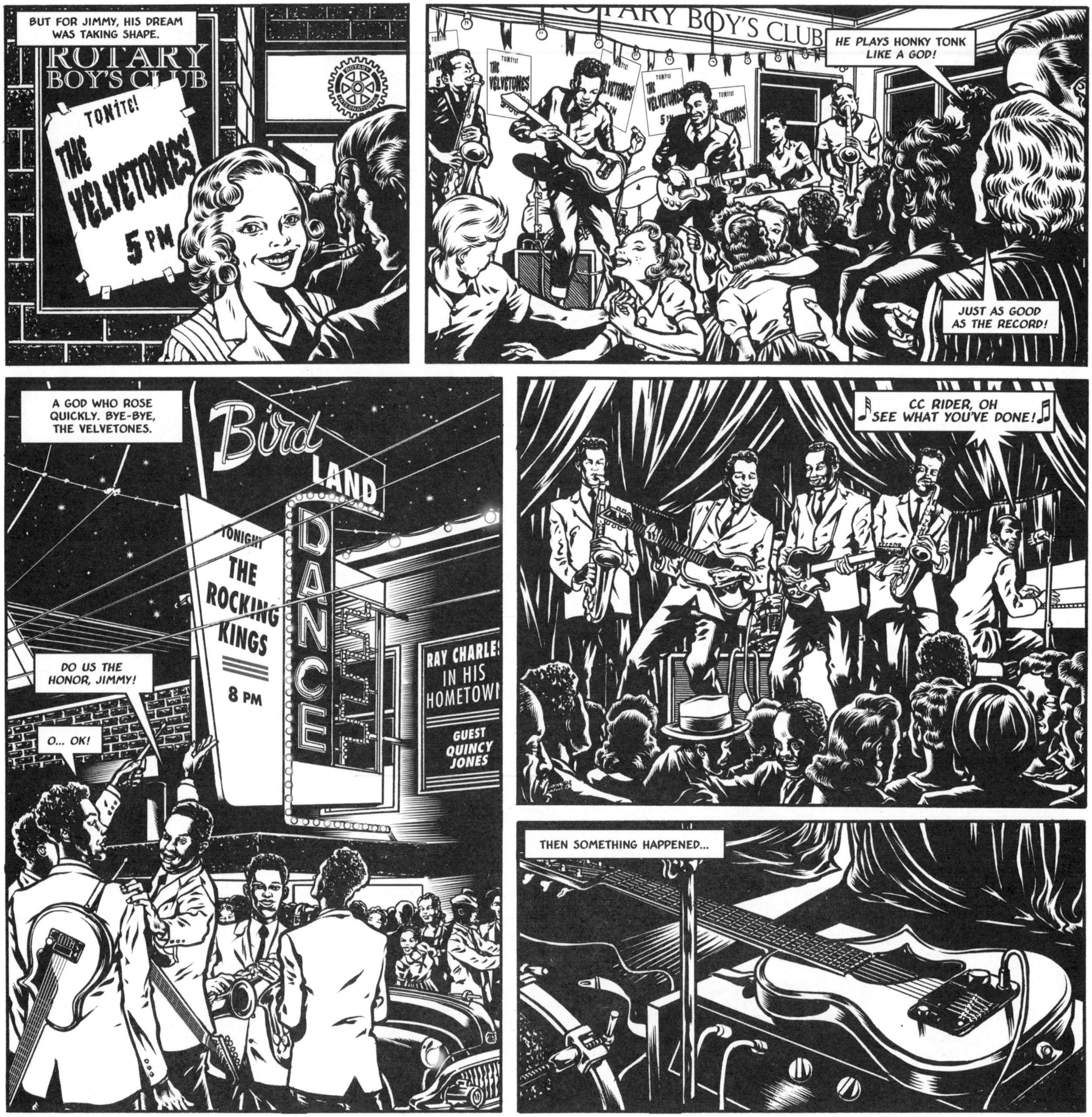
BUT FOR JIMMY, HIS DREAM WAS TAKING SHAPE.
ROTARY BOY'S CLUB
TONITE! THE VELVETONES! 5 PM
ROTARY BOY'S CLUB
HE PLAYS HONKY TONK LIKE A GOD!
JUST AS GOOD AS THE RECORD!
A GOD WHO ROSE QUICKLY. BYE-BYE, THE VELVETONES.
Bird LAND
TONIGHT THE ROCKING KINGS 8 PM
DANCE
RAY CHARLES IN HIS HOMETOWN
GUEST QUINCY JONES
DO US THE HONOR, JIMMY!
O... OK!
CC RIDER, OH SEE WHAT YOU'VE DONE!
THEN SOMETHING HAPPENED...

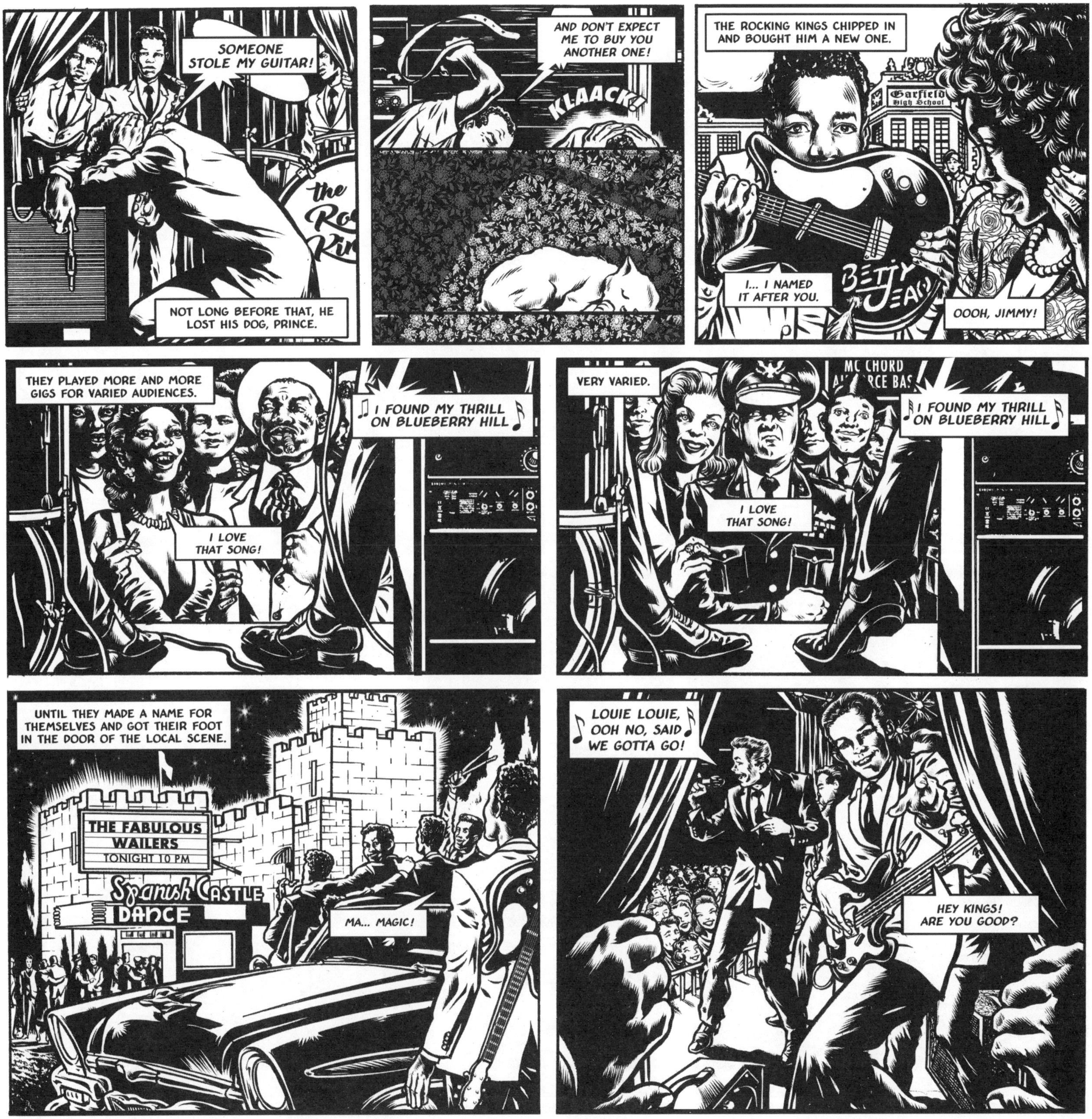
SOMEONE STOLE MY GUITAR!
NOT LONG BEFORE THAT, HE LOST HIS DOG, PRINCE.
AND DON'T EXPECT ME TO BUY YOU ANOTHER ONE!
KLAACK!
THE ROCKING KINGS CHIPPED IN AND BOUGHT HIM A NEW ONE.
Garfield High School
I... I NAMED IT AFTER YOU.
BETTY JEAN
OOOH, JIMMY!
THEY PLAYED MORE AND MORE GIGS FOR VARIED AUDIENCES.
I FOUND MY THRILL ON BLUEBERRY HILL
I LOVE THAT SONG!
VERY VARIED.
MC CHORD
I FOUND MY THRILL ON BLUEBERRY HILL
I LOVE THAT SONG!
UNTIL THEY MADE A NAME FOR THEMSELVES AND GOT THEIR FOOT IN THE DOOR OF THE LOCAL SCENE.
THE FABULOUS WAILERS
TONIGHT 10 PM
Spanish CASTLE
DANCE
MA... MAGIC!
LOUIE LOUIE, OOH NO, SAID WE GOTTA GO!
HEY KINGS! ARE YOU GOOD?

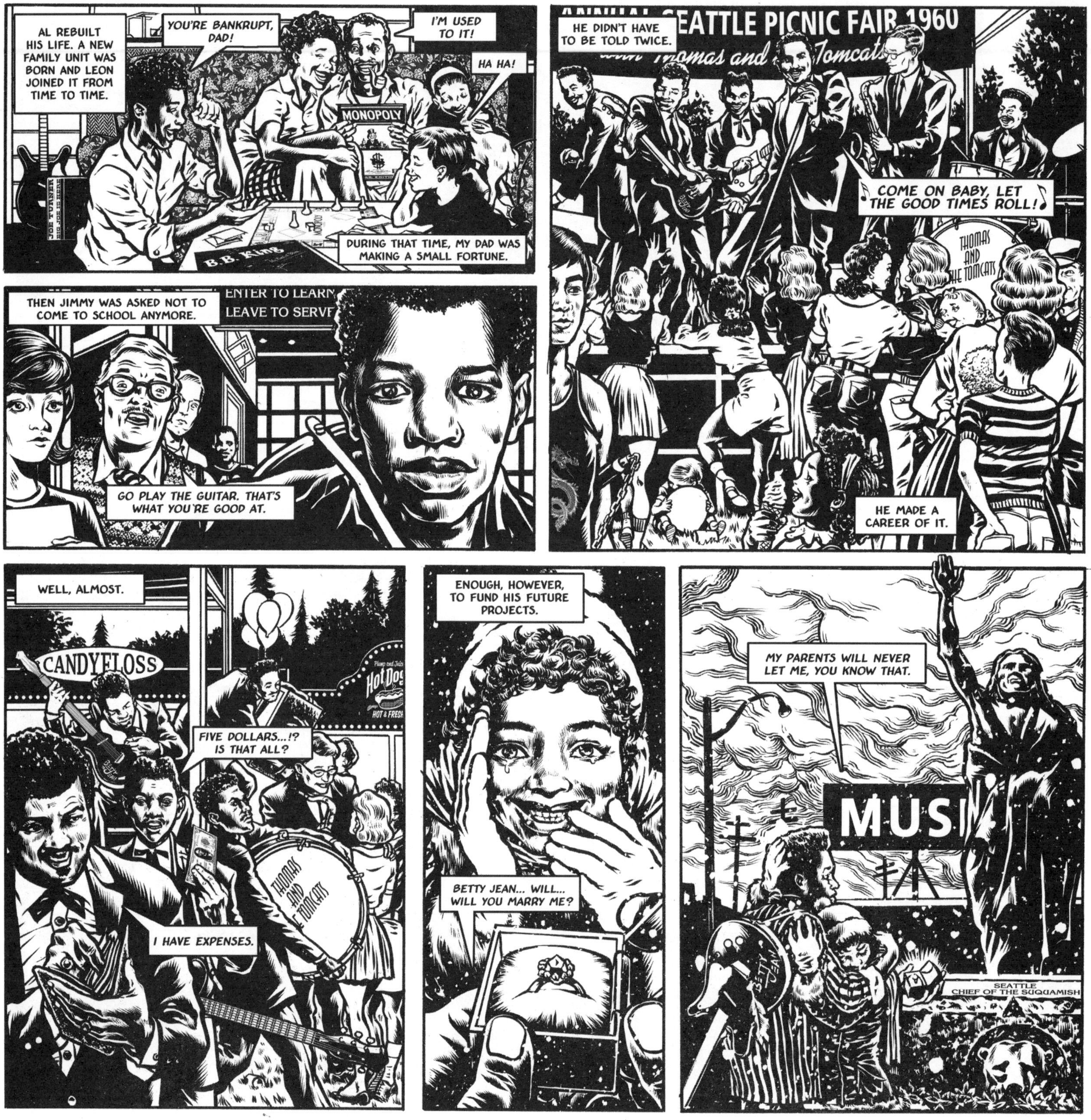
AL REBUILT HIS LIFE. A NEW FAMILY UNIT WAS BORN AND LEON JOINED IT FROM TIME TO TIME.
YOU'RE BANKRUPT, DAD!
I'M USED TO IT!
HA HA!
MONOPOLY
B.B. King
DURING THAT TIME, MY DAD WAS MAKING A SMALL FORTUNE.
THEN JIMMY WAS ASKED NOT TO COME TO SCHOOL ANYMORE.
ENTER TO LEARN
GO PLAY THE GUITAR. THAT'S WHAT YOU'RE GOOD AT.
HE DIDN'T HAVE TO BE TOLD TWICE.
SEATTLE PICNIC FAIR 1960
COME ON BABY, LET THE GOOD TIMES ROLL!
THOMAS AND THE TOMCATS
HE MADE A CAREER OF IT.
WELL, ALMOST.
CANDYFLOSS
Hot Dog
FIVE DOLLARS...!? IS THAT ALL?
I HAVE EXPENSES.
ENOUGH, HOWEVER, TO FUND HIS FUTURE PROJECTS.
BETTY JEAN... WILL... WILL YOU MARRY ME?
MY PARENTS WILL NEVER LET ME, YOU KNOW THAT.
MUSI
SEATTLE
CHIEF OF THE SUQUAMISH

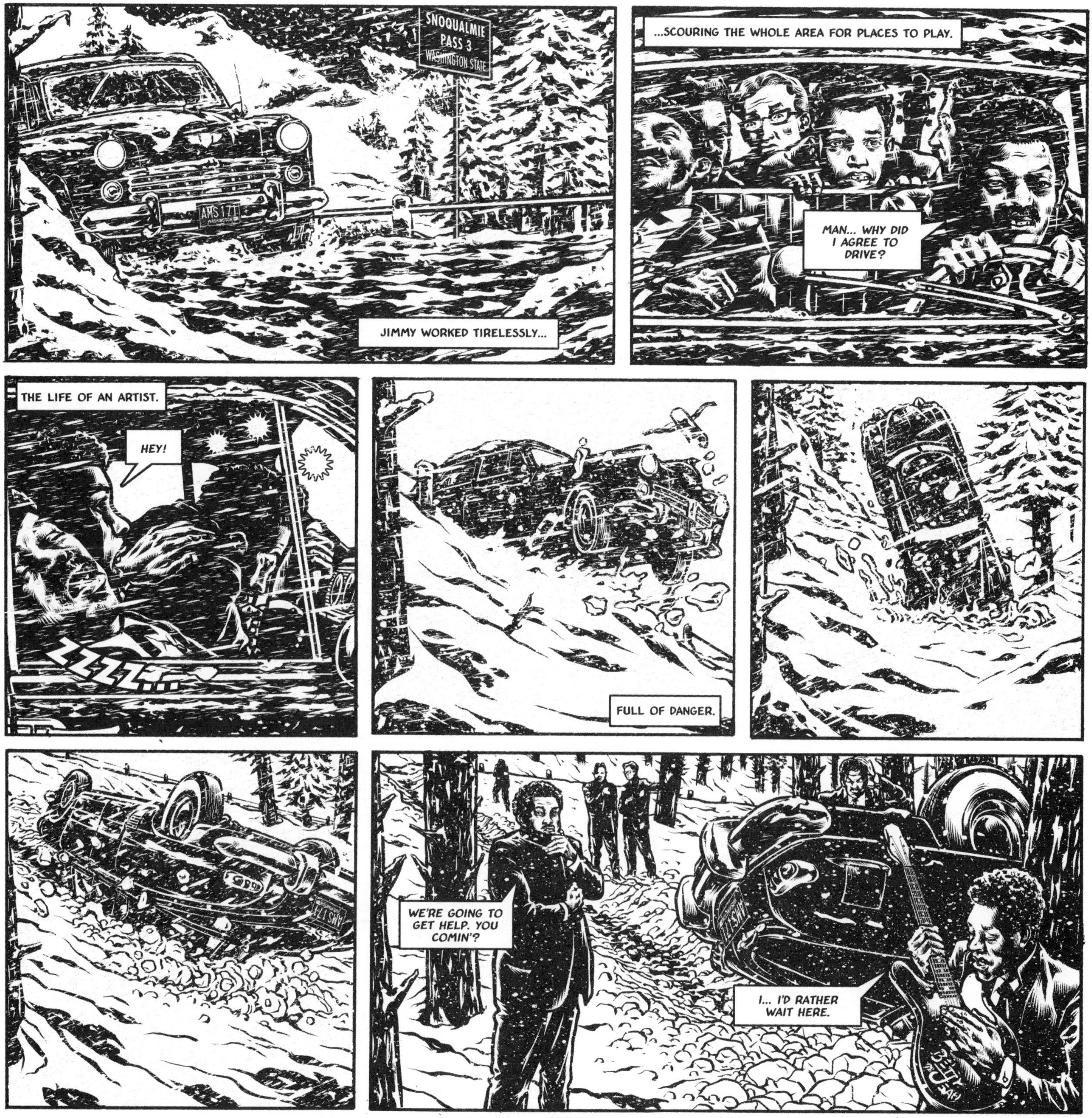
SNOQUALMIE
PASS 3
WASHINGTON STATE
JIMMY WORKED TIRELESSLY...
...SCOURING THE WHOLE AREA FOR PLACES TO PLAY.
MAN... WHY DID I AGREE TO DRIVE?
THE LIFE OF AN ARTIST.
HEY!
ZZZZ...
FULL OF DANGER.
WE'RE GOING TO GET HELP. YOU COMIN'?
I... I'D RATHER WAIT HERE.

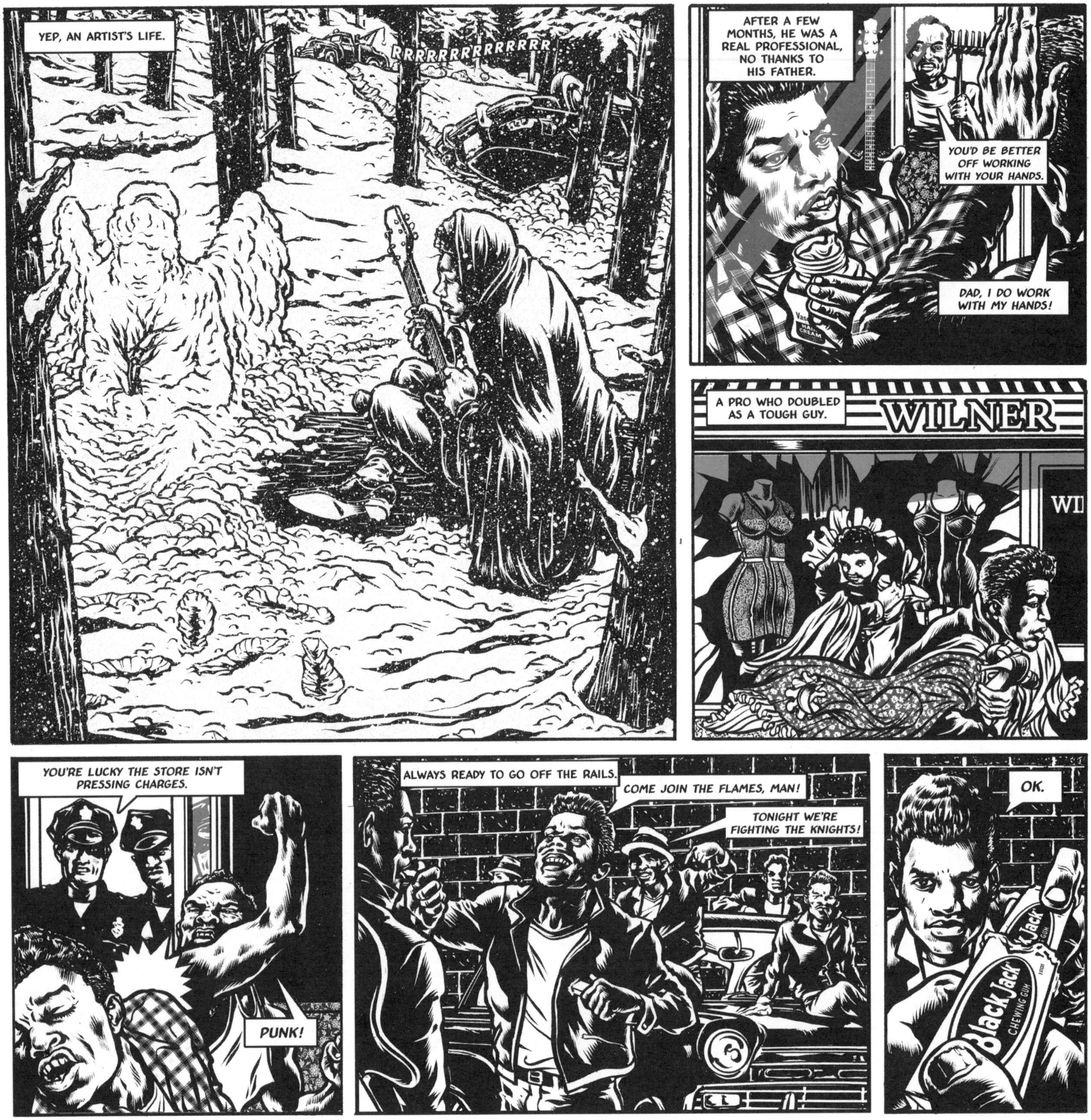
YEP, AN ARTIST'S LIFE.
RRRRRRRRRRRRRR
AFTER A FEW MONTHS, HE WAS A REAL PROFESSIONAL, NO THANKS TO HIS FATHER.
YOU'D BE BETTER OFF WORKING WITH YOUR HANDS.
DAD, I DO WORK WITH MY HANDS!
A PRO WHO DOUBLED AS A TOUGH GUY.
WILNER
YOU'RE LUCKY THE STORE ISN'T PRESSING CHARGES.
PUNK!
ALWAYS READY TO GO OFF THE RAILS.
COME JOIN THE FLAMES, MAN!
TONIGHT WE'RE FIGHTING THE KNIGHTS!
OK.
Black Jack
CHEWING GUM

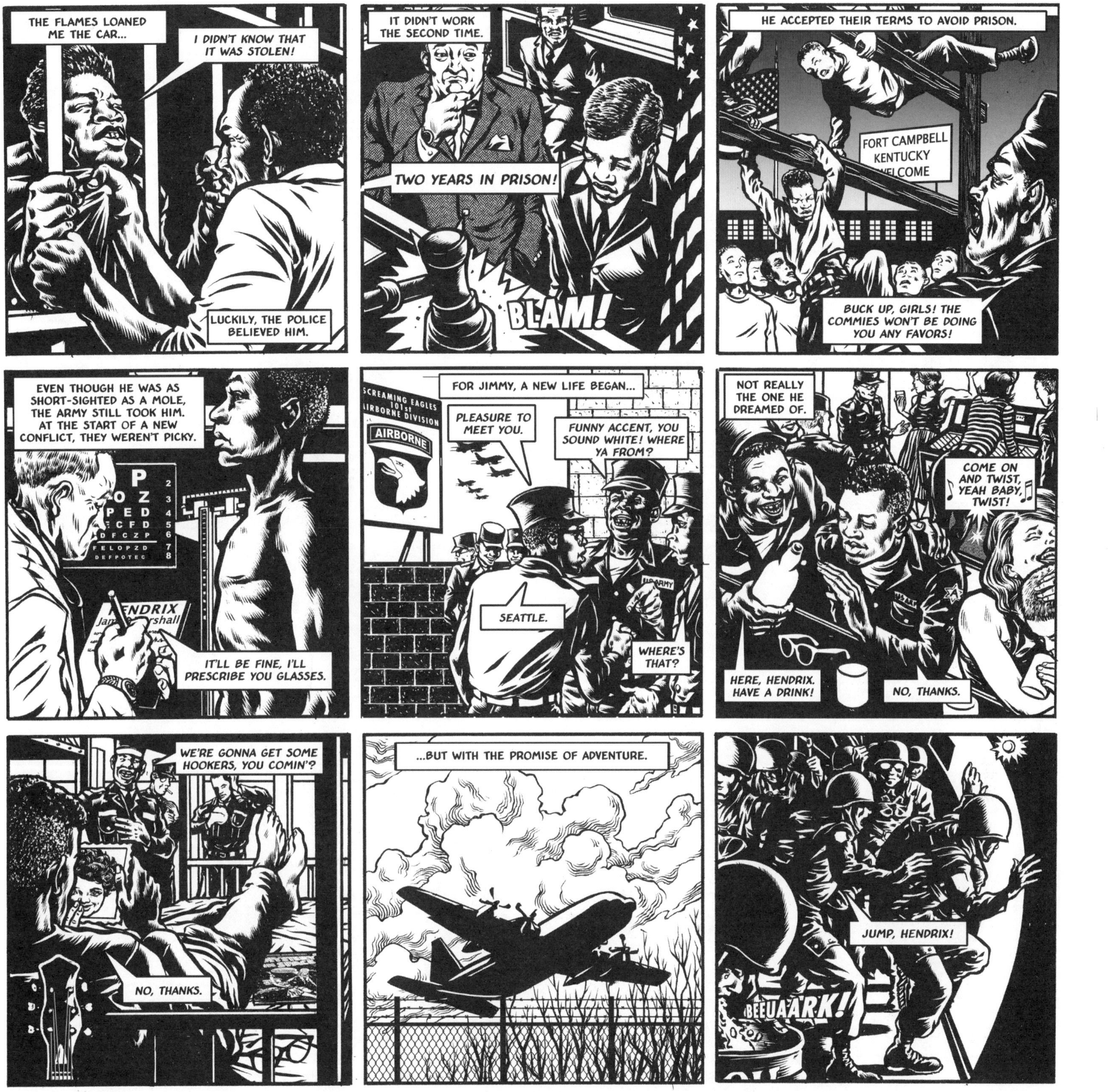

THE FLAMES LOANED ME THE CAR...
I DIDN'T KNOW THAT IT WAS STOLEN!
LUCKILY, THE POLICE BELIEVED HIM.
IT DIDN'T WORK THE SECOND TIME.
TWO YEARS IN PRISON!
BLAM!
HE ACCEPTED THEIR TERMS TO AVOID PRISON.
FORT CAMPBELL
KENTUCKY
BUCK UP, GIRLS! THE COMMIES WON'T BE DOING YOU ANY FAVORS!
EVEN THOUGH HE WAS AS SHORT-SIGHTED AS A MOLE, THE ARMY STILL TOOK HIM. AT THE START OF A NEW CONFLICT, THEY WEREN'T PICKY.
HENDRIX
IT'LL BE FINE, I'LL PRESCRIBE YOU GLASSES.
SCREAMING EAGLES 101st AIRBORNE DIVISION
AIRBORNE
FOR JIMMY, A NEW LIFE BEGAN...
PLEASURE TO MEET YOU.
FUNNY ACCENT, YOU SOUND WHITE! WHERE YA FROM?
SEATTLE.
WHERE'S THAT?
NOT REALLY THE ONE HE DREAMED OF.
COME ON AND TWIST, YEAH BABY, TWIST!
HERE, HENDRIX. HAVE A DRINK!
NO, THANKS.
WE'RE GONNA GET SOME HOOKERS, YOU COMIN'?
NO, THANKS.
...BUT WITH THE PROMISE OF ADVENTURE.
JUMP, HENDRIX!
BEEUAARK!

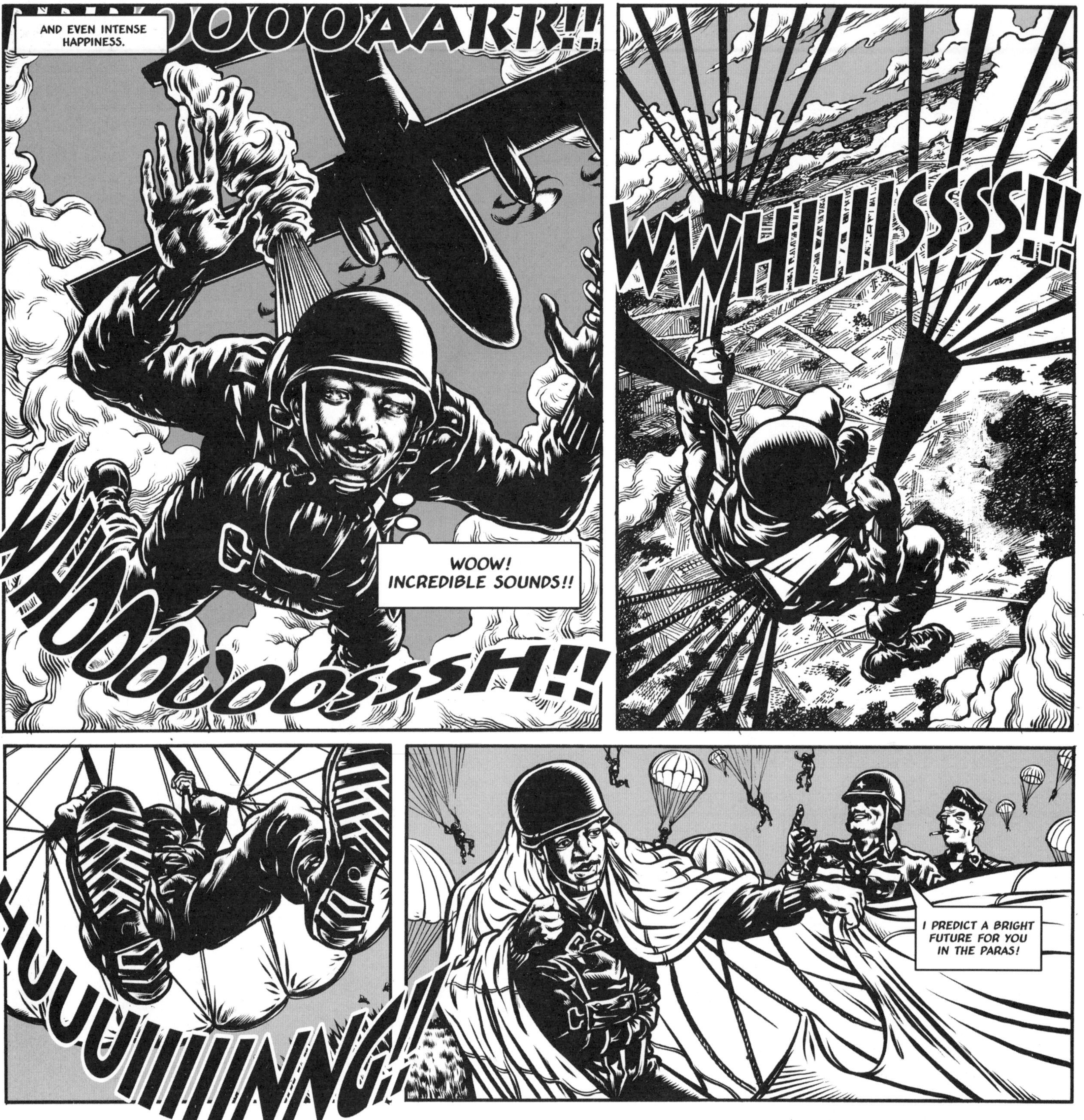
AND EVEN INTENSE HAPPINESS.
OOOOOAARR!!
WOOW! INCREDIBLE SOUNDS!!
WHOOOOOOOSSSH!!
WWHIIIIISSSS!!!
HUUUIIIIIINNG!!
I PREDICT A BRIGHT FUTURE FOR YOU IN THE PARAS!

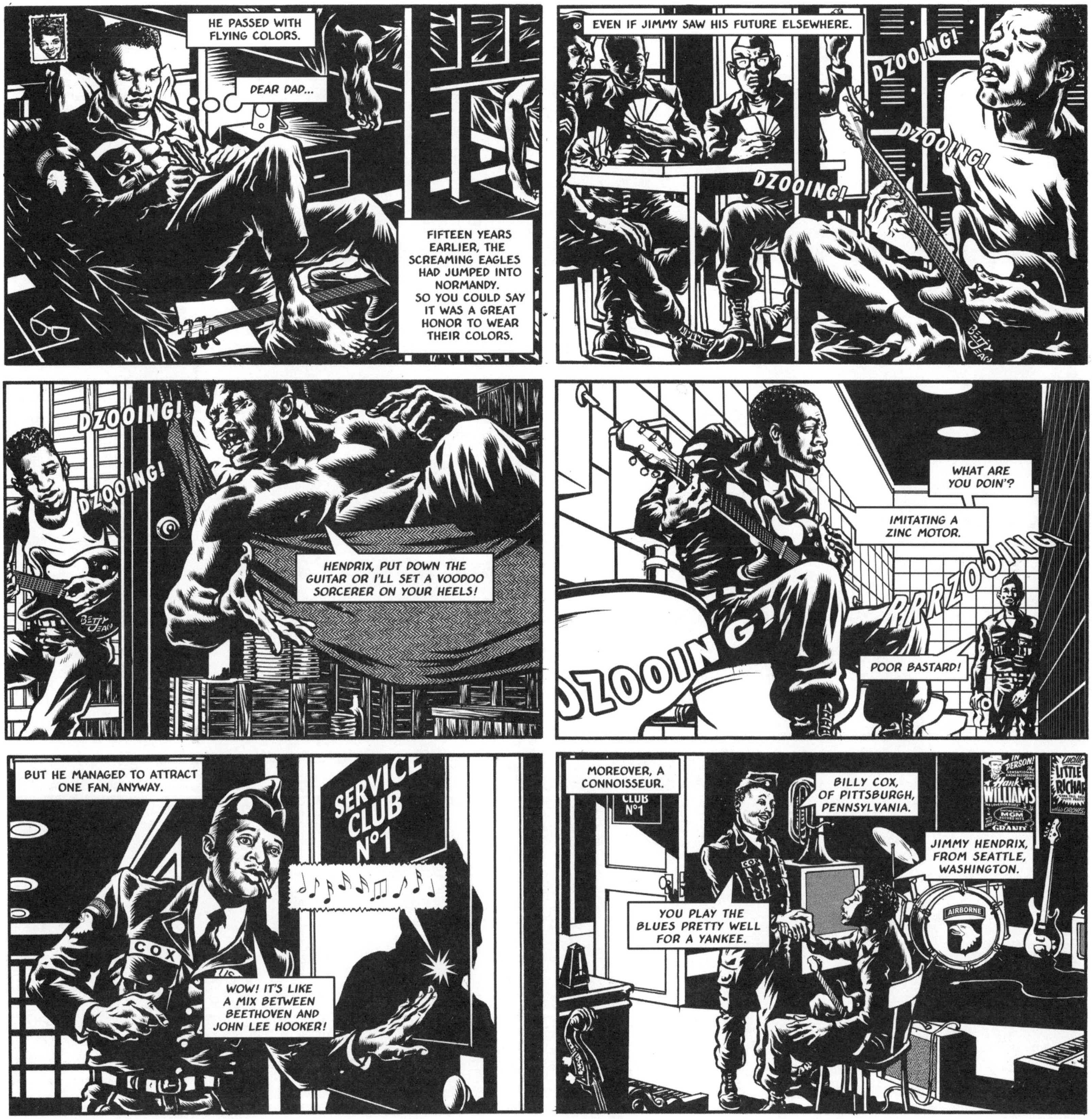
HE PASSED WITH FLYING COLORS.
DEAR DAD...
FIFTEEN YEARS EARLIER, THE SCREAMING EAGLES HAD JUMPED INTO NORMANDY. SO YOU COULD SAY IT WAS A GREAT HONOR TO WEAR THEIR COLORS.
EVEN IF JIMMY SAW HIS FUTURE ELSEWHERE.
DZOOING!
DZOOING!
DZOOING!
DZOOING!
DZOOING!
HENDRIX, PUT DOWN THE GUITAR OR I'LL SET A VOODOO SORCERER ON YOUR HEELS!
WHAT ARE YOU DOIN'?
IMITATING A ZINC MOTOR.
RRRZOOING
DZOOING
POOR BASTARD!
BUT HE MANAGED TO ATTRACT ONE FAN, ANYWAY.
SERVICE CLUB Nº1
COX
WOW! IT'S LIKE A MIX BETWEEN BEETHOVEN AND JOHN LEE HOOKER!
MOREOVER, A CONNOISSEUR.
BILLY COX, OF PITTSBURGH, PENNSYLVANIA.
JIMMY HENDRIX, FROM SEATTLE, WASHINGTON.
YOU PLAY THE BLUES PRETTY WELL FOR A YANKEE.
AIRBORNE

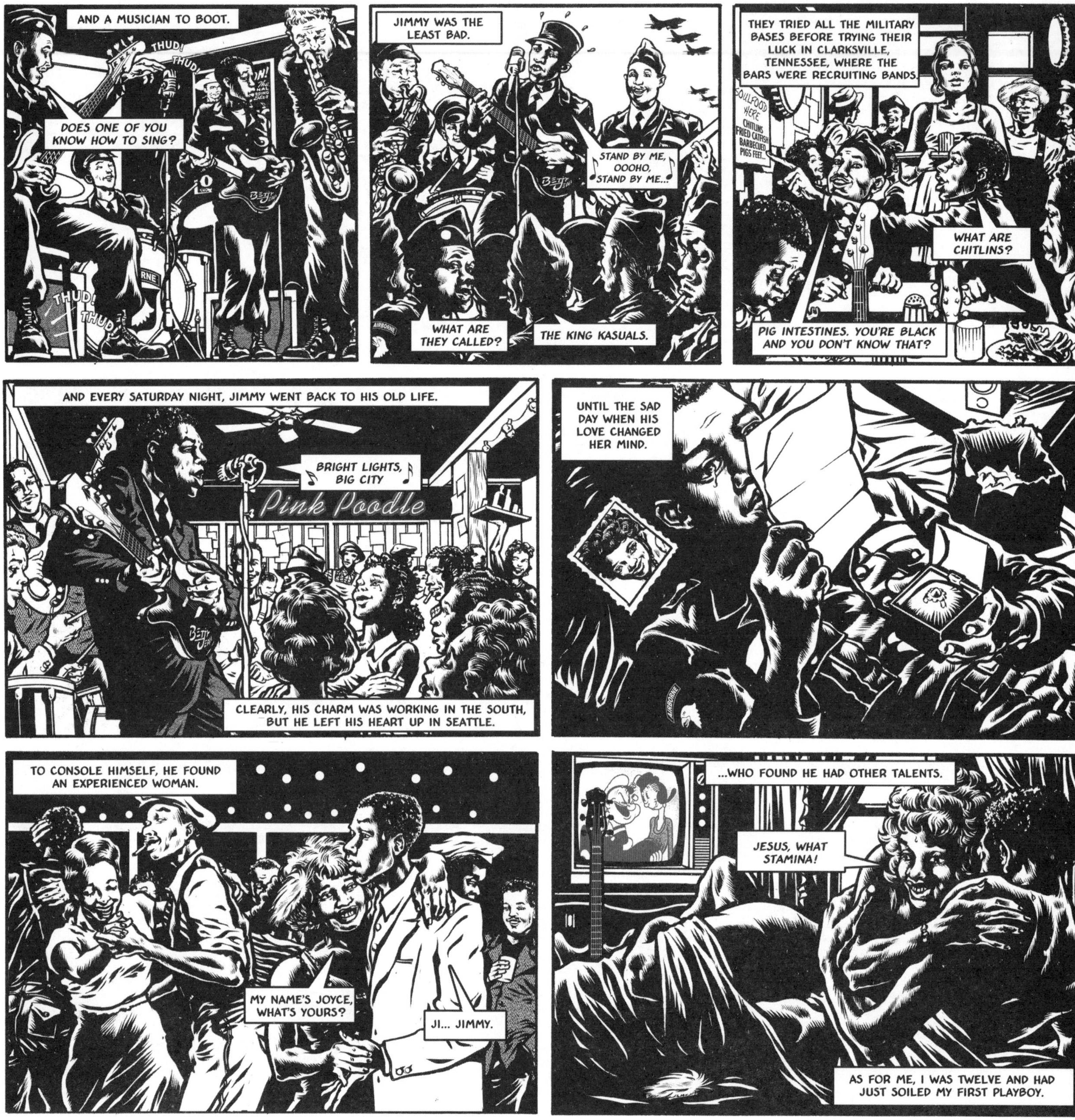
AND A MUSICIAN TO BOOT.
THUD! THUD!
DOES ONE OF YOU KNOW HOW TO SING?
THUD! THUD!
JIMMY WAS THE LEAST BAD.
STAND BY ME, OOOHO, STAND BY ME...
WHAT ARE THEY CALLED?
THE KING KASUALS.
THEY TRIED ALL THE MILITARY BASES BEFORE TRYING THEIR LUCK IN CLARKSVILLE, TENNESSEE, WHERE THE BARS WERE RECRUITING BANDS.
SOULFOOD HERE
CHITLINS FRIED CATFISH BARBECUED PIGS FEET...
WHAT ARE CHITLINS?
PIG INTESTINES. YOU'RE BLACK AND YOU DON'T KNOW THAT?
AND EVERY SATURDAY NIGHT, JIMMY WENT BACK TO HIS OLD LIFE.
BRIGHT LIGHTS, BIG CITY
Pink Poodle
CLEARLY, HIS CHARM WAS WORKING IN THE SOUTH, BUT HE LEFT HIS HEART UP IN SEATTLE.
UNTIL THE SAD DAY WHEN HIS LOVE CHANGED HER MIND.
AIRBORNE
TO CONSOLE HIMSELF, HE FOUND AN EXPERIENCED WOMAN.
MY NAME'S JOYCE, WHAT'S YOURS?
JI... JIMMY.
...WHO FOUND HE HAD OTHER TALENTS.
JESUS, WHAT STAMINA!
AS FOR ME, I WAS TWELVE AND HAD JUST SOILED MY FIRST PLAYBOY.

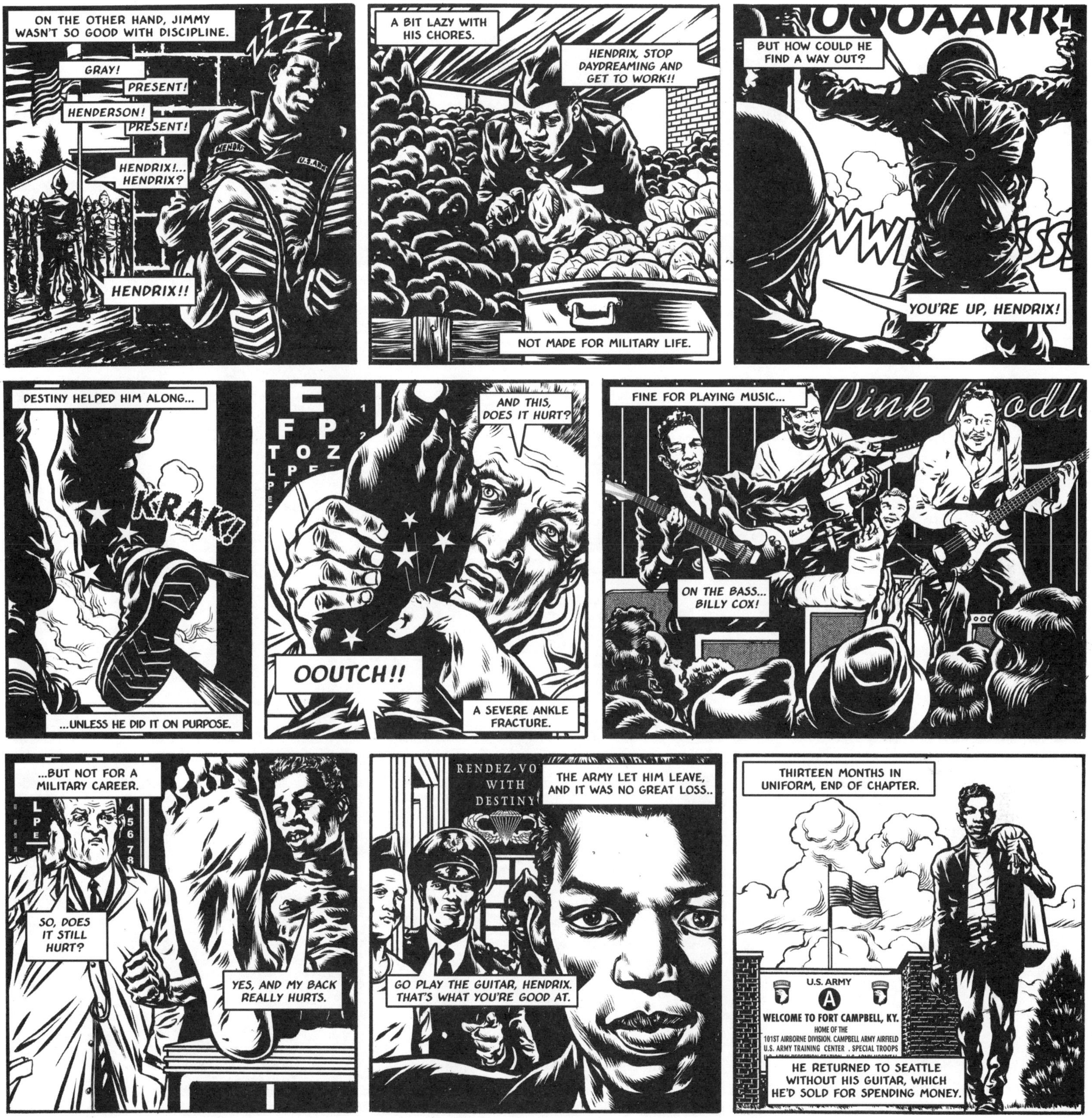

ON THE OTHER HAND, JIMMY WASN'T SO GOOD WITH DISCIPLINE.
ZZZZ...
GRAY!
PRESENT!
HENDERSON!
PRESENT!
HENDRIX!... HENDRIX?
HENDRIX!!
A BIT LAZY WITH HIS CHORES.
HENDRIX, STOP DAYDREAMING AND GET TO WORK!!
NOT MADE FOR MILITARY LIFE.
BUT HOW COULD HE FIND A WAY OUT?
YOU'RE UP, HENDRIX!
DESTINY HELPED HIM ALONG...
KRAK!
...UNLESS HE DID IT ON PURPOSE.
AND THIS, DOES IT HURT?
OOUTCH!!
A SEVERE ANKLE FRACTURE.
FINE FOR PLAYING MUSIC...
ON THE BASS... BILLY COX!
...BUT NOT FOR A MILITARY CAREER.
SO, DOES IT STILL HURT?
YES, AND MY BACK REALLY HURTS.
RENDEZ-VO WITH DESTINY
THE ARMY LET HIM LEAVE, AND IT WAS NO GREAT LOSS..
GO PLAY THE GUITAR, HENDRIX. THAT'S WHAT YOU'RE GOOD AT.
THIRTEEN MONTHS IN UNIFORM, END OF CHAPTER.
U.S. ARMY
WELCOME TO FORT CAMPBELL, KY.
HOME OF THE
101ST AIRBORNE DIVISION. CAMPBELL ARMY AIRFIELD
U.S. ARMY TRAINING CENTER . SPECIAL TROOPS
HE RETURNED TO SEATTLE WITHOUT HIS GUITAR, WHICH HE'D SOLD FOR SPENDING MONEY.

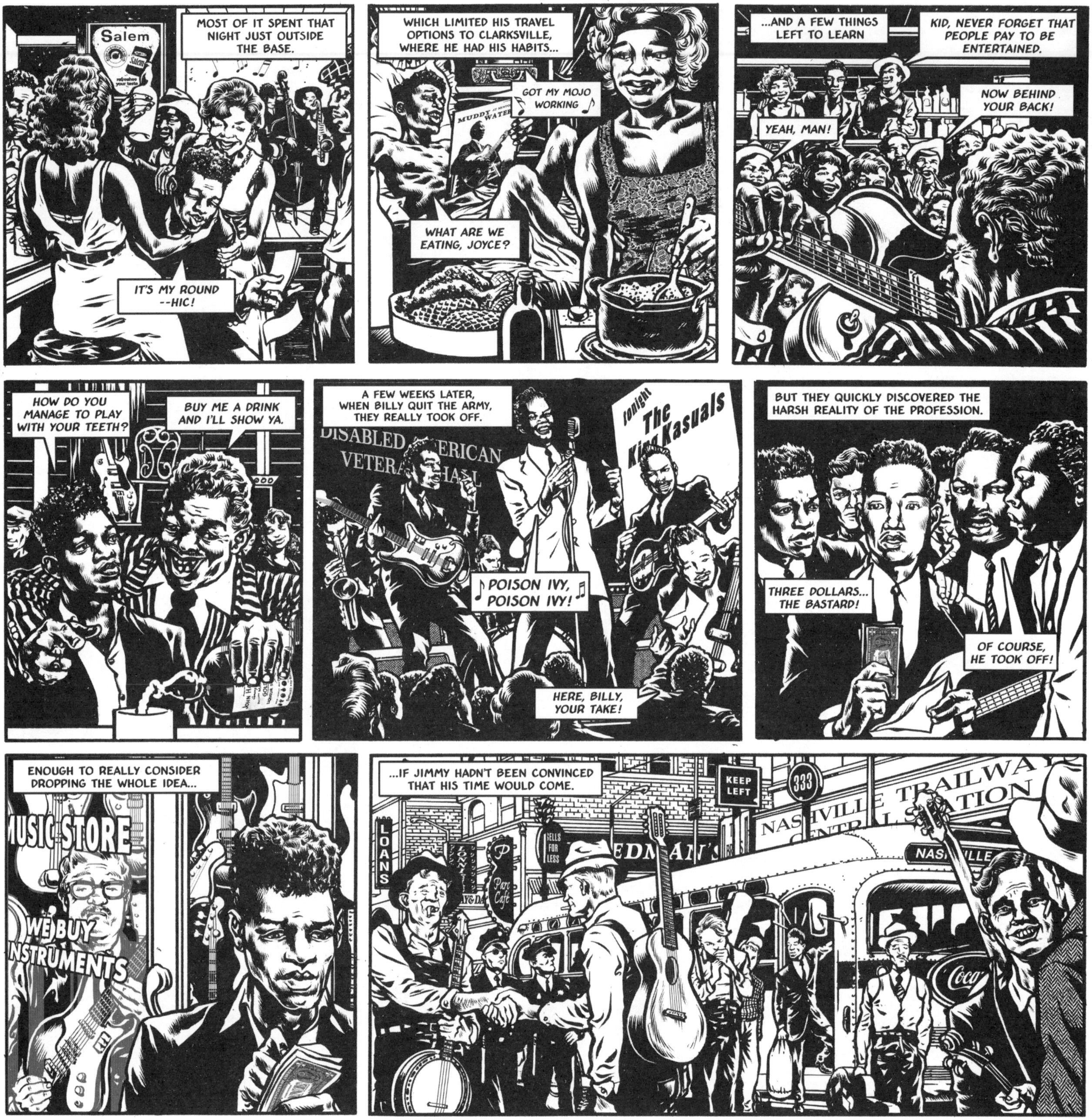
MOST OF IT SPENT THAT NIGHT JUST OUTSIDE THE BASE.
Salem
IT'S MY ROUND --HIC!
WHICH LIMITED HIS TRAVEL OPTIONS TO CLARKSVILLE, WHERE HE HAD HIS HABITS...
GOT MY MOJO WORKING
WHAT ARE WE EATING, JOYCE?
...AND A FEW THINGS LEFT TO LEARN
KID, NEVER FORGET THAT PEOPLE PAY TO BE ENTERTAINED.
NOW BEHIND YOUR BACK!
YEAH, MAN!
HOW DO YOU MANAGE TO PLAY WITH YOUR TEETH?
BUY ME A DRINK AND I'LL SHOW YA.
A FEW WEEKS LATER, WHEN BILLY QUIT THE ARMY, THEY REALLY TOOK OFF.
tonight The King Kasuals
POISON IVY, POISON IVY!
HERE, BILLY, YOUR TAKE!
BUT THEY QUICKLY DISCOVERED THE HARSH REALITY OF THE PROFESSION.
THREE DOLLARS... THE BASTARD!
OF COURSE, HE TOOK OFF!
ENOUGH TO REALLY CONSIDER DROPPING THE WHOLE IDEA...
MUSIC STORE
WE BUY INSTRUMENTS
...IF JIMMY HADN'T BEEN CONVINCED THAT HIS TIME WOULD COME.
KEEP LEFT
333
LOANS
NASHVILLE

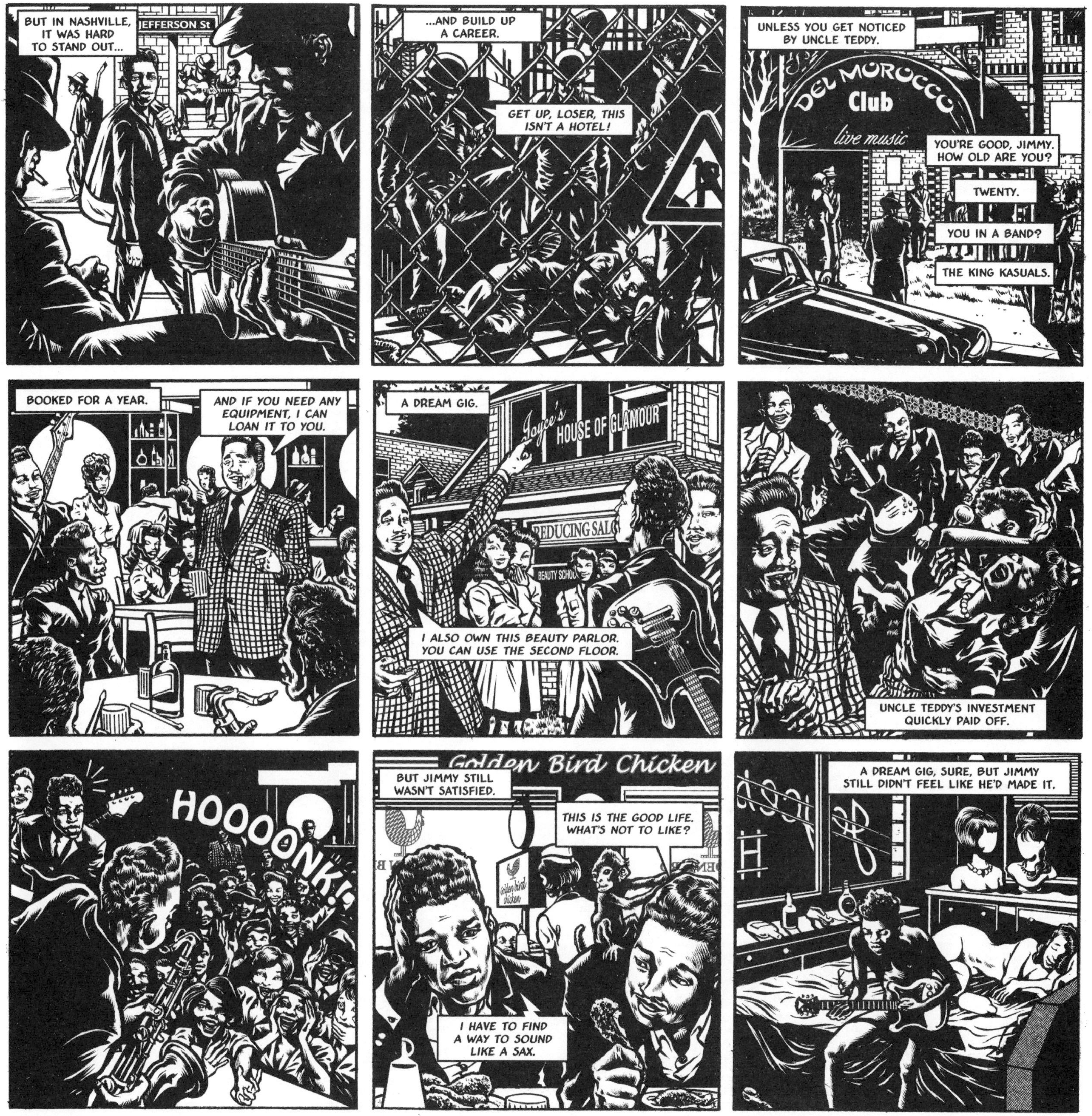
BUT IN NASHVILLE, IT WAS HARD TO STAND OUT...
JEFFERSON St
...AND BUILD UP A CAREER.
GET UP, LOSER, THIS ISN'T A HOTEL!
UNLESS YOU GET NOTICED BY UNCLE TEDDY.
DEL MOROCCO Club
live music
YOU'RE GOOD, JIMMY. HOW OLD ARE YOU?
TWENTY.
YOU IN A BAND?
THE KING KASUALS.
BOOKED FOR A YEAR.
AND IF YOU NEED ANY EQUIPMENT, I CAN LOAN IT TO YOU.
A DREAM GIG.
Joyce's HOUSE OF GLAMOUR
I ALSO OWN THIS BEAUTY PARLOR. YOU CAN USE THE SECOND FLOOR.
UNCLE TEDDY'S INVESTMENT QUICKLY PAID OFF.
HOOOONK!
Golden Bird Chicken
BUT JIMMY STILL WASN'T SATISFIED.
THIS IS THE GOOD LIFE. WHAT'S NOT TO LIKE?
golden bird chicken
I HAVE TO FIND A WAY TO SOUND LIKE A SAX.
A DREAM GIG, SURE, BUT JIMMY STILL DIDN'T FEEL LIKE HE'D MADE IT.

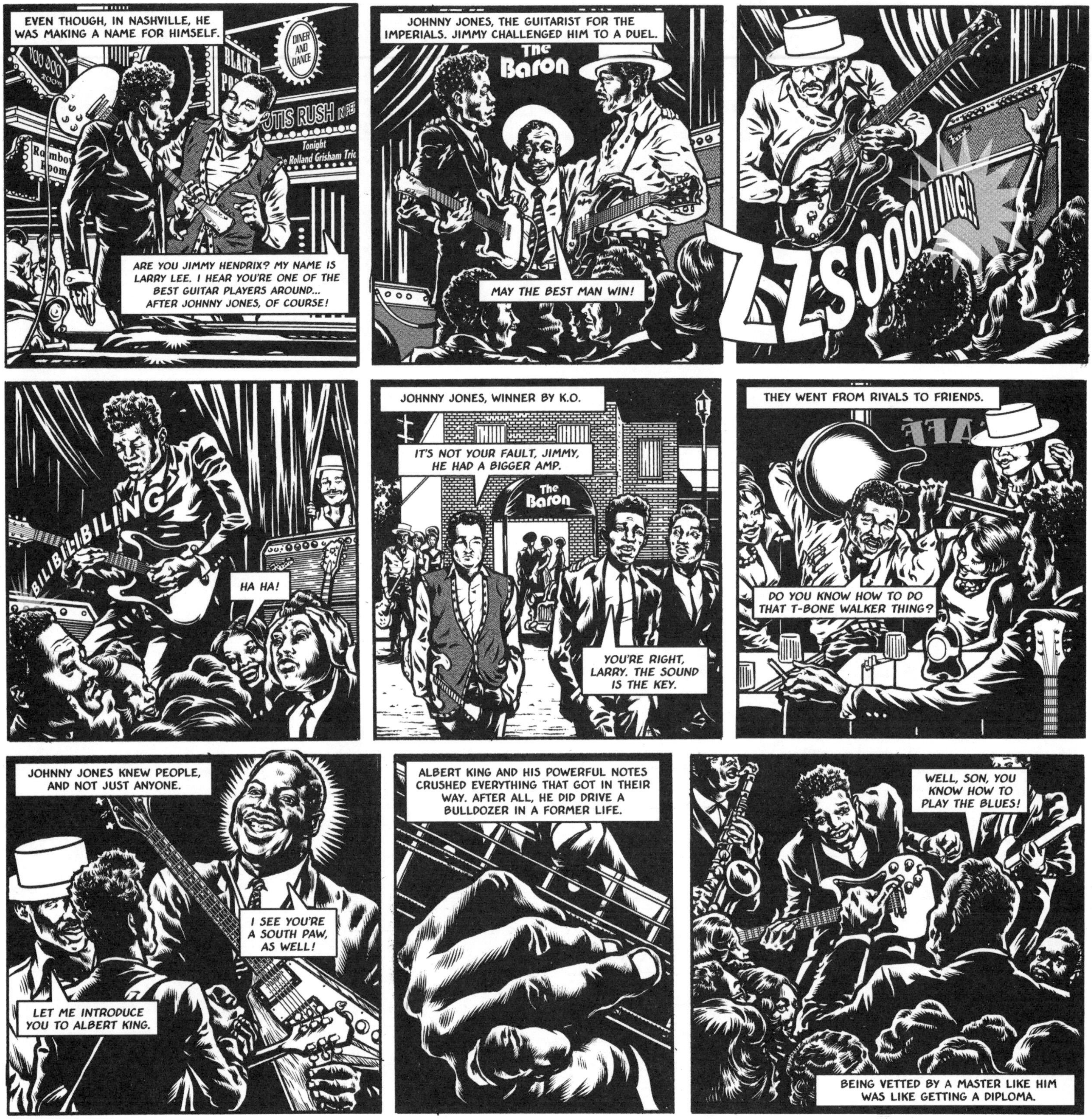
EVEN THOUGH, IN NASHVILLE, HE WAS MAKING A NAME FOR HIMSELF.
DINER AND DANCE
Tonight
ARE YOU JIMMY HENDRIX? MY NAME IS LARRY LEE. I HEAR YOU'RE ONE OF THE BEST GUITAR PLAYERS AROUND... AFTER JOHNNY JONES, OF COURSE!
JOHNNY JONES, THE GUITARIST FOR THE IMPERIALS. JIMMY CHALLENGED HIM TO A DUEL.
The Baron
MAY THE BEST MAN WIN!
ZZSOOOIIING!!
BILIBILIBILING
HA HA!
JOHNNY JONES, WINNER BY K.O.
IT'S NOT YOUR FAULT, JIMMY, HE HAD A BIGGER AMP.
The Baron
YOU'RE RIGHT, LARRY. THE SOUND IS THE KEY.
THEY WENT FROM RIVALS TO FRIENDS.
DO YOU KNOW HOW TO DO THAT T-BONE WALKER THING?
JOHNNY JONES KNEW PEOPLE, AND NOT JUST ANYONE.
I SEE YOU'RE A SOUTH PAW, AS WELL!
LET ME INTRODUCE YOU TO ALBERT KING.
ALBERT KING AND HIS POWERFUL NOTES CRUSHED EVERYTHING THAT GOT IN THEIR WAY. AFTER ALL, HE DID DRIVE A BULLDOZER IN A FORMER LIFE.
WELL, SON, YOU KNOW HOW TO PLAY THE BLUES!
BEING VETTED BY A MASTER LIKE HIM WAS LIKE GETTING A DIPLOMA.

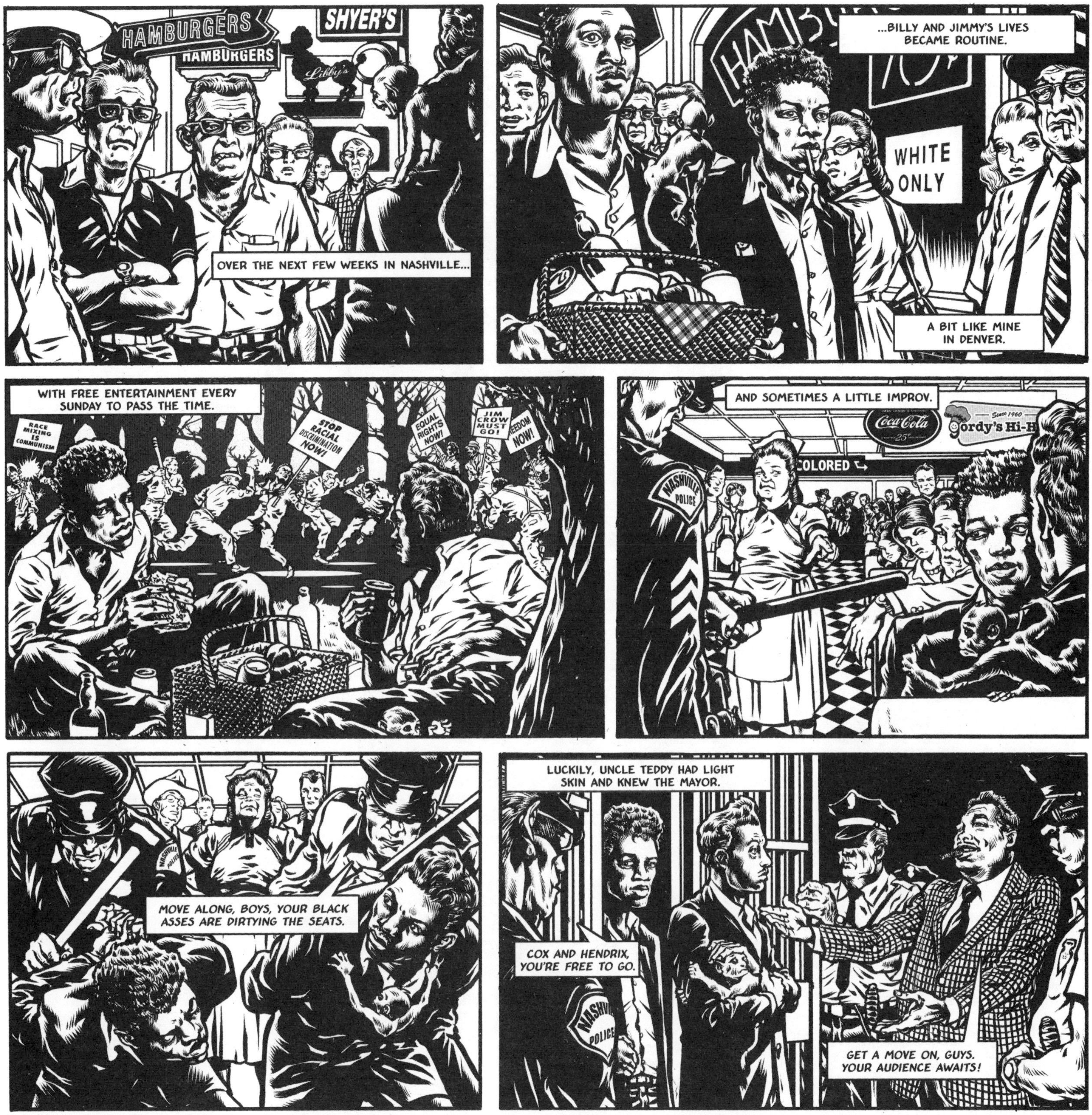
HAMBURGERS
HAMBURGERS
SHYER'S
OVER THE NEXT FEW WEEKS IN NASHVILLE...
...BILLY AND JIMMY'S LIVES BECAME ROUTINE.
WHITE ONLY
A BIT LIKE MINE IN DENVER.
WITH FREE ENTERTAINMENT EVERY SUNDAY TO PASS THE TIME.
RACE MIXING IS COMMUNISM
STOP RACIAL DISCRIMINATION NOW!
EQUAL RIGHTS NOW!
JIM CROW MUST GO!
AND SOMETIMES A LITTLE IMPROV.
Coca-Cola
Since 1960
COLORED
NASHVILLE POLICE
MOVE ALONG, BOYS, YOUR BLACK ASSES ARE DIRTYING THE SEATS.
LUCKILY, UNCLE TEDDY HAD LIGHT SKIN AND KNEW THE MAYOR.
COX AND HENDRIX, YOU'RE FREE TO GO.
GET A MOVE ON, GUYS. YOUR AUDIENCE AWAITS!

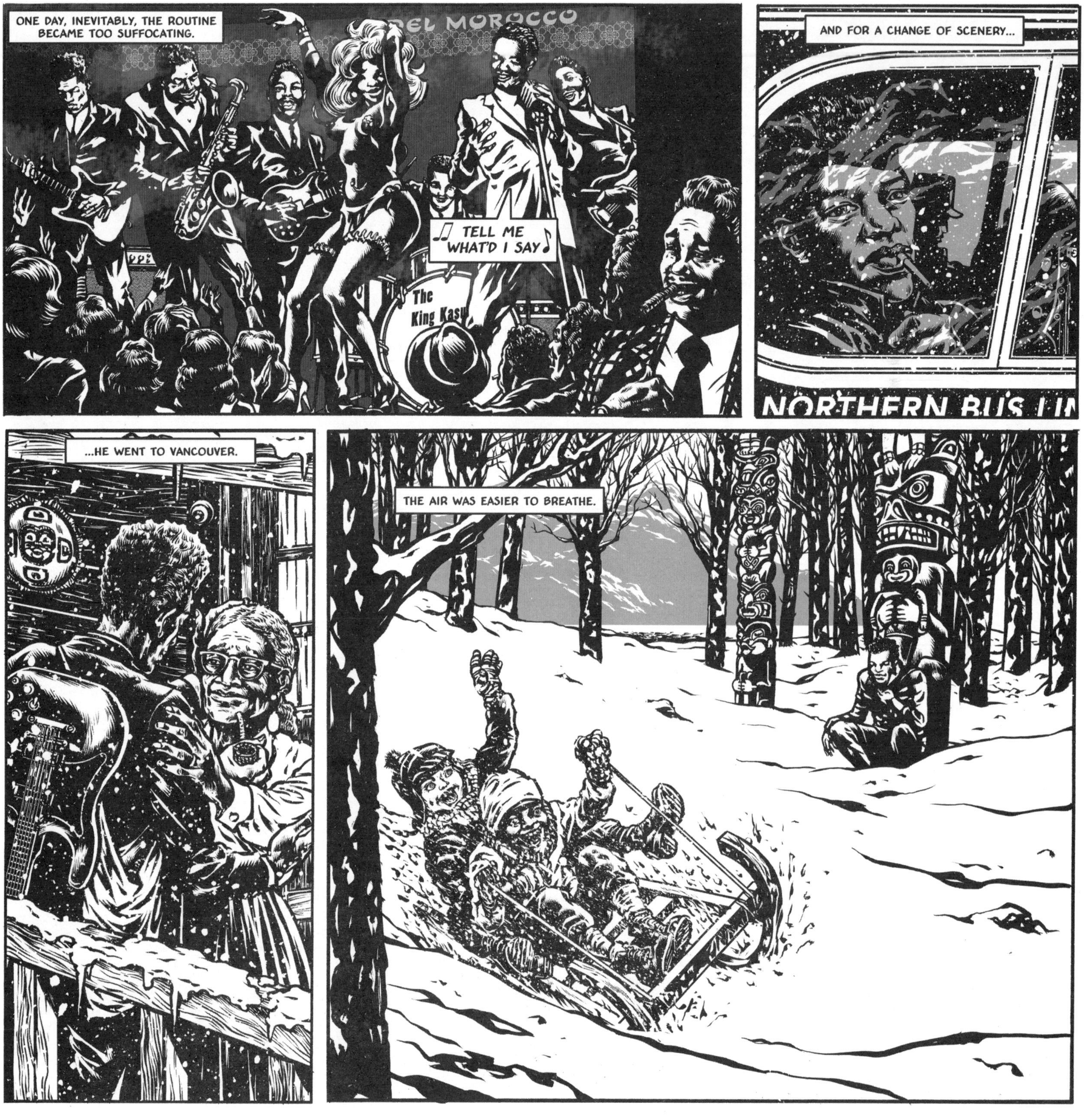
ONE DAY, INEVITABLY, THE ROUTINE BECAME TOO SUFFOCATING.
TELL ME WHAT'D I SAY
AND FOR A CHANGE OF SCENERY...
NORTHERN BUS LIN
...HE WENT TO VANCOUVER.
THE AIR WAS EASIER TO BREATHE.

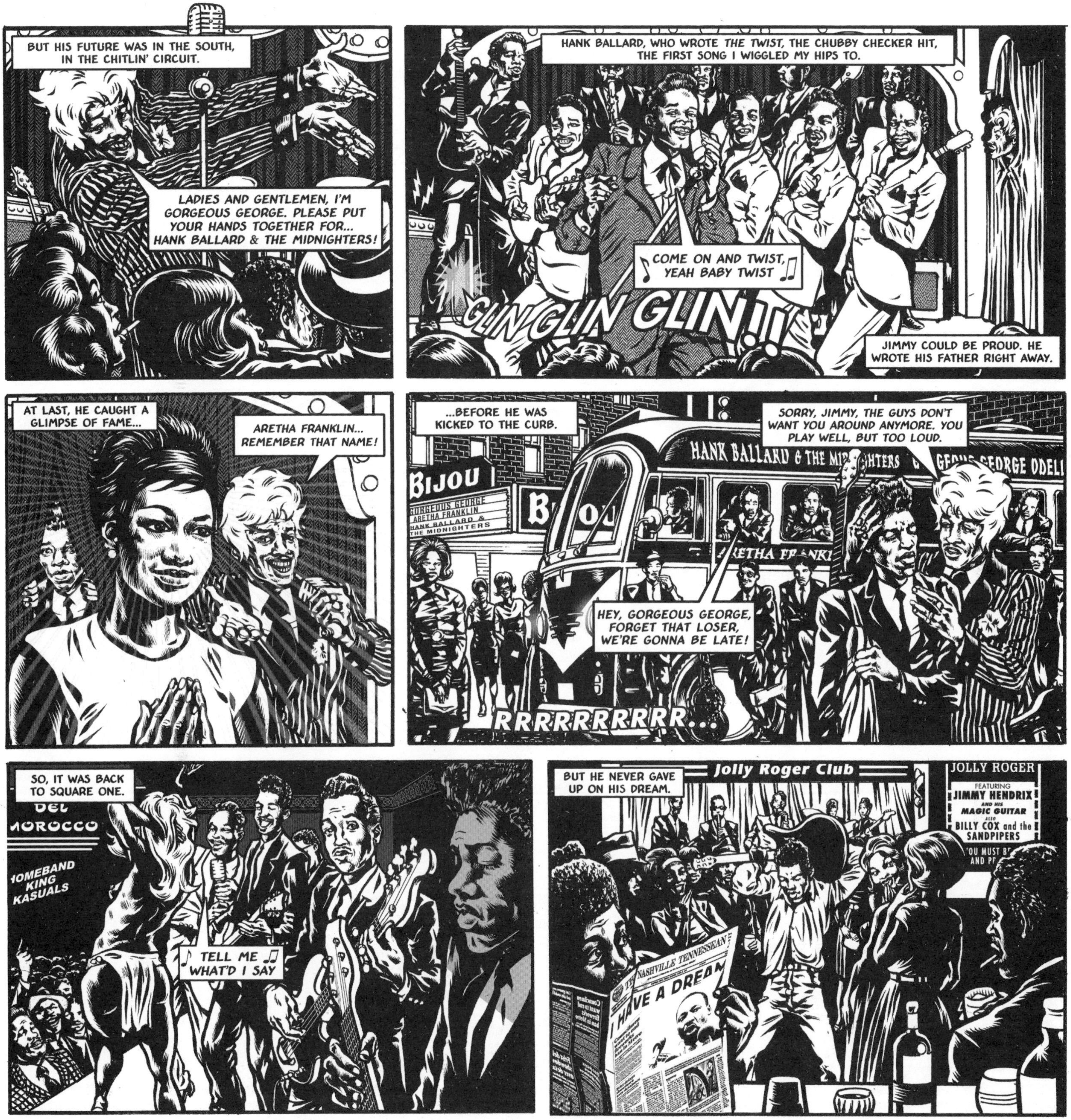
BUT HIS FUTURE WAS IN THE SOUTH, IN THE CHITLIN' CIRCUIT.
LADIES AND GENTLEMEN, I'M GORGEOUS GEORGE. PLEASE PUT YOUR HANDS TOGETHER FOR... HANK BALLARD & THE MIDNIGHTERS!
HANK BALLARD, WHO WROTE *THE TWIST*, THE CHUBBY CHECKER HIT, THE FIRST SONG I WIGGLED MY HIPS TO.
♪ COME ON AND TWIST, YEAH BABY TWIST ♫
GLIN GLIN GLIN!!!
JIMMY COULD BE PROUD. HE WROTE HIS FATHER RIGHT AWAY.
AT LAST, HE CAUGHT A GLIMPSE OF FAME...
ARETHA FRANKLIN... REMEMBER THAT NAME!
...BEFORE HE WAS KICKED TO THE CURB.
BIJOU
GORGEOUS GEORGE
ARETHA FRANKLIN
HANK BALLARD & THE MIDNIGHTERS
HANK BALLARD & THE MIDNIGHTERS
SORRY, JIMMY, THE GUYS DON'T WANT YOU AROUND ANYMORE. YOU PLAY WELL, BUT TOO LOUD.
HEY, GORGEOUS GEORGE, FORGET THAT LOSER, WE'RE GONNA BE LATE!
RRRRRRRRRRR...
SO, IT WAS BACK TO SQUARE ONE.
DEL MOROCCO
HOMEBAND
KING KASUALS
♪ TELL ME ♫ WHAT'D I SAY
BUT HE NEVER GAVE UP ON HIS DREAM.
Jolly Roger Club
JOLLY ROGER
FEATURING
JIMMY HENDRIX
AND HIS
MAGIC GUITAR
ALSO
BILLY COX and the SANDPIPERS
NASHVILLE TENNESSEAN
I HAVE A DREAM

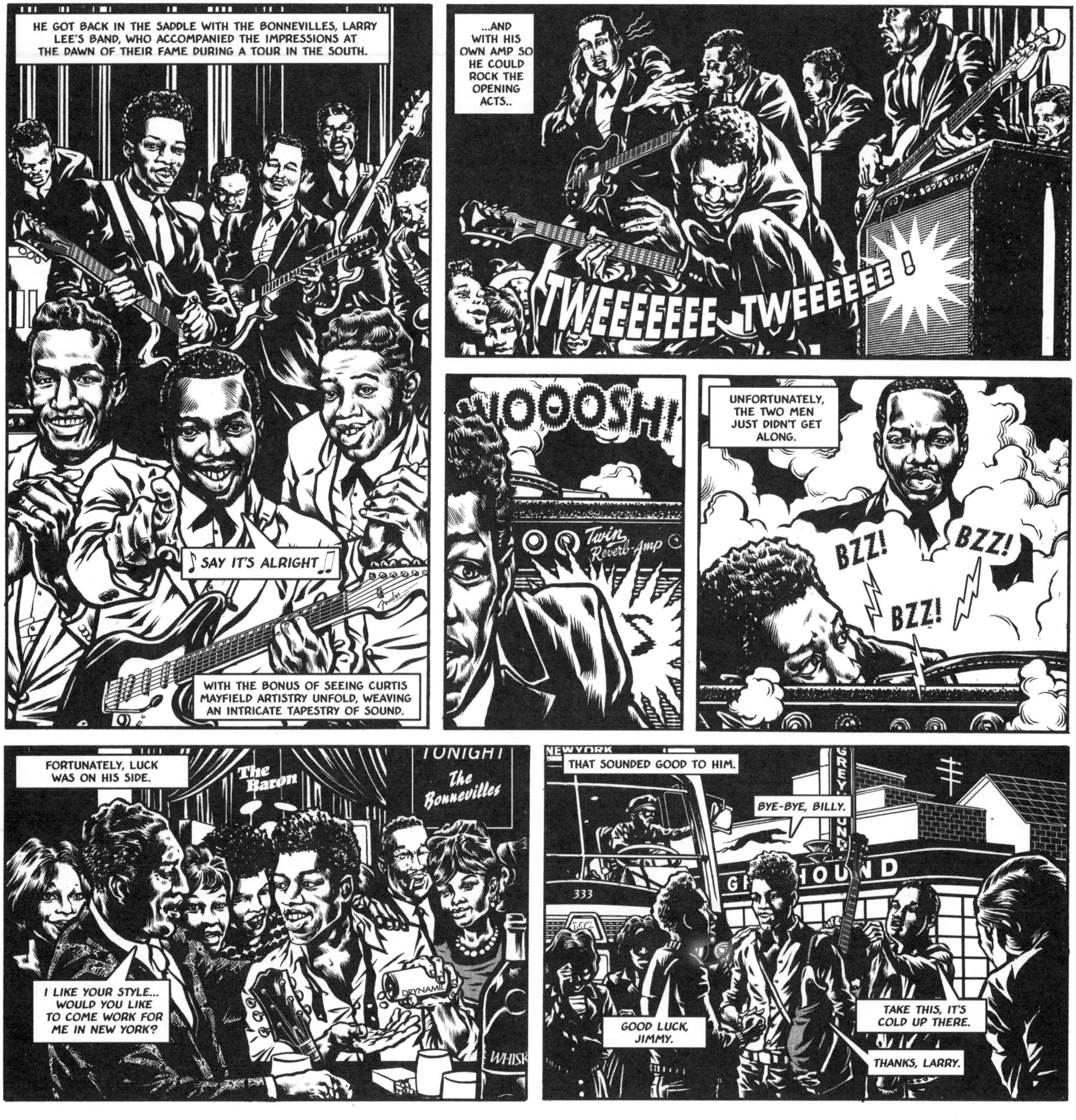

HE GOT BACK IN THE SADDLE WITH THE BONNEVILLES, LARRY LEE'S BAND, WHO ACCOMPANIED THE IMPRESSIONS AT THE DAWN OF THEIR FAME DURING A TOUR IN THE SOUTH.
♪ SAY IT'S ALRIGHT ♫
WITH THE BONUS OF SEEING CURTIS MAYFIELD ARTISTRY UNFOLD, WEAVING AN INTRICATE TAPESTRY OF SOUND.
...AND WITH HIS OWN AMP SO HE COULD ROCK THE OPENING ACTS..
TWEEEEEEE... TWEEEEEEE!
Twin Reverb-Amp
UNFORTUNATELY, THE TWO MEN JUST DIDN'T GET ALONG.
BZZ!
BZZ!
BZZ!
FORTUNATELY, LUCK WAS ON HIS SIDE.
The Baron
TONIGHT The Bonnevilles
I LIKE YOUR STYLE... WOULD YOU LIKE TO COME WORK FOR ME IN NEW YORK?
THAT SOUNDED GOOD TO HIM.
BYE-BYE, BILLY.
333
GREYHOUND
GOOD LUCK, JIMMY.
TAKE THIS, IT'S COLD UP THERE.
THANKS, LARRY.

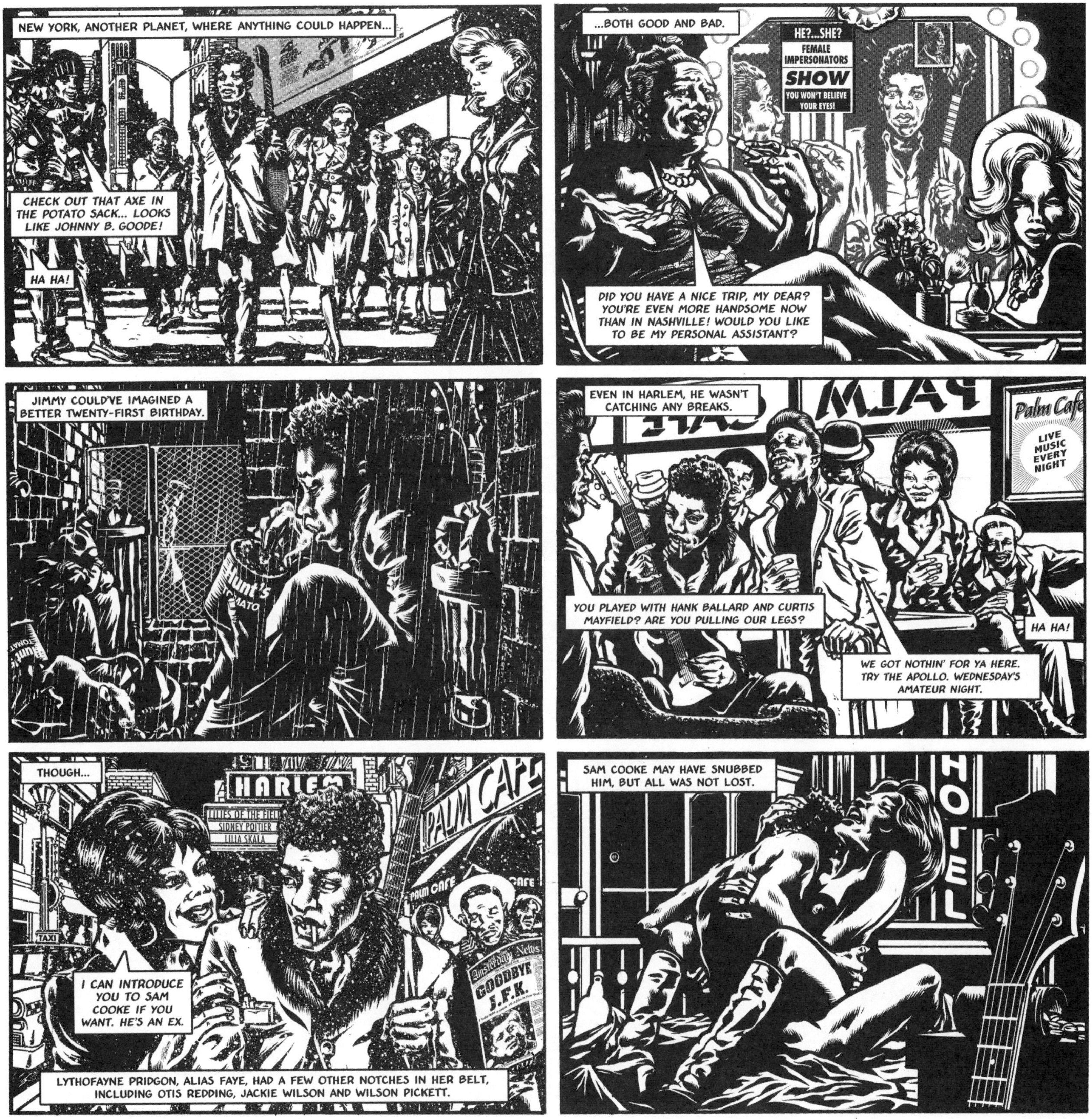
NEW YORK, ANOTHER PLANET, WHERE ANYTHING COULD HAPPEN...
CHECK OUT THAT AXE IN THE POTATO SACK... LOOKS LIKE JOHNNY B. GOODE!
HA HA!
...BOTH GOOD AND BAD.
HE?...SHE?
FEMALE IMPERSONATORS
SHOW
YOU WON'T BELIEVE YOUR EYES!
DID YOU HAVE A NICE TRIP, MY DEAR? YOU'RE EVEN MORE HANDSOME NOW THAN IN NASHVILLE! WOULD YOU LIKE TO BE MY PERSONAL ASSISTANT?
JIMMY COULD'VE IMAGINED A BETTER TWENTY-FIRST BIRTHDAY.
EVEN IN HARLEM, HE WASN'T CATCHING ANY BREAKS.
Palm Cafe
LIVE MUSIC EVERY NIGHT
YOU PLAYED WITH HANK BALLARD AND CURTIS MAYFIELD? ARE YOU PULLING OUR LEGS?
HA HA!
WE GOT NOTHIN' FOR YA HERE. TRY THE APOLLO. WEDNESDAY'S AMATEUR NIGHT.
THOUGH...
HARLEM
LILIES OF THE FIELD
SIDNEY POITIER
LILIA SKALA
PALM CAFE
TAXI
I CAN INTRODUCE YOU TO SAM COOKE IF YOU WANT. HE'S AN EX.
GOODBYE J.F.K.
LYTHOFAYNE PRIDGON, ALIAS FAYE, HAD A FEW OTHER NOTCHES IN HER BELT, INCLUDING OTIS REDDING, JACKIE WILSON AND WILSON PICKETT.
SAM COOKE MAY HAVE SNUBBED HIM, BUT ALL WAS NOT LOST.
HOTEL

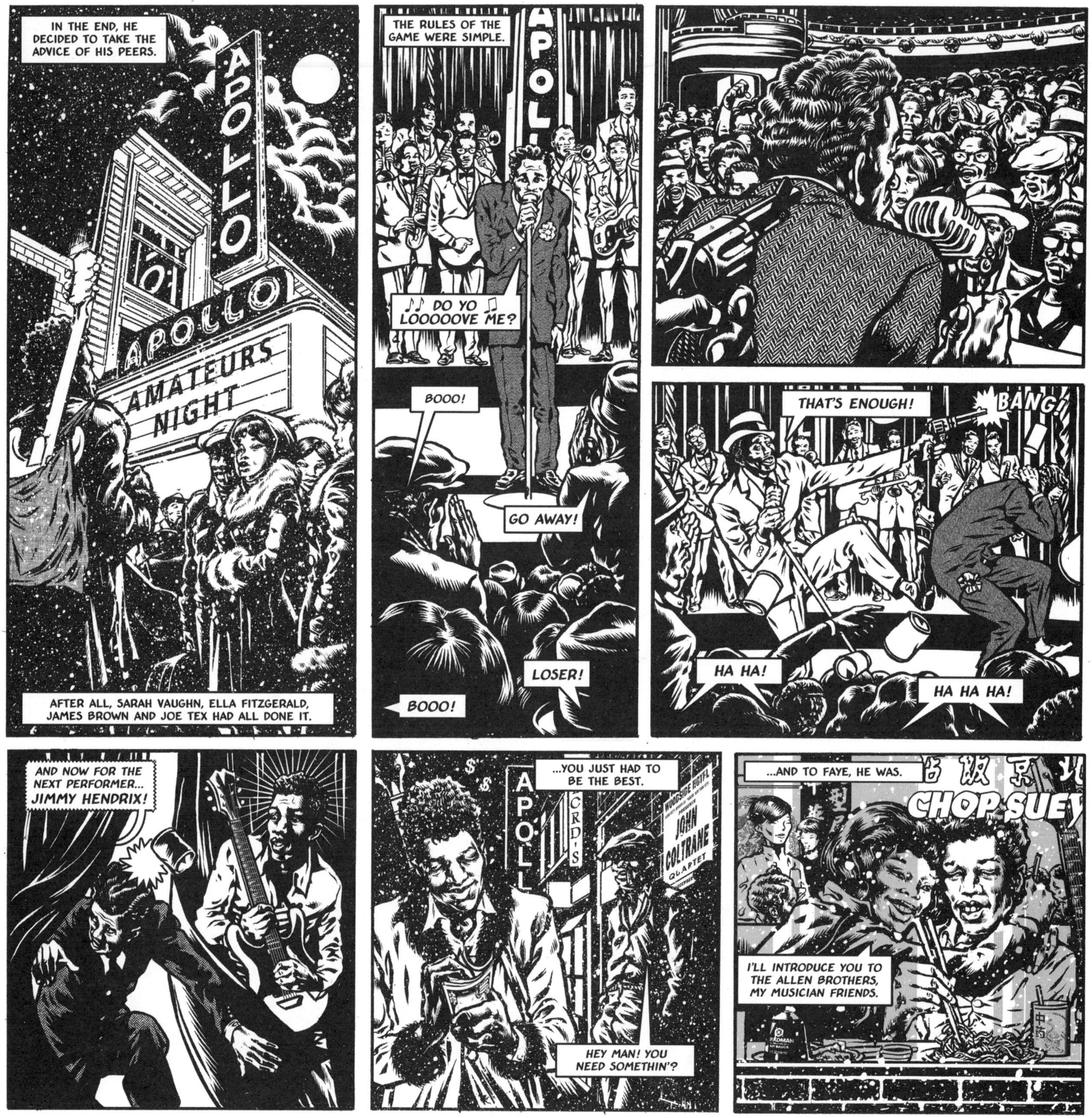
IN THE END, HE DECIDED TO TAKE THE ADVICE OF HIS PEERS.
APOLLO
APOLLO
AMATEURS NIGHT
AFTER ALL, SARAH VAUGHN, ELLA FITZGERALD, JAMES BROWN AND JOE TEX HAD ALL DONE IT.
THE RULES OF THE GAME WERE SIMPLE.
♪♪ DO YO ♫ LOOOOOVE ME?
BOOO!
GO AWAY!
LOSER!
BOOO!
THAT'S ENOUGH!
BANG!
HA HA!
HA HA HA!
AND NOW FOR THE NEXT PERFORMER... JIMMY HENDRIX!
...YOU JUST HAD TO BE THE BEST.
JOHN COLTRANE QUARTET
HEY MAN! YOU NEED SOMETHIN'?
...AND TO FAYE, HE WAS.
CHOP SUEY
I'LL INTRODUCE YOU TO THE ALLEN BROTHERS, MY MUSICIAN FRIENDS.

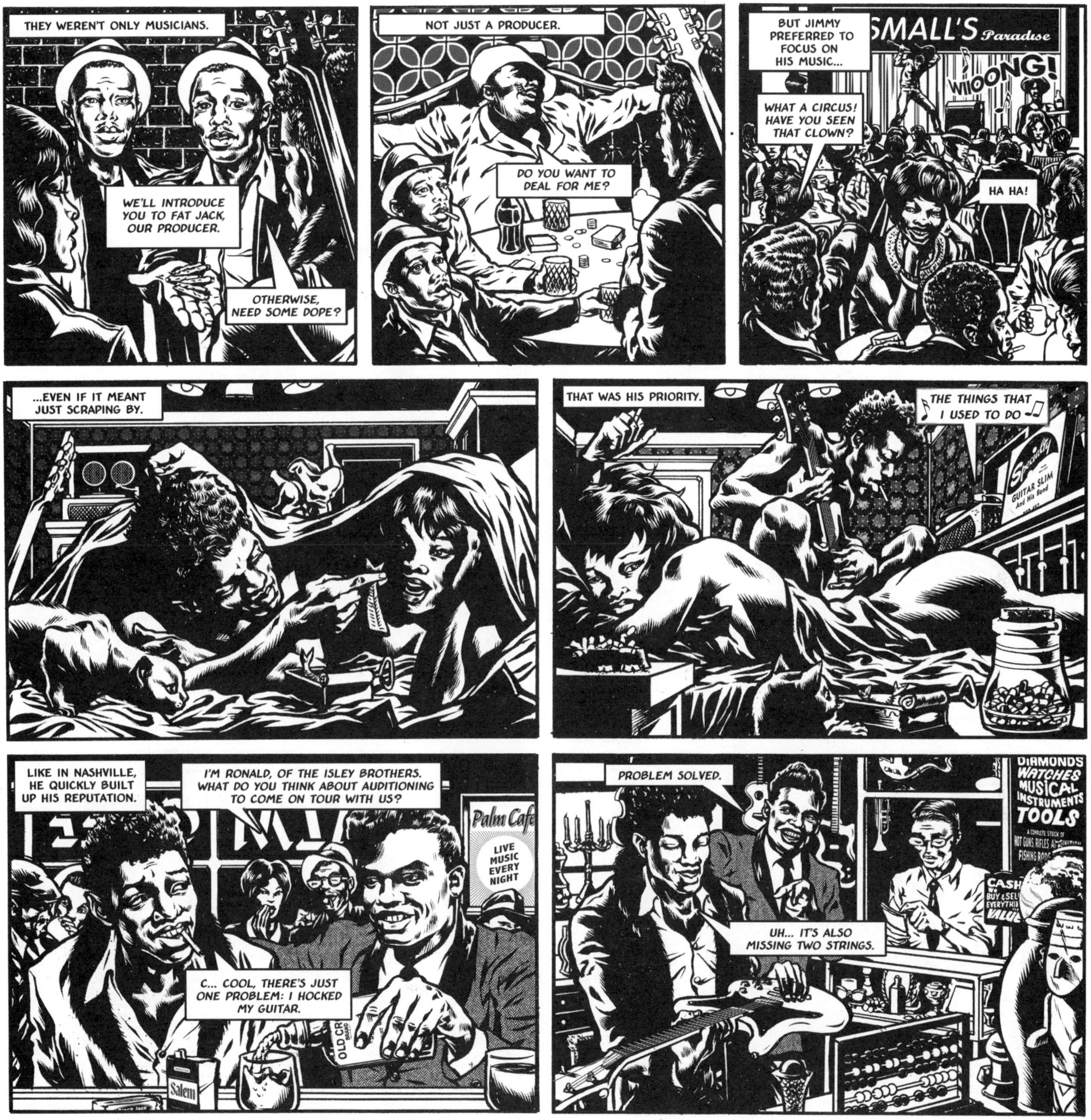
THEY WEREN'T ONLY MUSICIANS.
WE'LL INTRODUCE YOU TO FAT JACK, OUR PRODUCER.
OTHERWISE, NEED SOME DOPE?
NOT JUST A PRODUCER.
DO YOU WANT TO DEAL FOR ME?
BUT JIMMY PREFERRED TO FOCUS ON HIS MUSIC...
SMALL'S Paradise
WIOONG!
WHAT A CIRCUS! HAVE YOU SEEN THAT CLOWN?
HA HA!
...EVEN IF IT MEANT JUST SCRAPING BY.
THAT WAS HIS PRIORITY.
THE THINGS THAT I USED TO DO
Specialty
GUITAR SLIM And His Band
LIKE IN NASHVILLE, HE QUICKLY BUILT UP HIS REPUTATION.
I'M RONALD, OF THE ISLEY BROTHERS. WHAT DO YOU THINK ABOUT AUDITIONING TO COME ON TOUR WITH US?
Palm Cafe
LIVE MUSIC EVERY NIGHT
C... COOL, THERE'S JUST ONE PROBLEM: I HOCKED MY GUITAR.
Salem
PROBLEM SOLVED.
DIAMONDS WATCHES MUSICAL INSTRUMENTS TOOLS
UH... IT'S ALSO MISSING TWO STRINGS.

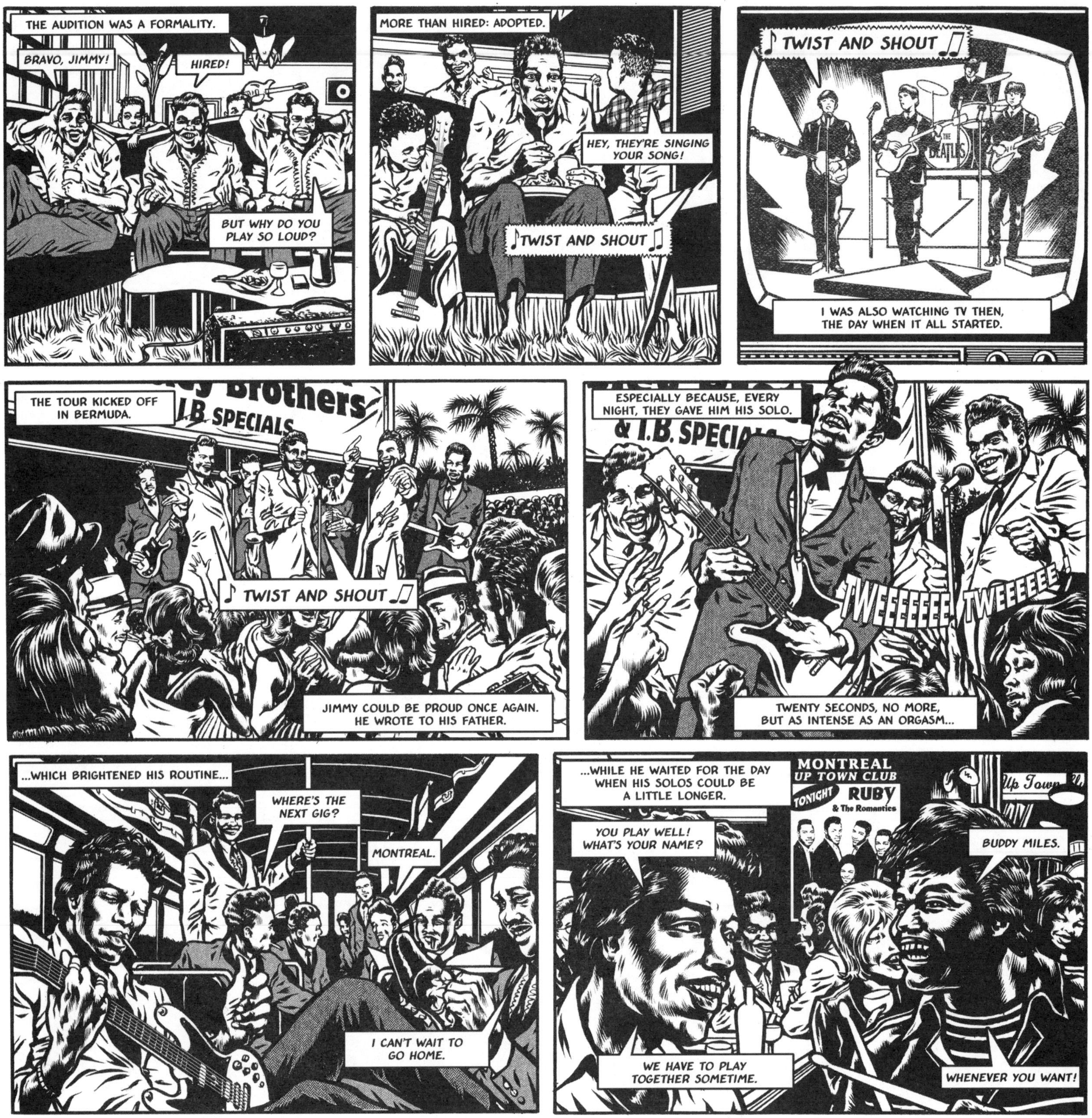

THE AUDITION WAS A FORMALITY.
BRAVO, JIMMY!
HIRED!
BUT WHY DO YOU PLAY SO LOUD?
MORE THAN HIRED: ADOPTED.
HEY, THEY'RE SINGING YOUR SONG!
♪TWIST AND SHOUT♫
♪ TWIST AND SHOUT ♫
THE BEATLES
I WAS ALSO WATCHING TV THEN, THE DAY WHEN IT ALL STARTED.
THE TOUR KICKED OFF IN BERMUDA.
I.B. SPECIALS
♪ TWIST AND SHOUT ♫
JIMMY COULD BE PROUD ONCE AGAIN. HE WROTE TO HIS FATHER.
ESPECIALLY BECAUSE, EVERY NIGHT, THEY GAVE HIM HIS SOLO.
& I.B. SPECIAL
TWEEEEEEE TWEEEEEE
TWENTY SECONDS, NO MORE, BUT AS INTENSE AS AN ORGASM...
...WHICH BRIGHTENED HIS ROUTINE...
WHERE'S THE NEXT GIG?
MONTREAL.
I CAN'T WAIT TO GO HOME.
...WHILE HE WAITED FOR THE DAY WHEN HIS SOLOS COULD BE A LITTLE LONGER.
MONTREAL
UP TOWN CLUB
TONIGHT
RUBY
YOU PLAY WELL! WHAT'S YOUR NAME?
BUDDY MILES.
WE HAVE TO PLAY TOGETHER SOMETIME.
WHENEVER YOU WANT!

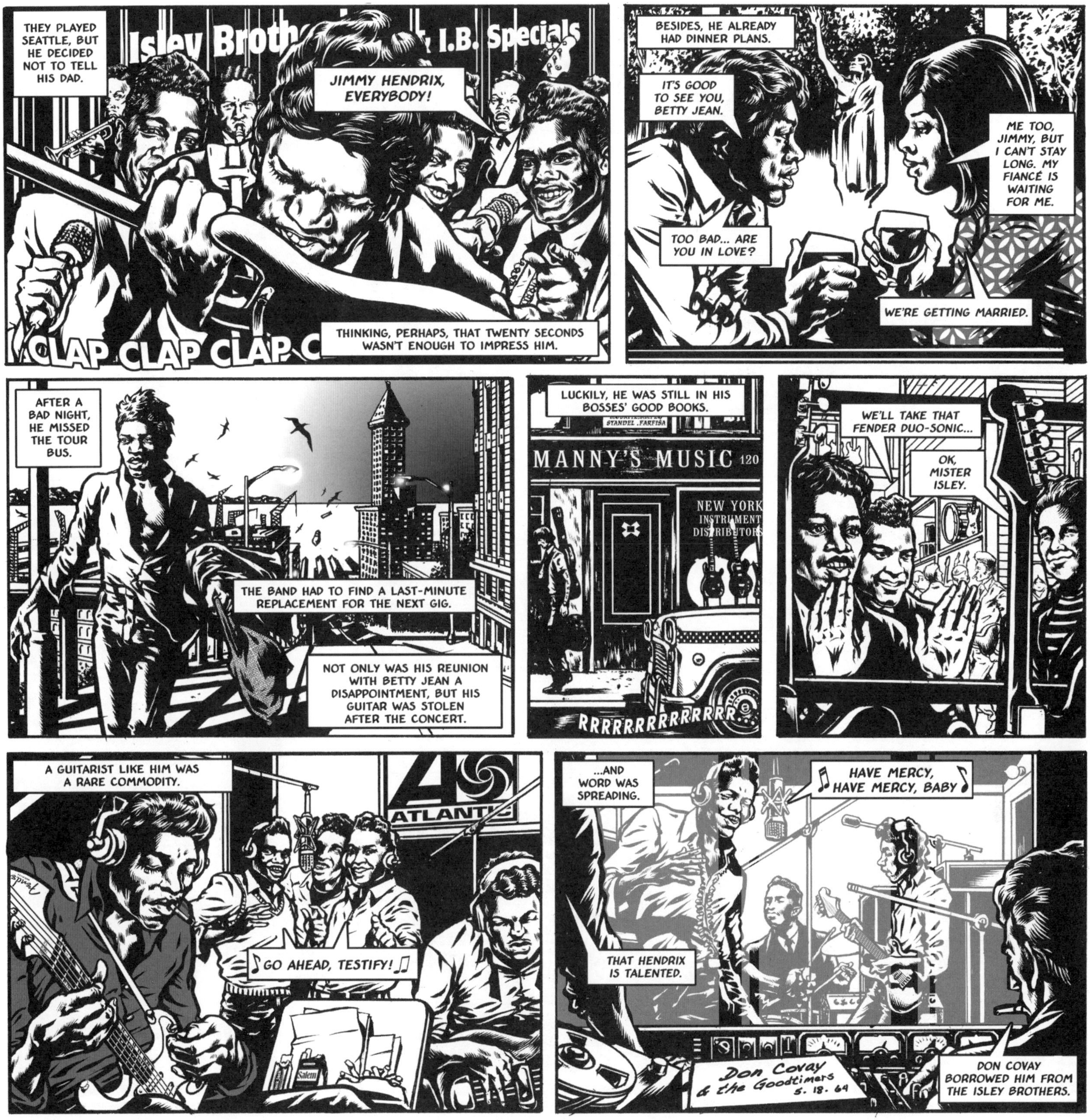
THEY PLAYED SEATTLE, BUT HE DECIDED NOT TO TELL HIS DAD.
Isley Broth
I.B. Specials
JIMMY HENDRIX, EVERYBODY!
CLAP CLAP CLAP C
THINKING, PERHAPS, THAT TWENTY SECONDS WASN'T ENOUGH TO IMPRESS HIM.
BESIDES, HE ALREADY HAD DINNER PLANS.
IT'S GOOD TO SEE YOU, BETTY JEAN.
ME TOO, JIMMY, BUT I CAN'T STAY LONG. MY FIANCÉ IS WAITING FOR ME.
TOO BAD... ARE YOU IN LOVE?
WE'RE GETTING MARRIED.
AFTER A BAD NIGHT, HE MISSED THE TOUR BUS.
THE BAND HAD TO FIND A LAST-MINUTE REPLACEMENT FOR THE NEXT GIG.
NOT ONLY WAS HIS REUNION WITH BETTY JEAN A DISAPPOINTMENT, BUT HIS GUITAR WAS STOLEN AFTER THE CONCERT.
LUCKILY, HE WAS STILL IN HIS BOSSES' GOOD BOOKS.
STANDEL, FARFISA
MANNY'S MUSIC 120
NEW YORK INSTRUMENT DISTRIBUTORS
RRRRRRRRRRRRR
WE'LL TAKE THAT FENDER DUO-SONIC...
OK, MISTER ISLEY.
A GUITARIST LIKE HIM WAS A RARE COMMODITY.
ATLANTIC
♪GO AHEAD, TESTIFY!♫
Salem
...AND WORD WAS SPREADING.
♪HAVE MERCY, HAVE MERCY, BABY♪
THAT HENDRIX IS TALENTED.
Don Covay & the Goodtimers 5. 18. 64
DON COVAY BORROWED HIM FROM THE ISLEY BROTHERS.

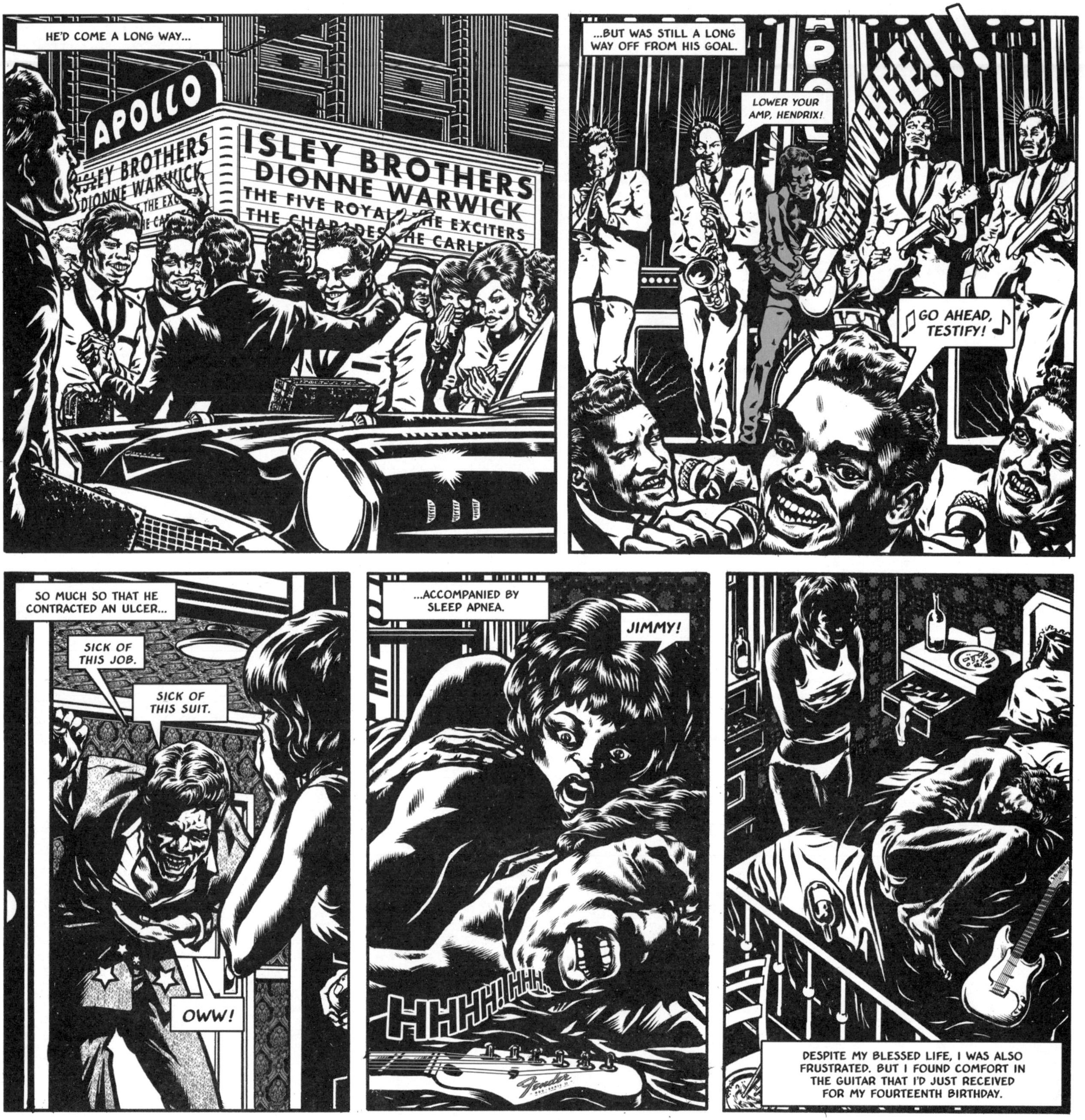
HE'D COME A LONG WAY...
APOLLO
ISLEY BROTHERS
DIONNE WARWICK
...BUT WAS STILL A LONG WAY OFF FROM HIS GOAL.
LOWER YOUR AMP, HENDRIX!
GO AHEAD, TESTIFY!
SO MUCH SO THAT HE CONTRACTED AN ULCER...
SICK OF THIS JOB.
SICK OF THIS SUIT.
OWW!
...ACCOMPANIED BY SLEEP APNEA.
JIMMY!
DESPITE MY BLESSED LIFE, I WAS ALSO FRUSTRATED. BUT I FOUND COMFORT IN THE GUITAR THAT I'D JUST RECEIVED FOR MY FOURTEENTH BIRTHDAY.

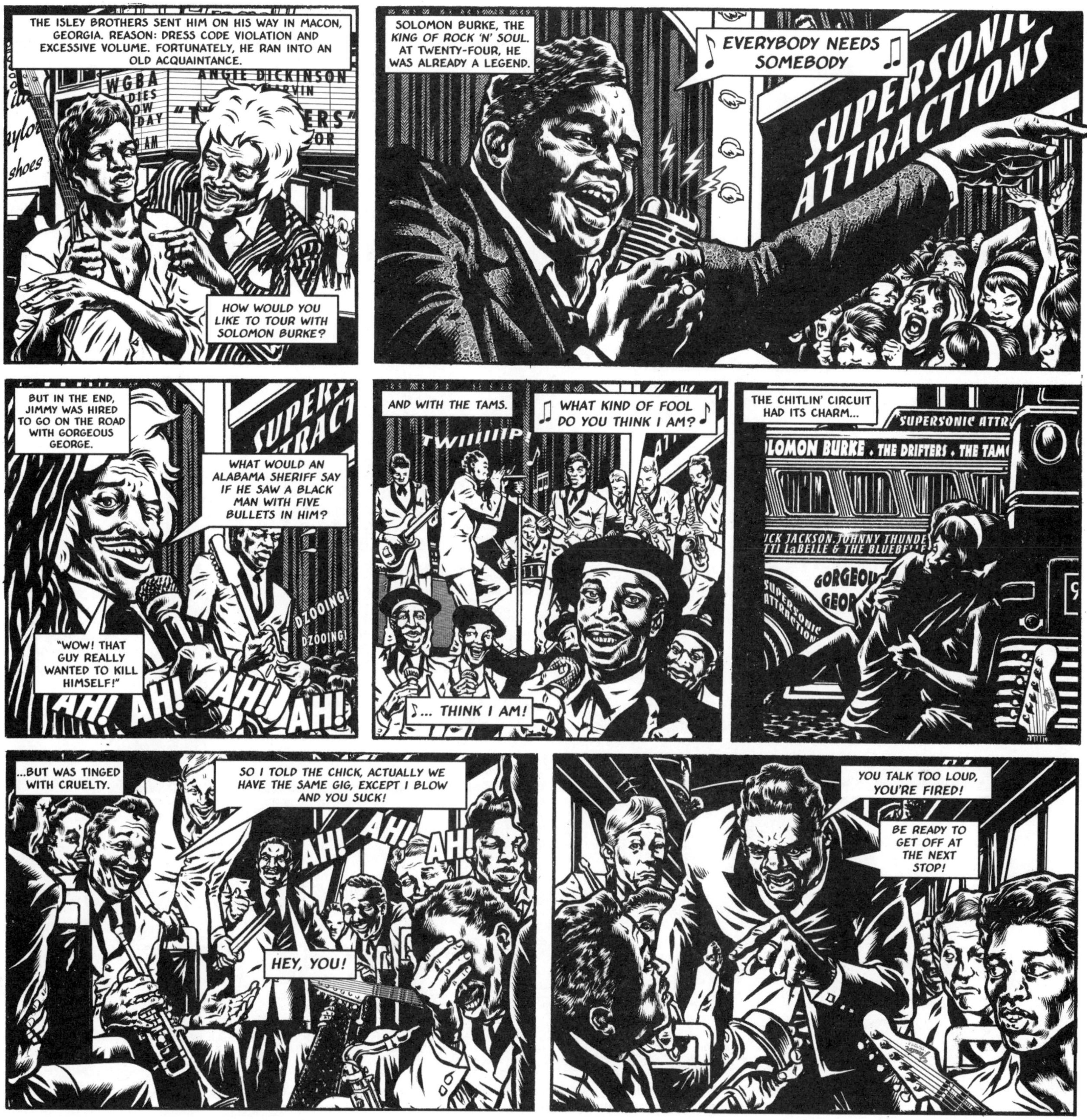
THE ISLEY BROTHERS SENT HIM ON HIS WAY IN MACON, GEORGIA. REASON: DRESS CODE VIOLATION AND EXCESSIVE VOLUME. FORTUNATELY, HE RAN INTO AN OLD ACQUAINTANCE.
ANGIE DICKINSON
WGBA
HOW WOULD YOU LIKE TO TOUR WITH SOLOMON BURKE?
SOLOMON BURKE, THE KING OF ROCK 'N' SOUL. AT TWENTY-FOUR, HE WAS ALREADY A LEGEND.
♪ EVERYBODY NEEDS SOMEBODY ♫
SUPERSONIC ATTRACTIONS
BUT IN THE END, JIMMY WAS HIRED TO GO ON THE ROAD WITH GORGEOUS GEORGE.
WHAT WOULD AN ALABAMA SHERIFF SAY IF HE SAW A BLACK MAN WITH FIVE BULLETS IN HIM?
DZOOING! DZOOING!
"WOW! THAT GUY REALLY WANTED TO KILL HIMSELF!"
AH! AH! AH! AH!
AND WITH THE TAMS.
♫ WHAT KIND OF FOOL DO YOU THINK I AM? ♪
TWIIIIIP!
♪... THINK I AM!
THE CHITLIN' CIRCUIT HAD ITS CHARM...
SUPERSONIC ATTR
OLOMON BURKE . THE DRIFTERS . THE TAM
...BUT WAS TINGED WITH CRUELTY.
SO I TOLD THE CHICK, ACTUALLY WE HAVE THE SAME GIG, EXCEPT I BLOW AND YOU SUCK!
AH! AH! AH!
HEY, YOU!
YOU TALK TOO LOUD, YOU'RE FIRED!
BE READY TO GET OFF AT THE NEXT STOP!

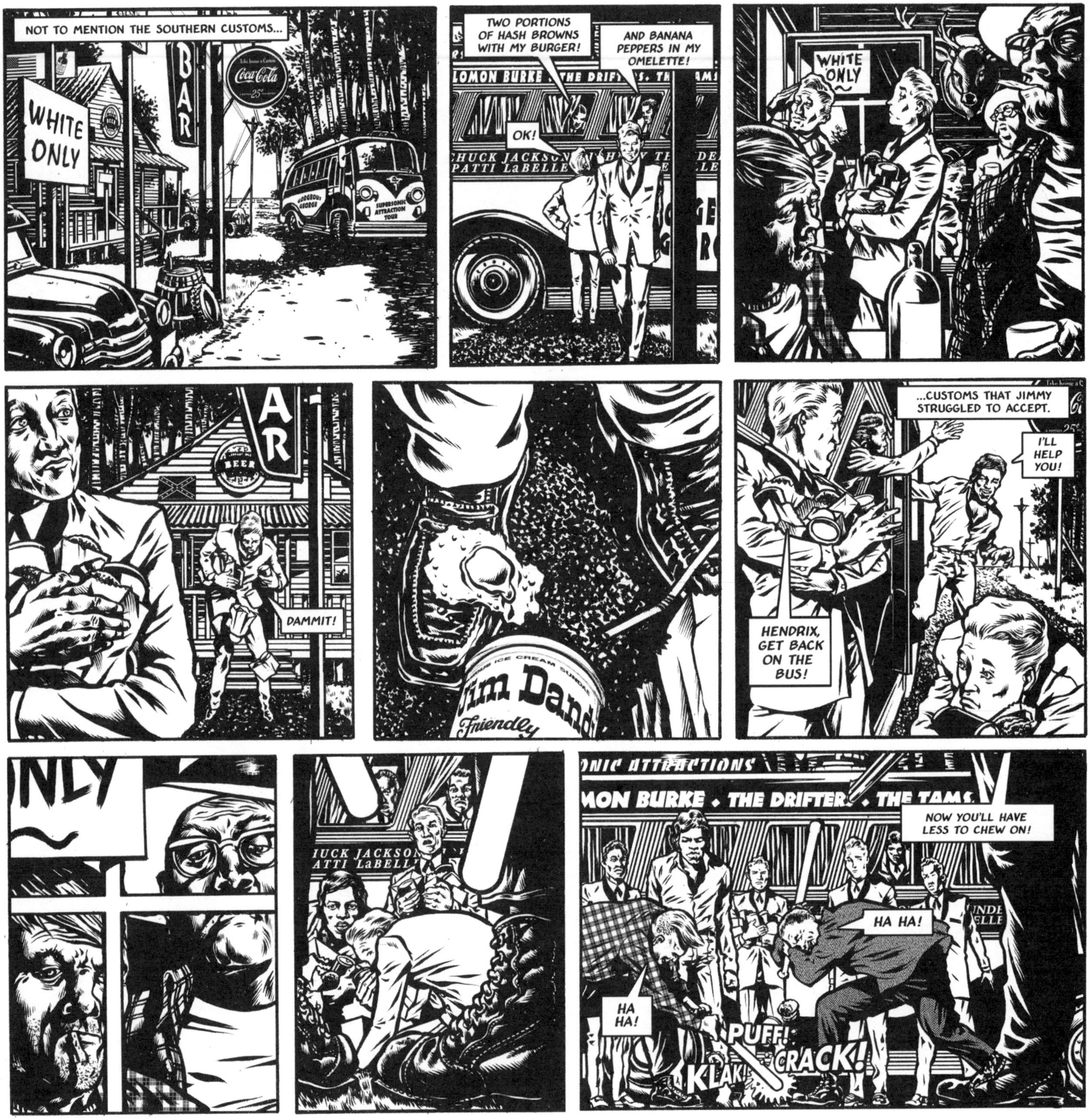
NOT TO MENTION THE SOUTHERN CUSTOMS...
WHITE ONLY
BAR
TWO PORTIONS OF HASH BROWNS WITH MY BURGER!
AND BANANA PEPPERS IN MY OMELETTE!
OK!
WHITE ONLY
DAMMIT!
...CUSTOMS THAT JIMMY STRUGGLED TO ACCEPT.
I'LL HELP YOU!
HENDRIX, GET BACK ON THE BUS!
NOW YOU'LL HAVE LESS TO CHEW ON!
HA HA!
HA HA!
PUFF!
CRACK!
KLAK!

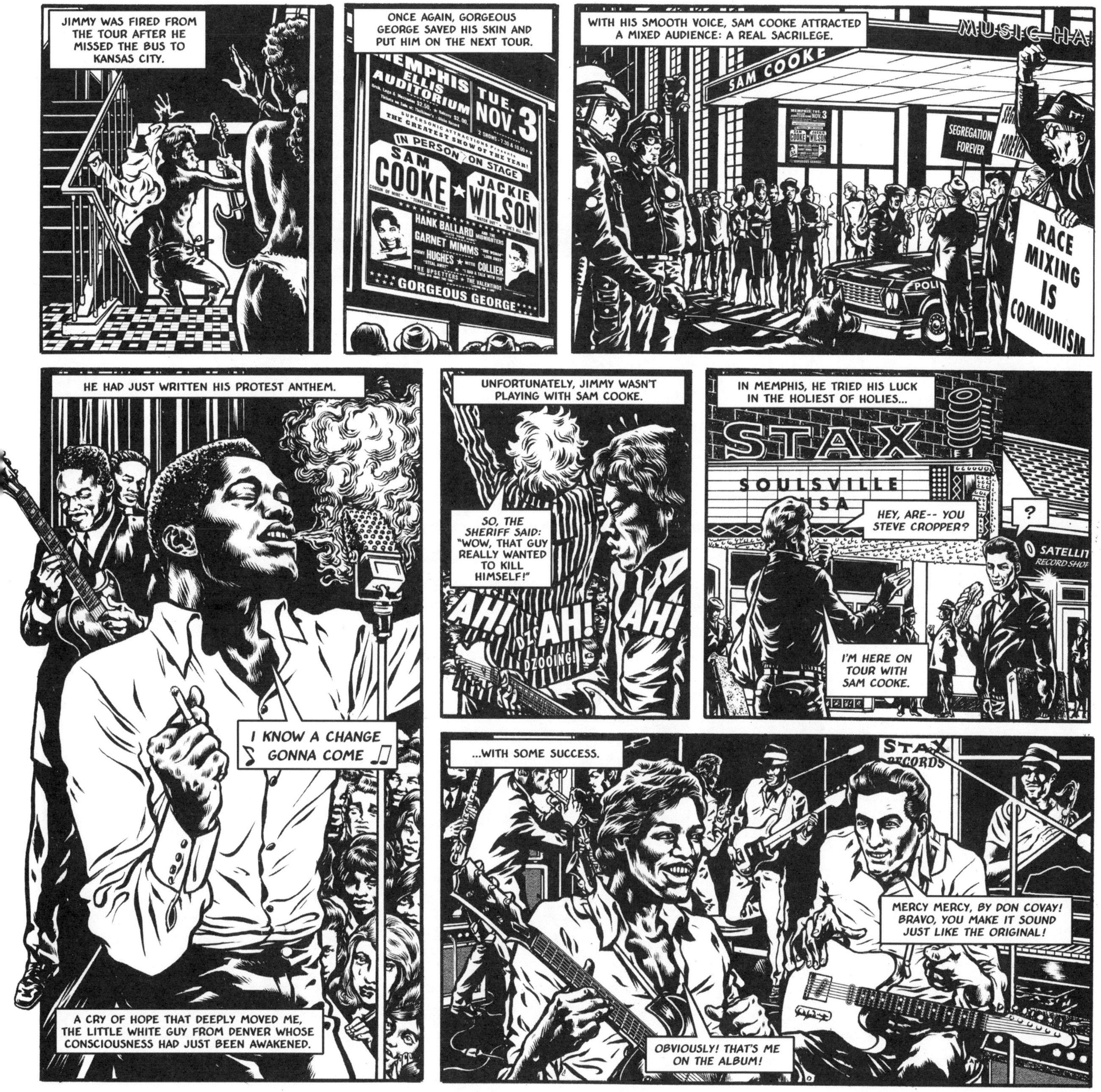
JIMMY WAS FIRED FROM THE TOUR AFTER HE MISSED THE BUS TO KANSAS CITY.
ONCE AGAIN, GORGEOUS GEORGE SAVED HIS SKIN AND PUT HIM ON THE NEXT TOUR.
MEMPHIS ELLIS AUDITORIUM
TUE. NOV. 3
THE GREATEST SHOW OF THE YEAR!
IN PERSON ON STAGE
SAM COOKE
JACKIE WILSON
HANK BALLARD
GARNET MIMMS
JIMMY HUGHES
COLLIER
THE UPSETTERS
THE VALENTINOS
GORGEOUS GEORGE
WITH HIS SMOOTH VOICE, SAM COOKE ATTRACTED A MIXED AUDIENCE: A REAL SACRILEGE.
MUSIC HA
SAM COOKE
SEGREGATION FOREVER
RACE MIXING IS COMMUNISM
HE HAD JUST WRITTEN HIS PROTEST ANTHEM.
I KNOW A CHANGE GONNA COME
A CRY OF HOPE THAT DEEPLY MOVED ME, THE LITTLE WHITE GUY FROM DENVER WHOSE CONSCIOUSNESS HAD JUST BEEN AWAKENED.
UNFORTUNATELY, JIMMY WASN'T PLAYING WITH SAM COOKE.
SO, THE SHERIFF SAID: "WOW, THAT GUY REALLY WANTED TO KILL HIMSELF!"
AH! AH! AH!
DZOOING!
IN MEMPHIS, HE TRIED HIS LUCK IN THE HOLIEST OF HOLIES...
STAX
SOULSVILLE
HEY, ARE-- YOU STEVE CROPPER?
?
SATELLIT
RECORD SHOP
I'M HERE ON TOUR WITH SAM COOKE.
...WITH SOME SUCCESS.
STAX RECORDS
MERCY MERCY, BY DON COVAY! BRAVO, YOU MAKE IT SOUND JUST LIKE THE ORIGINAL!
OBVIOUSLY! THAT'S ME ON THE ALBUM!

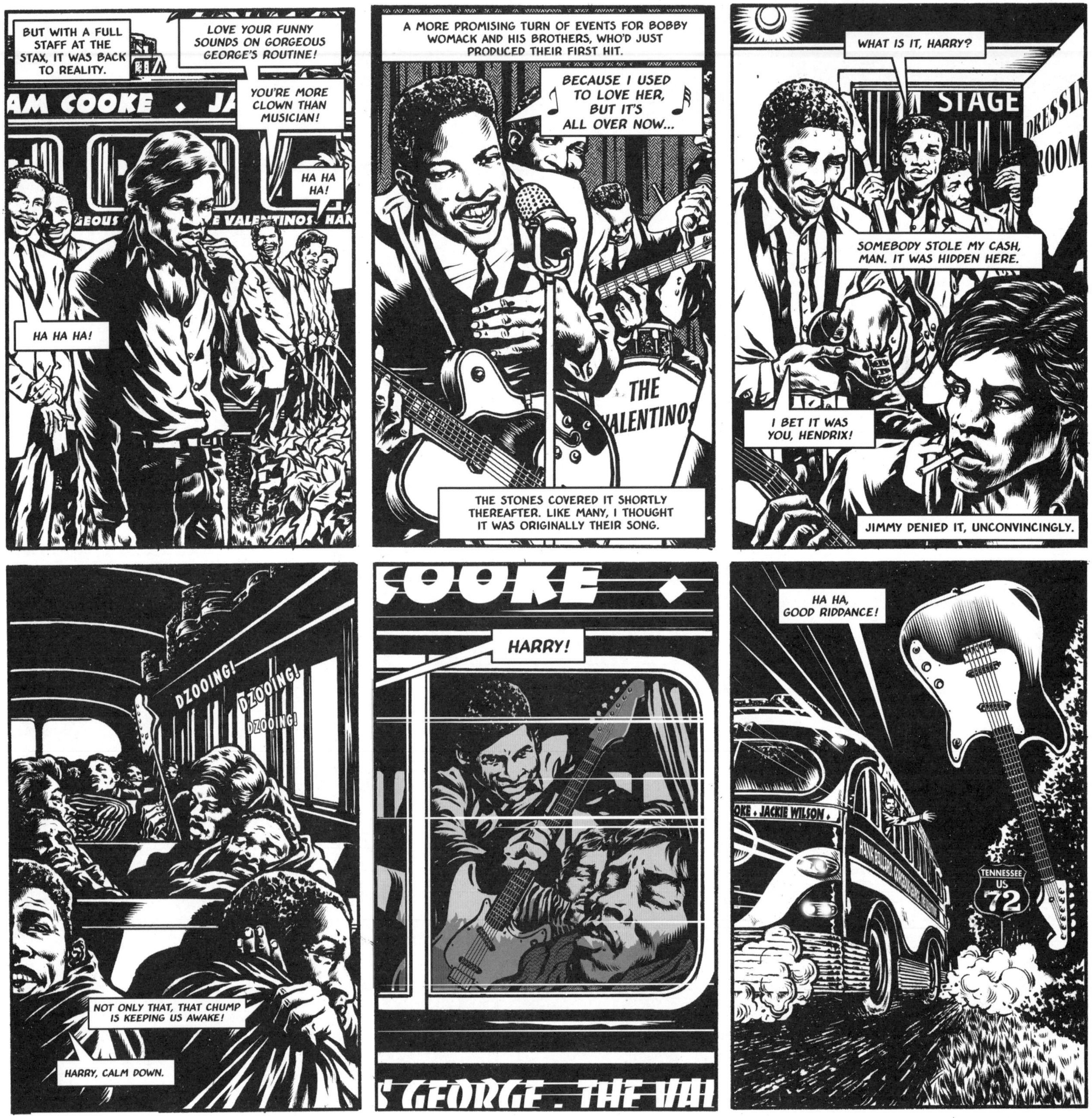
BUT WITH A FULL STAFF AT THE STAX, IT WAS BACK TO REALITY.
LOVE YOUR FUNNY SOUNDS ON GORGEOUS GEORGE'S ROUTINE!
YOU'RE MORE CLOWN THAN MUSICIAN!
HA HA HA!
HA HA HA!
A MORE PROMISING TURN OF EVENTS FOR BOBBY WOMACK AND HIS BROTHERS, WHO'D JUST PRODUCED THEIR FIRST HIT.
BECAUSE I USED TO LOVE HER, BUT IT'S ALL OVER NOW...
THE STONES COVERED IT SHORTLY THEREAFTER. LIKE MANY, I THOUGHT IT WAS ORIGINALLY THEIR SONG.
WHAT IS IT, HARRY?
SOMEBODY STOLE MY CASH, MAN. IT WAS HIDDEN HERE.
I BET IT WAS YOU, HENDRIX!
JIMMY DENIED IT, UNCONVINCINGLY.
DZOOING!
DZOOING!
DZOOING!
NOT ONLY THAT, THAT CHUMP IS KEEPING US AWAKE!
HARRY, CALM DOWN.
HARRY!
HA HA, GOOD RIDDANCE!
TENNESSEE
US
72

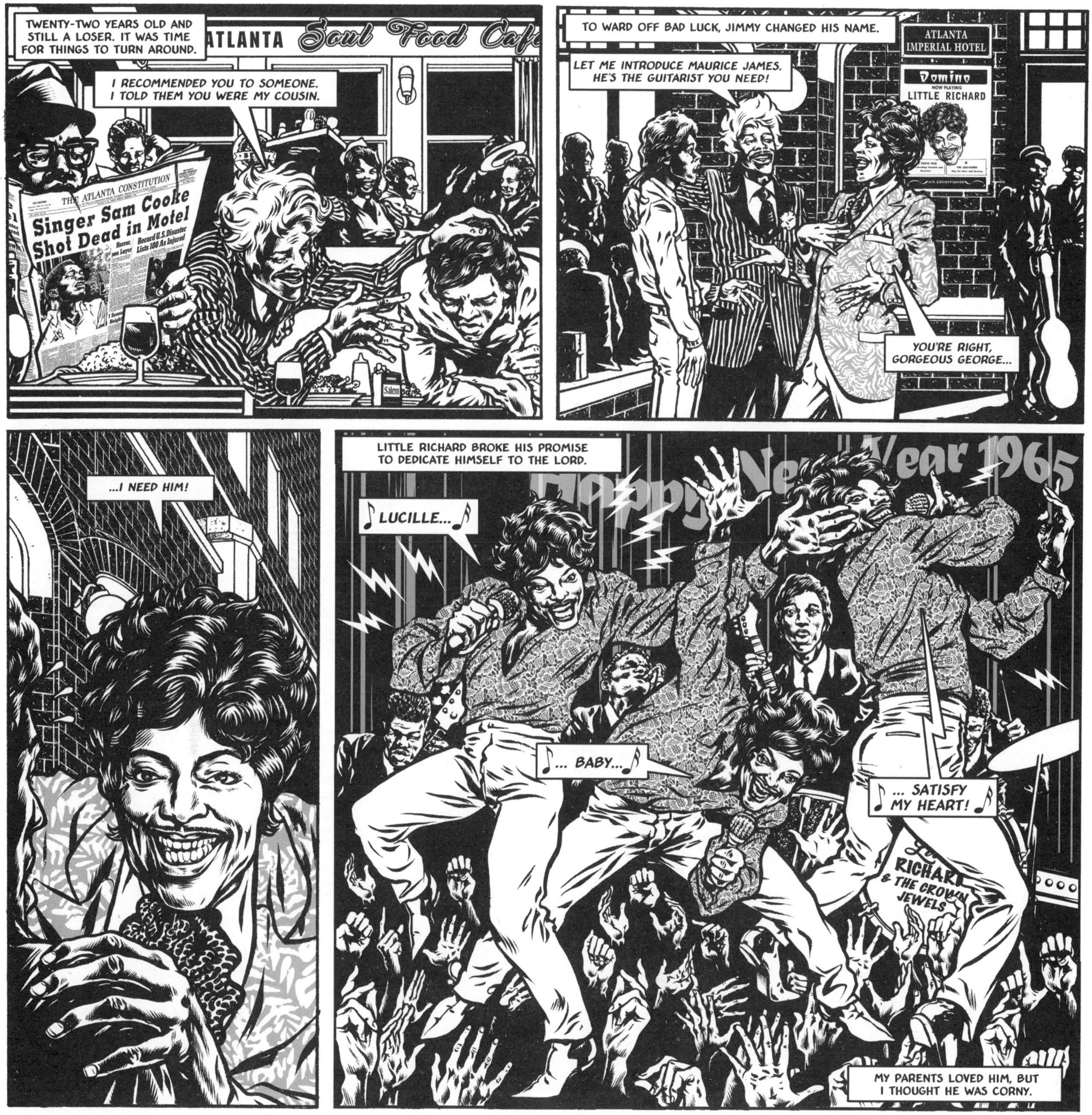
TWENTY-TWO YEARS OLD AND STILL A LOSER. IT WAS TIME FOR THINGS TO TURN AROUND.
ATLANTA Soul Food Cafe
I RECOMMENDED YOU TO SOMEONE. I TOLD THEM YOU WERE MY COUSIN.
THE ATLANTA CONSTITUTION
Singer Sam Cooke Shot Dead in Motel
Record U.S. Disaster Lists 100 As Injured
Salem
TO WARD OFF BAD LUCK, JIMMY CHANGED HIS NAME.
ATLANTA IMPERIAL HOTEL
Domino
NOW PLAYING
LITTLE RICHARD
AIR CONDITIONED
LET ME INTRODUCE MAURICE JAMES. HE'S THE GUITARIST YOU NEED!
YOU'RE RIGHT, GORGEOUS GEORGE...
...I NEED HIM!
LITTLE RICHARD BROKE HIS PROMISE TO DEDICATE HIMSELF TO THE LORD.
Year 1965
♪ LUCILLE... ♪
♪ ... BABY... ♪
♪ ... SATISFY MY HEART! ♪
RICHARD & THE CROWN JEWELS
MY PARENTS LOVED HIM, BUT I THOUGHT HE WAS CORNY.

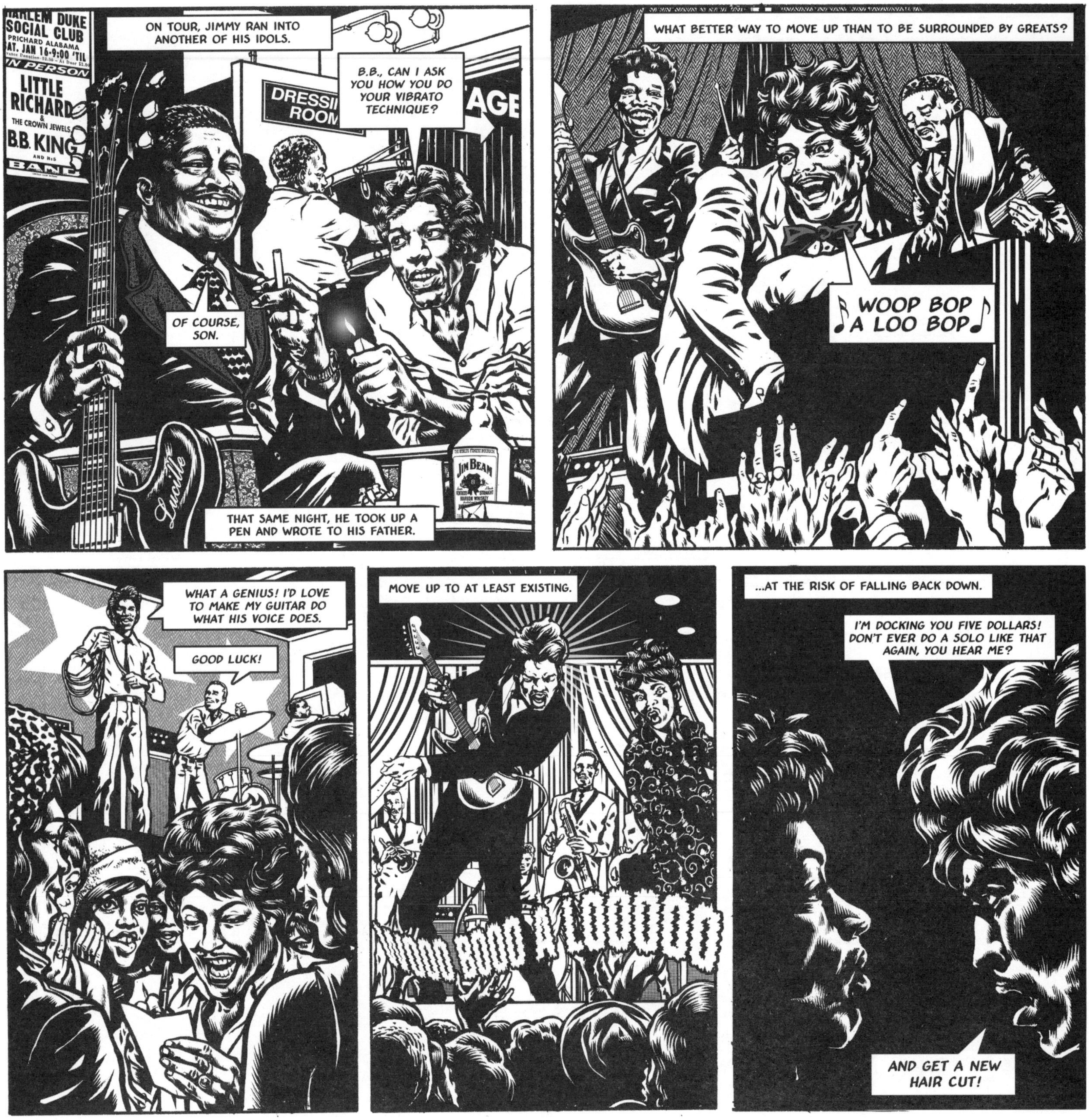
DUKE
SOCIAL CLUB
PRICHARD ALABAMA
JAN 16-9:00 'TIL
PERSON
LITTLE RICHARD
& THE CROWN JEWELS
B.B. KING
AND HIS
BAND
ON TOUR, JIMMY RAN INTO ANOTHER OF HIS IDOLS.
B.B., CAN I ASK YOU HOW YOU DO YOUR VIBRATO TECHNIQUE?
OF COURSE, SON.
THAT SAME NIGHT, HE TOOK UP A PEN AND WROTE TO HIS FATHER.
WHAT BETTER WAY TO MOVE UP THAN TO BE SURROUNDED BY GREATS?
♪ WOOP BOP A LOO BOP ♪
WHAT A GENIUS! I'D LOVE TO MAKE MY GUITAR DO WHAT HIS VOICE DOES.
GOOD LUCK!
MOVE UP TO AT LEAST EXISTING.
...AT THE RISK OF FALLING BACK DOWN.
I'M DOCKING YOU FIVE DOLLARS! DON'T EVER DO A SOLO LIKE THAT AGAIN, YOU HEAR ME?
AND GET A NEW HAIR CUT!

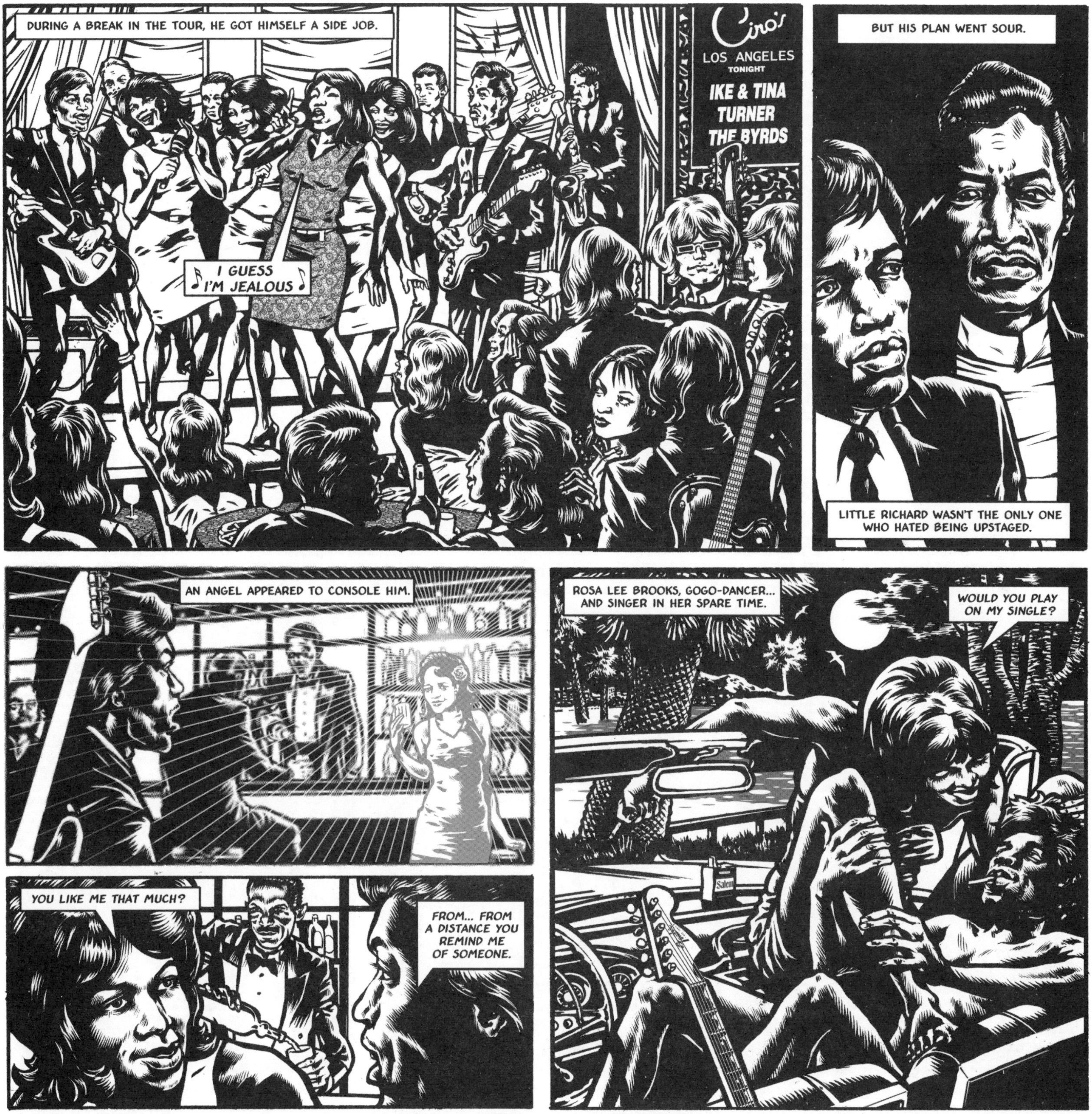
DURING A BREAK IN THE TOUR, HE GOT HIMSELF A SIDE JOB.
Ciro's
LOS ANGELES
TONIGHT
IKE & TINA
TURNER
THE BYRDS
♪ I GUESS
I'M JEALOUS ♪
BUT HIS PLAN WENT SOUR.
LITTLE RICHARD WASN'T THE ONLY ONE
WHO HATED BEING UPSTAGED.
AN ANGEL APPEARED TO CONSOLE HIM.
YOU LIKE ME THAT MUCH?
FROM... FROM
A DISTANCE YOU
REMIND ME
OF SOMEONE.
ROSA LEE BROOKS, GOGO-DANCER...
AND SINGER IN HER SPARE TIME.
WOULD YOU PLAY
ON MY SINGLE?
Salem

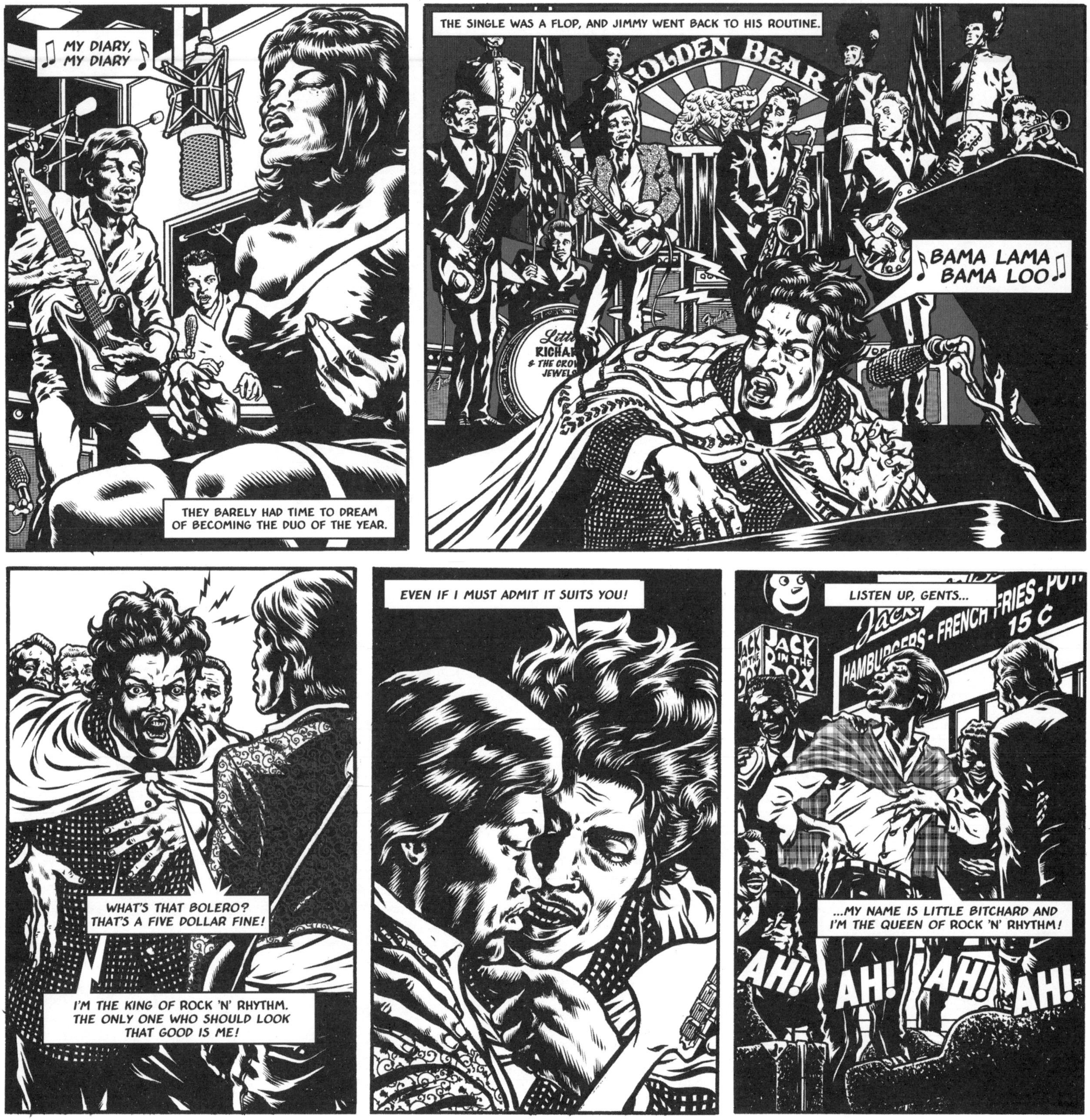
♫ MY DIARY, MY DIARY ♪
THEY BARELY HAD TIME TO DREAM OF BECOMING THE DUO OF THE YEAR.
THE SINGLE WAS A FLOP, AND JIMMY WENT BACK TO HIS ROUTINE.
♪ BAMA LAMA BAMA LOO ♫
WHAT'S THAT BOLERO? THAT'S A FIVE DOLLAR FINE!
I'M THE KING OF ROCK 'N' RHYTHM. THE ONLY ONE WHO SHOULD LOOK THAT GOOD IS ME!
EVEN IF I MUST ADMIT IT SUITS YOU!
LISTEN UP, GENTS...
JACK IN THE BOX
15 C
...MY NAME IS LITTLE BITCHARD AND I'M THE QUEEN OF ROCK 'N' RHYTHM!
AH! AH! AH! AH!

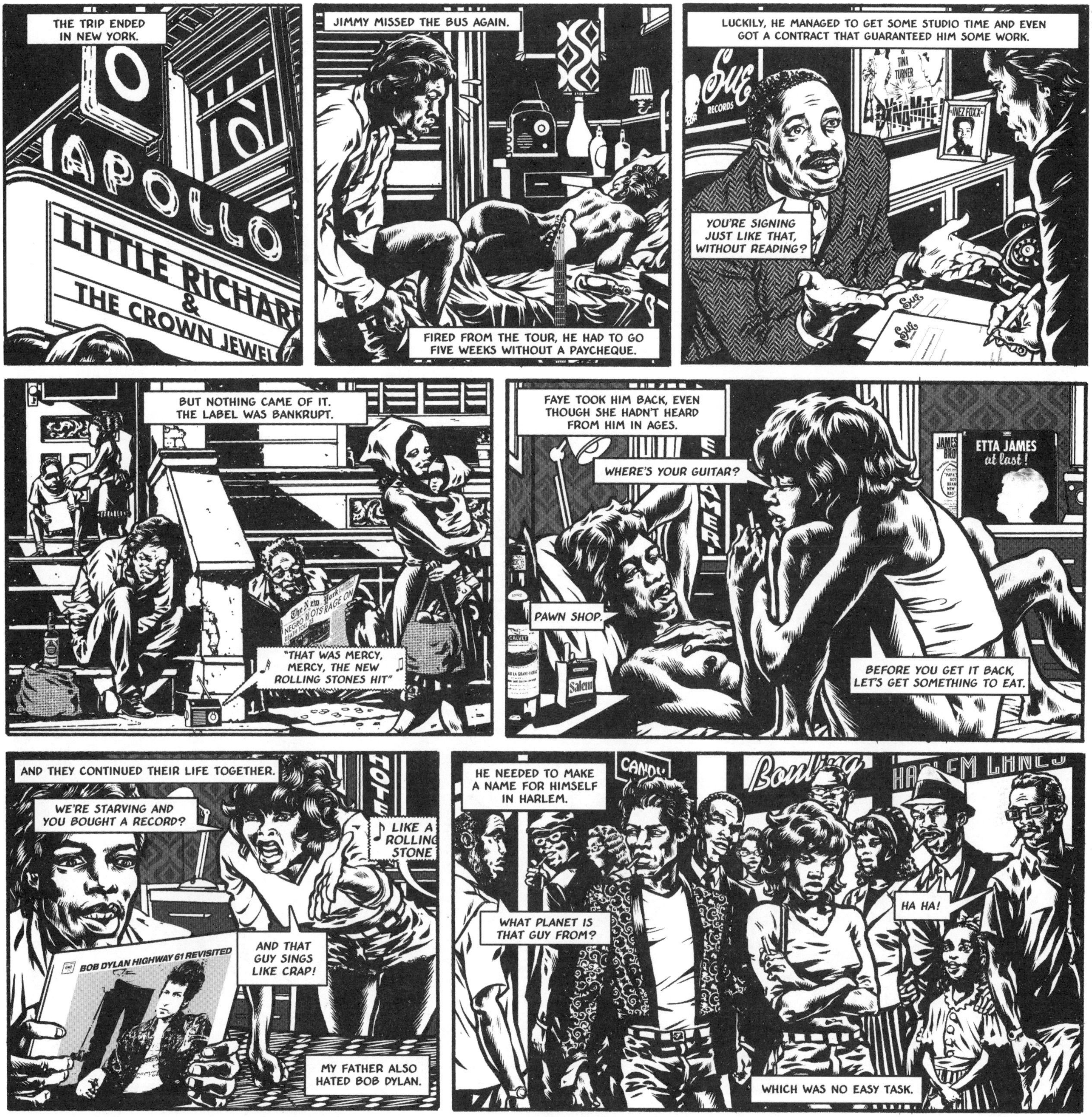
THE TRIP ENDED IN NEW YORK.
APOLLO
JIMMY MISSED THE BUS AGAIN.
FIRED FROM THE TOUR, HE HAD TO GO FIVE WEEKS WITHOUT A PAYCHEQUE.
LUCKILY, HE MANAGED TO GET SOME STUDIO TIME AND EVEN GOT A CONTRACT THAT GUARANTEED HIM SOME WORK.
Sue RECORDS
TINA TURNER
INEZ FOXX
YOU'RE SIGNING JUST LIKE THAT, WITHOUT READING?
BUT NOTHING CAME OF IT. THE LABEL WAS BANKRUPT.
NEGRO RIOTS RAGE ON
"THAT WAS MERCY, MERCY, THE NEW ROLLING STONES HIT"
FAYE TOOK HIM BACK, EVEN THOUGH SHE HADN'T HEARD FROM HIM IN AGES.
ETTA JAMES at last!
WHERE'S YOUR GUITAR?
PAWN SHOP.
CALVET
Salem
BEFORE YOU GET IT BACK, LET'S GET SOMETHING TO EAT.
AND THEY CONTINUED THEIR LIFE TOGETHER.
WE'RE STARVING AND YOU BOUGHT A RECORD?
♪ LIKE A ROLLING STONE
BOB DYLAN HIGHWAY 61 REVISITED
AND THAT GUY SINGS LIKE CRAP!
MY FATHER ALSO HATED BOB DYLAN.
HE NEEDED TO MAKE A NAME FOR HIMSELF IN HARLEM.
Bowling
WHAT PLANET IS THAT GUY FROM?
HA HA!
WHICH WAS NO EASY TASK.

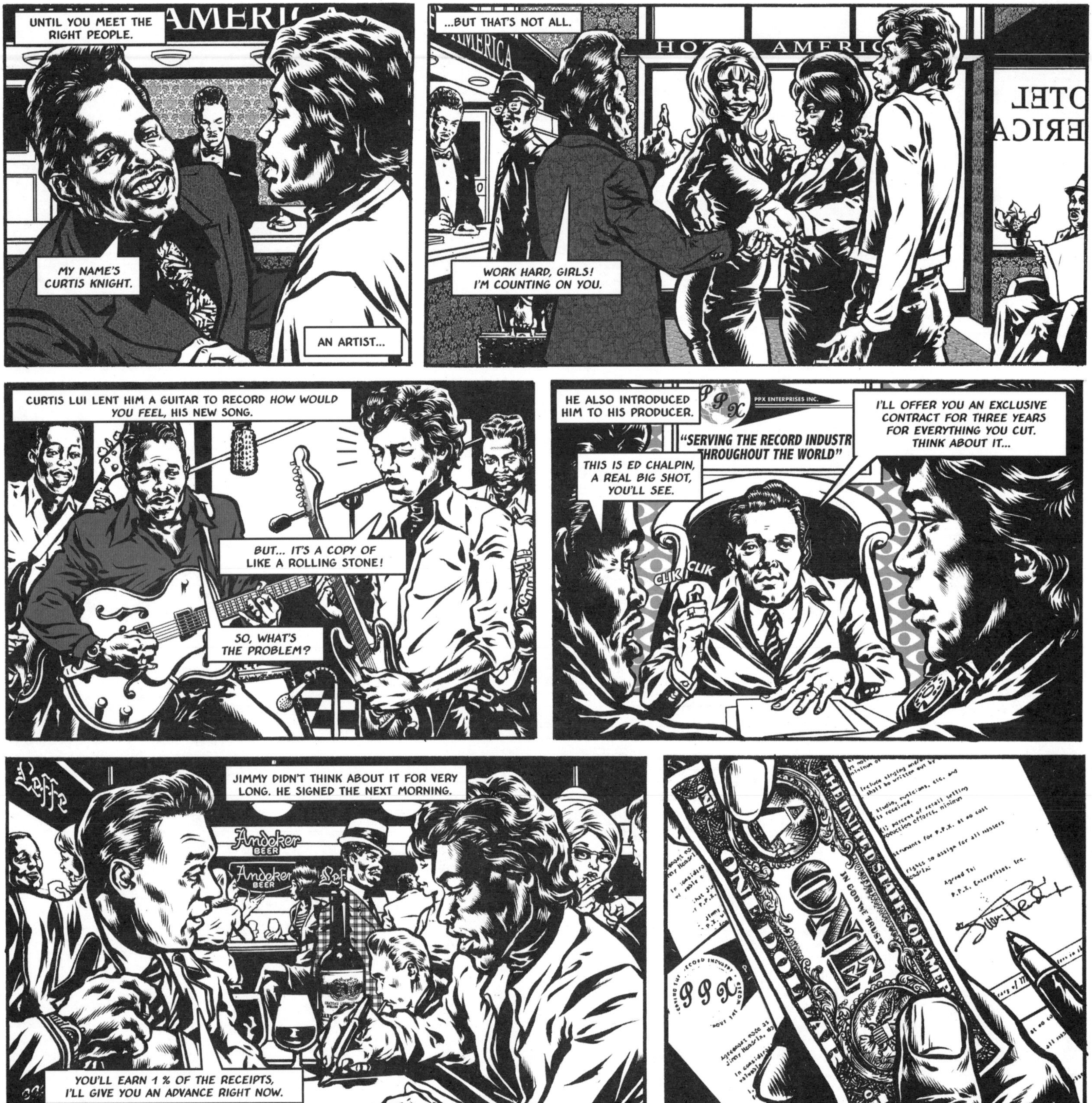
UNTIL YOU MEET THE RIGHT PEOPLE.
MY NAME'S CURTIS KNIGHT.
AN ARTIST...
...BUT THAT'S NOT ALL.
WORK HARD, GIRLS! I'M COUNTING ON YOU.
CURTIS LUI LENT HIM A GUITAR TO RECORD *HOW WOULD YOU FEEL*, HIS NEW SONG.
BUT... IT'S A COPY OF LIKE A ROLLING STONE!
SO, WHAT'S THE PROBLEM?
HE ALSO INTRODUCED HIM TO HIS PRODUCER.
PPX ENTERPRISES INC.
"SERVING THE RECORD INDUSTR THROUGHOUT THE WORLD"
THIS IS ED CHALPIN, A REAL BIG SHOT, YOU'LL SEE.
I'LL OFFER YOU AN EXCLUSIVE CONTRACT FOR THREE YEARS FOR EVERYTHING YOU CUT. THINK ABOUT IT...
CLIK CLIK
JIMMY DIDN'T THINK ABOUT IT FOR VERY LONG. HE SIGNED THE NEXT MORNING.
YOU'LL EARN 1 % OF THE RECEIPTS, I'LL GIVE YOU AN ADVANCE RIGHT NOW.

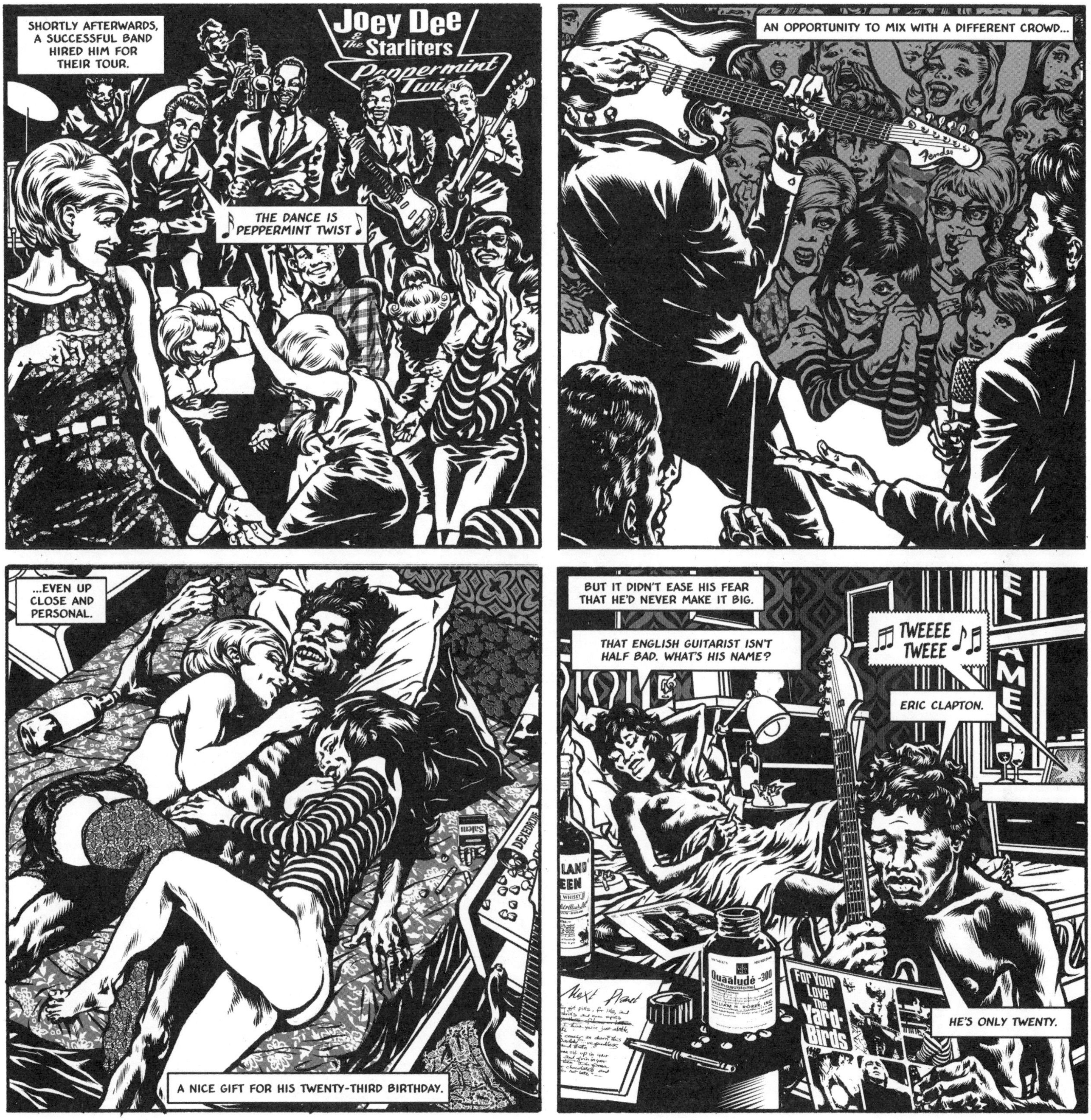
SHORTLY AFTERWARDS, A SUCCESSFUL BAND HIRED HIM FOR THEIR TOUR.
Joey Dee
& The Starliters
THE DANCE IS PEPPERMINT TWIST
AN OPPORTUNITY TO MIX WITH A DIFFERENT CROWD...
Fender
...EVEN UP CLOSE AND PERSONAL.
Salem
DEXEDRINE
A NICE GIFT FOR HIS TWENTY-THIRD BIRTHDAY.
BUT IT DIDN'T EASE HIS FEAR THAT HE'D NEVER MAKE IT BIG.
THAT ENGLISH GUITARIST ISN'T HALF BAD. WHAT'S HIS NAME?
TWEEEE TWEEE
ERIC CLAPTON.
Quaalude -300
For Your Love The Yard-Birds
HE'S ONLY TWENTY.

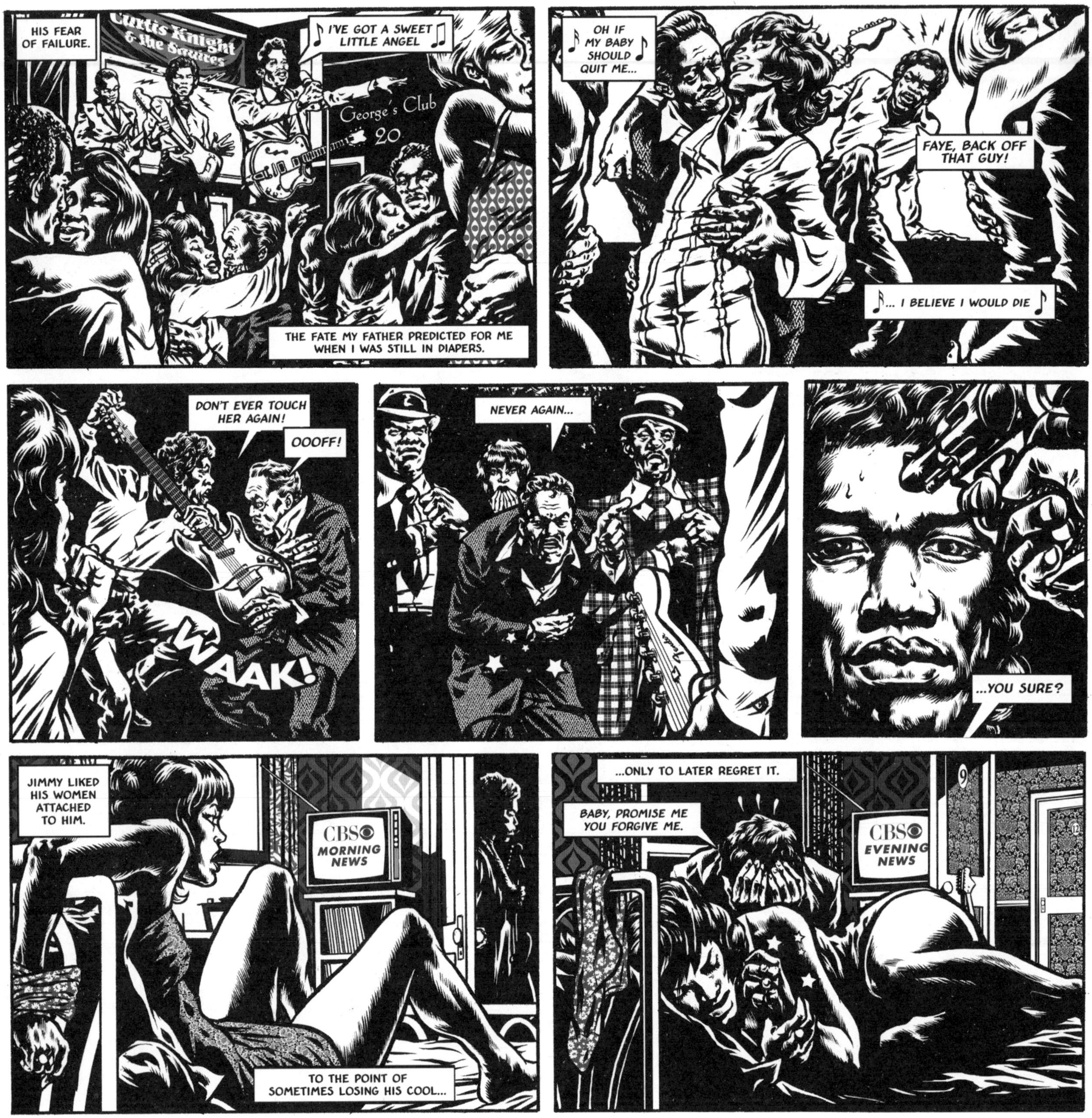
HIS FEAR OF FAILURE.
Curtis Knight & the Squires
♪ I'VE GOT A SWEET LITTLE ANGEL ♫
George's Club 20
THE FATE MY FATHER PREDICTED FOR ME WHEN I WAS STILL IN DIAPERS.
♪ OH IF MY BABY SHOULD QUIT ME... ♪
FAYE, BACK OFF THAT GUY!
♪... I BELIEVE I WOULD DIE ♪
DON'T EVER TOUCH HER AGAIN!
OOOFF!
WAAK!
NEVER AGAIN...
...YOU SURE?
JIMMY LIKED HIS WOMEN ATTACHED TO HIM.
CBS MORNING NEWS
TO THE POINT OF SOMETIMES LOSING HIS COOL...
...ONLY TO LATER REGRET IT.
BABY, PROMISE ME YOU FORGIVE ME.
CBS EVENING NEWS

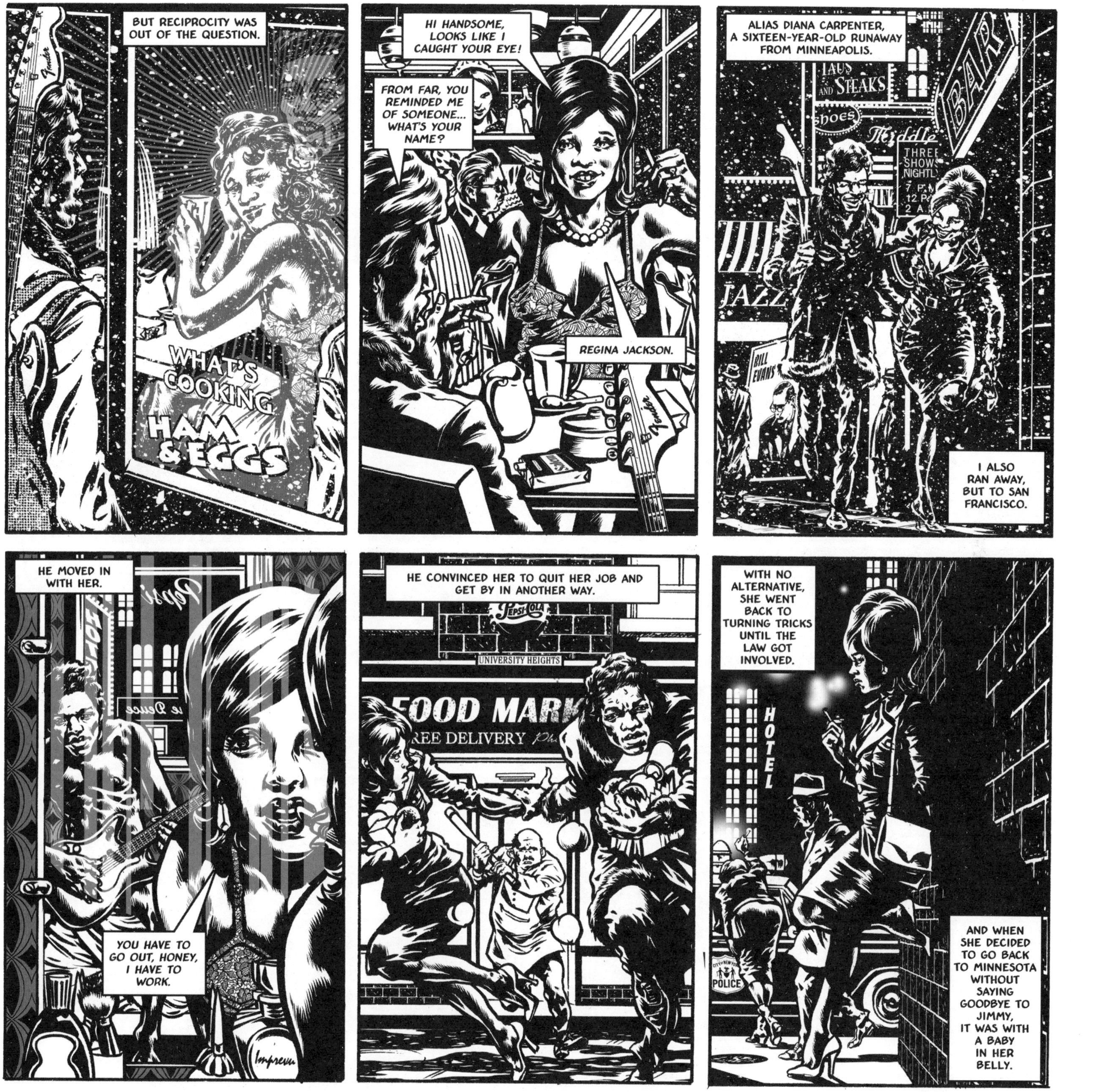

BUT RECIPROCITY WAS OUT OF THE QUESTION.
WHAT'S COOKING
HAM & EGGS
HI HANDSOME, LOOKS LIKE I CAUGHT YOUR EYE!
FROM FAR, YOU REMINDED ME OF SOMEONE... WHAT'S YOUR NAME?
REGINA JACKSON.
ALIAS DIANA CARPENTER, A SIXTEEN-YEAR-OLD RUNAWAY FROM MINNEAPOLIS.
BAR
STEAKS
shoes
THREE SHOWS NIGHTLY
JAZZ
BILL EVANS
I ALSO RAN AWAY, BUT TO SAN FRANCISCO.
HE MOVED IN WITH HER.
YOU HAVE TO GO OUT, HONEY, I HAVE TO WORK.
HE CONVINCED HER TO QUIT HER JOB AND GET BY IN ANOTHER WAY.
UNIVERSITY HEIGHTS
FOOD MARK
REE DELIVERY
WITH NO ALTERNATIVE, SHE WENT BACK TO TURNING TRICKS UNTIL THE LAW GOT INVOLVED.
HOTEL
POLICE
AND WHEN SHE DECIDED TO GO BACK TO MINNESOTA WITHOUT SAYING GOODBYE TO JIMMY, IT WAS WITH A BABY IN HER BELLY.

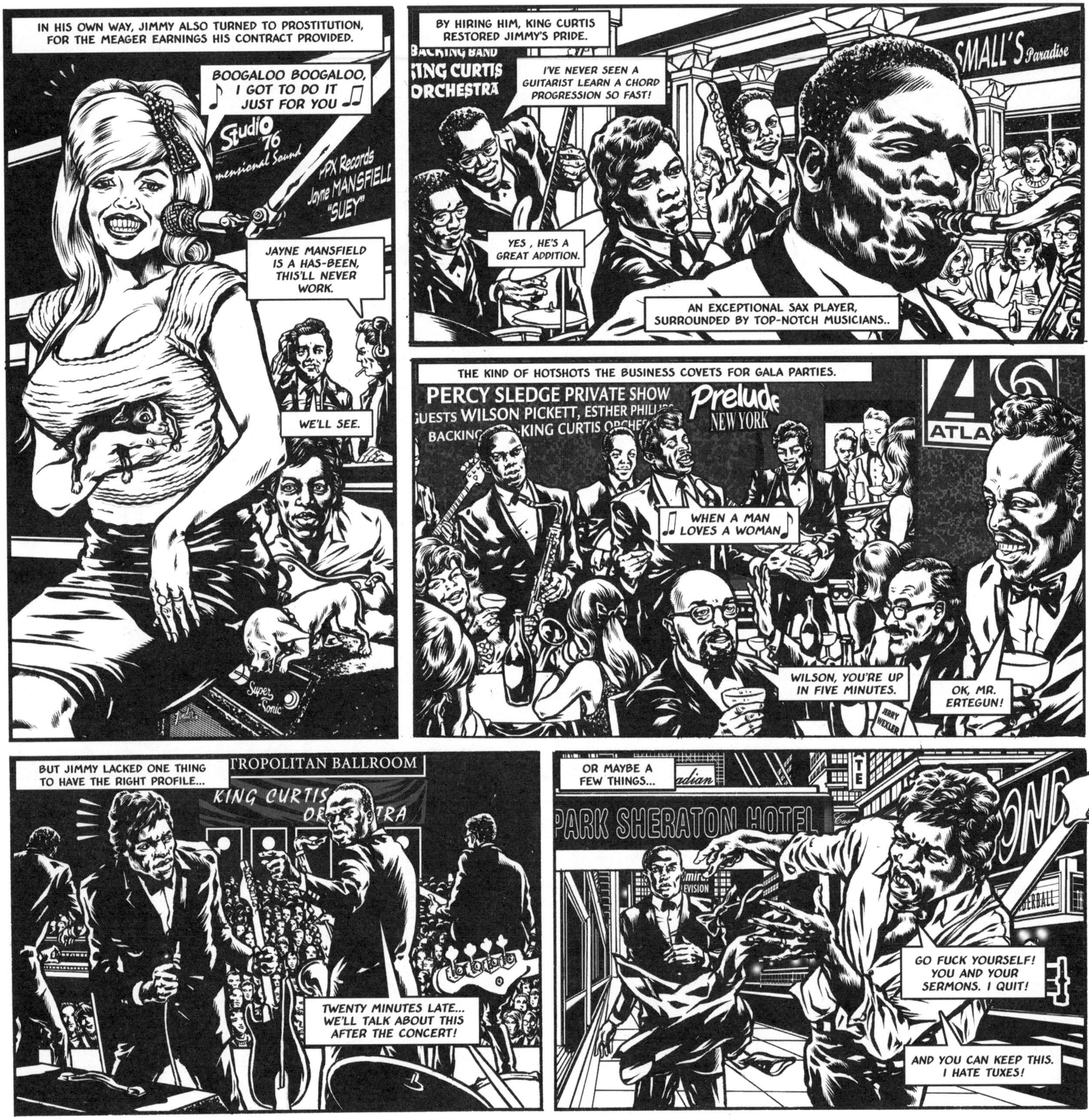
IN HIS OWN WAY, JIMMY ALSO TURNED TO PROSTITUTION, FOR THE MEAGER EARNINGS HIS CONTRACT PROVIDED.
BOOGALOO BOOGALOO, I GOT TO DO IT JUST FOR YOU
Studio 76
PPX Records Jayne MANSFIELD "SUEY"
JAYNE MANSFIELD IS A HAS-BEEN, THIS'LL NEVER WORK.
WE'LL SEE.
Super Sonic
BY HIRING HIM, KING CURTIS RESTORED JIMMY'S PRIDE.
KING CURTIS ORCHESTRA
SMALL'S Paradise
I'VE NEVER SEEN A GUITARIST LEARN A CHORD PROGRESSION SO FAST!
YES , HE'S A GREAT ADDITION.
AN EXCEPTIONAL SAX PLAYER, SURROUNDED BY TOP-NOTCH MUSICIANS..
THE KIND OF HOTSHOTS THE BUSINESS COVETS FOR GALA PARTIES.
PERCY SLEDGE PRIVATE SHOW
Prelude NEW YORK
ATLA
WHEN A MAN LOVES A WOMAN
WILSON, YOU'RE UP IN FIVE MINUTES.
JERRY WEXLER
OK, MR. ERTEGUN!
BUT JIMMY LACKED ONE THING TO HAVE THE RIGHT PROFILE...
TROPOLITAN BALLROOM
KING CURTIS
TWENTY MINUTES LATE... WE'LL TALK ABOUT THIS AFTER THE CONCERT!
OR MAYBE A FEW THINGS...
PARK SHERATON HOTEL
GO FUCK YOURSELF! YOU AND YOUR SERMONS. I QUIT!
AND YOU CAN KEEP THIS. I HATE TUXES!

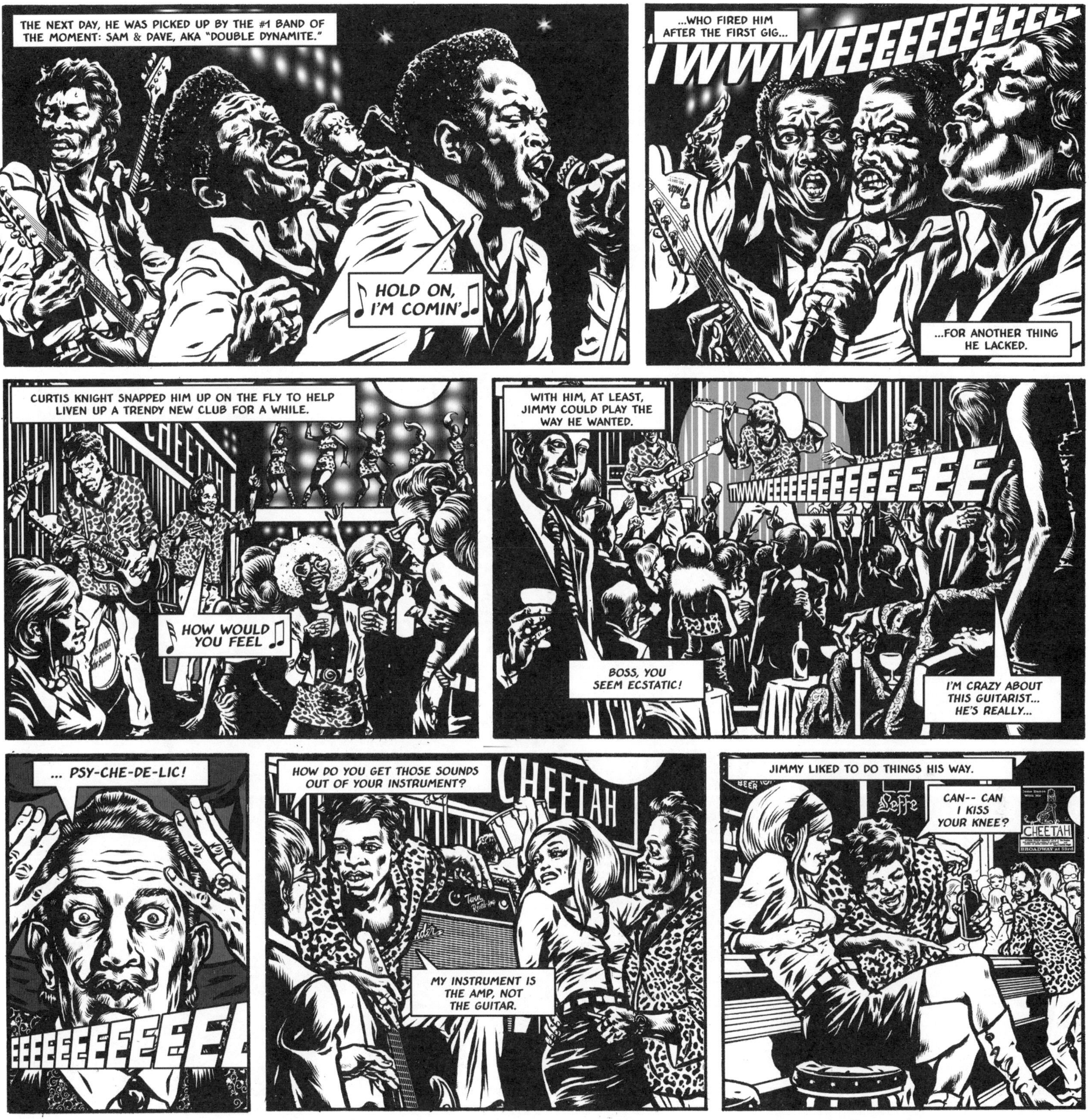
THE NEXT DAY, HE WAS PICKED UP BY THE #1 BAND OF THE MOMENT: SAM & DAVE, AKA "DOUBLE DYNAMITE."
♪ HOLD ON, I'M COMIN' ♫
...WHO FIRED HIM AFTER THE FIRST GIG...
TWWWEEEEEEEEEEEEL
...FOR ANOTHER THING HE LACKED.
CURTIS KNIGHT SNAPPED HIM UP ON THE FLY TO HELP LIVEN UP A TRENDY NEW CLUB FOR A WHILE.
CHEETAH
♪ HOW WOULD YOU FEEL ♫
WITH HIM, AT LEAST, JIMMY COULD PLAY THE WAY HE WANTED.
TWWWEEEEEEEEEEEEE
BOSS, YOU SEEM ECSTATIC!
I'M CRAZY ABOUT THIS GUITARIST... HE'S REALLY...
... PSY-CHE-DE-LIC!
EEEEEEEEEEEEL
HOW DO YOU GET THOSE SOUNDS OUT OF YOUR INSTRUMENT?
CHEETAH
MY INSTRUMENT IS THE AMP, NOT THE GUITAR.
JIMMY LIKED TO DO THINGS HIS WAY.
CAN-- CAN I KISS YOUR KNEE?
CHEETAH
BROADWAY at 53rd

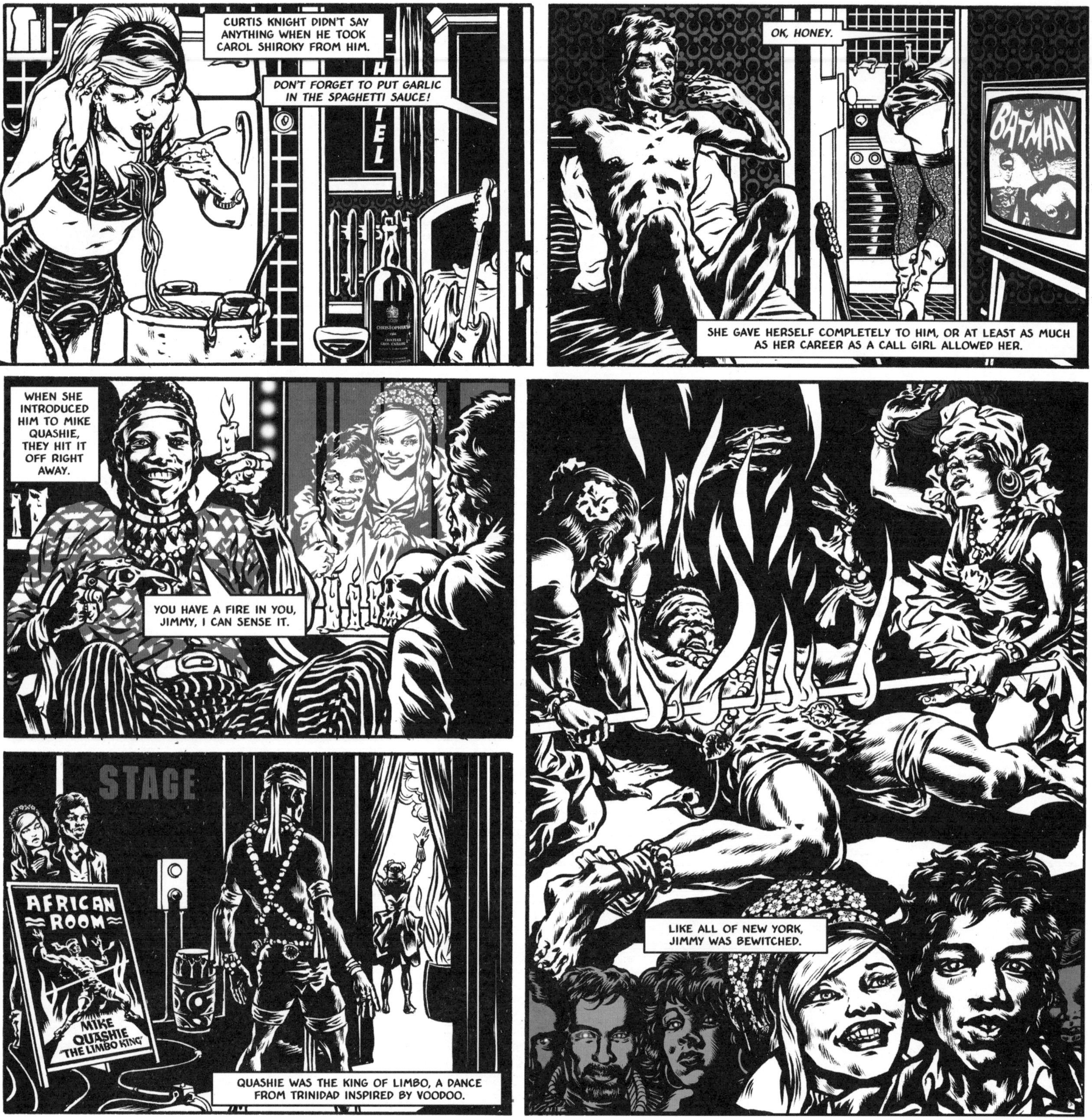
CURTIS KNIGHT DIDN'T SAY ANYTHING WHEN HE TOOK CAROL SHIROKY FROM HIM.
DON'T FORGET TO PUT GARLIC IN THE SPAGHETTI SAUCE!
OK, HONEY.
BATMAN
SHE GAVE HERSELF COMPLETELY TO HIM, OR AT LEAST AS MUCH AS HER CAREER AS A CALL GIRL ALLOWED HER.
WHEN SHE INTRODUCED HIM TO MIKE QUASHIE, THEY HIT IT OFF RIGHT AWAY.
YOU HAVE A FIRE IN YOU, JIMMY, I CAN SENSE IT.
STAGE
AFRICAN ROOM
MIKE QUASHIE "THE LIMBO KING"
QUASHIE WAS THE KING OF LIMBO, A DANCE FROM TRINIDAD INSPIRED BY VOODOO.
LIKE ALL OF NEW YORK, JIMMY WAS BEWITCHED.

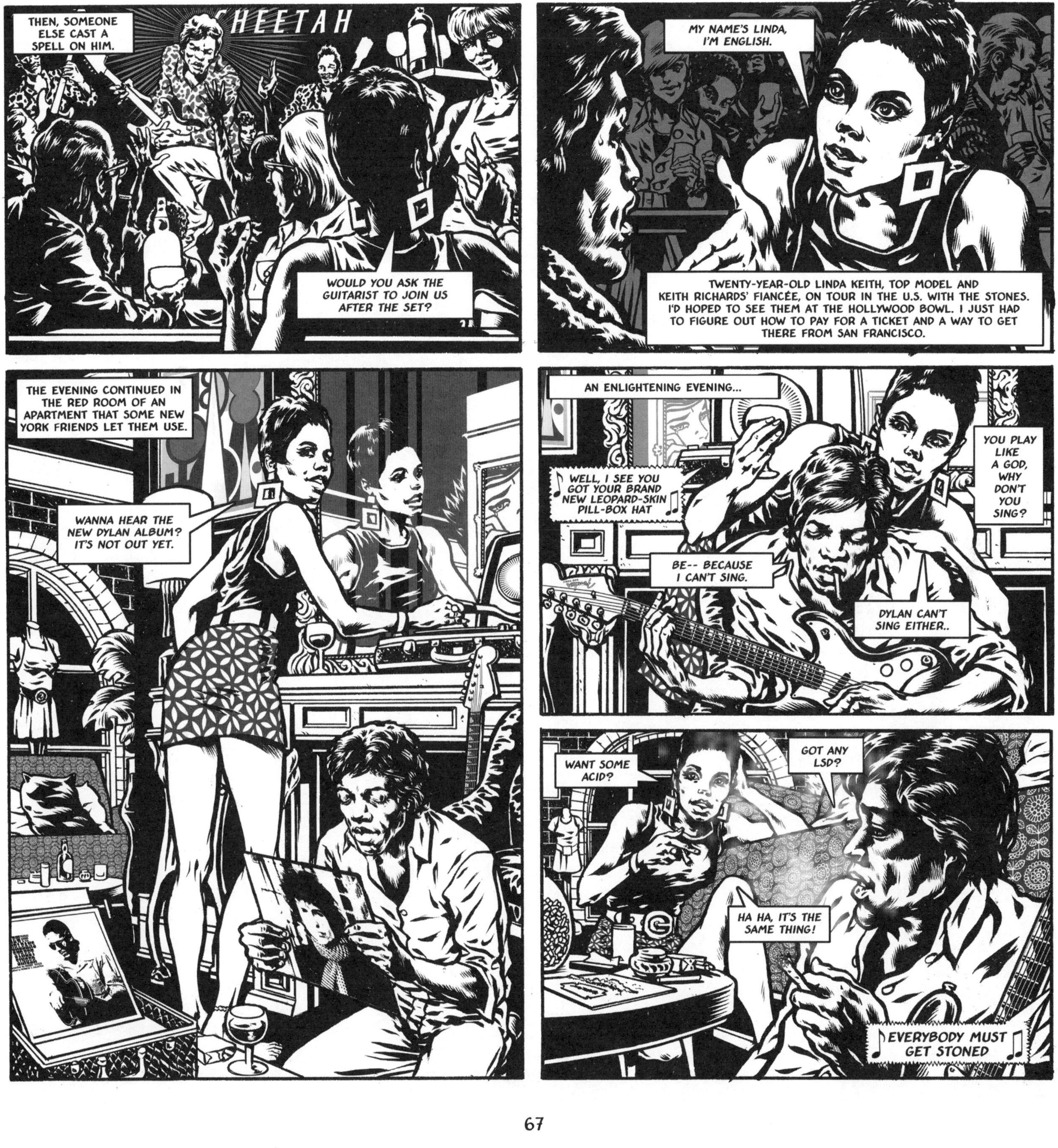
THEN, SOMEONE ELSE CAST A SPELL ON HIM.
CHEETAH
WOULD YOU ASK THE GUITARIST TO JOIN US AFTER THE SET?
MY NAME'S LINDA, I'M ENGLISH.
TWENTY-YEAR-OLD LINDA KEITH, TOP MODEL AND KEITH RICHARDS' FIANCÉE, ON TOUR IN THE U.S. WITH THE STONES. I'D HOPED TO SEE THEM AT THE HOLLYWOOD BOWL. I JUST HAD TO FIGURE OUT HOW TO PAY FOR A TICKET AND A WAY TO GET THERE FROM SAN FRANCISCO.
THE EVENING CONTINUED IN THE RED ROOM OF AN APARTMENT THAT SOME NEW YORK FRIENDS LET THEM USE.
WANNA HEAR THE NEW DYLAN ALBUM? IT'S NOT OUT YET.
AN ENLIGHTENING EVENING...
♪ WELL, I SEE YOU GOT YOUR BRAND NEW LEOPARD-SKIN PILL-BOX HAT ♪
YOU PLAY LIKE A GOD, WHY DON'T YOU SING?
BE-- BECAUSE I CAN'T SING.
DYLAN CAN'T SING EITHER..
WANT SOME ACID?
GOT ANY LSD?
HA HA, IT'S THE SAME THING!
♪ EVERYBODY MUST GET STONED ♪

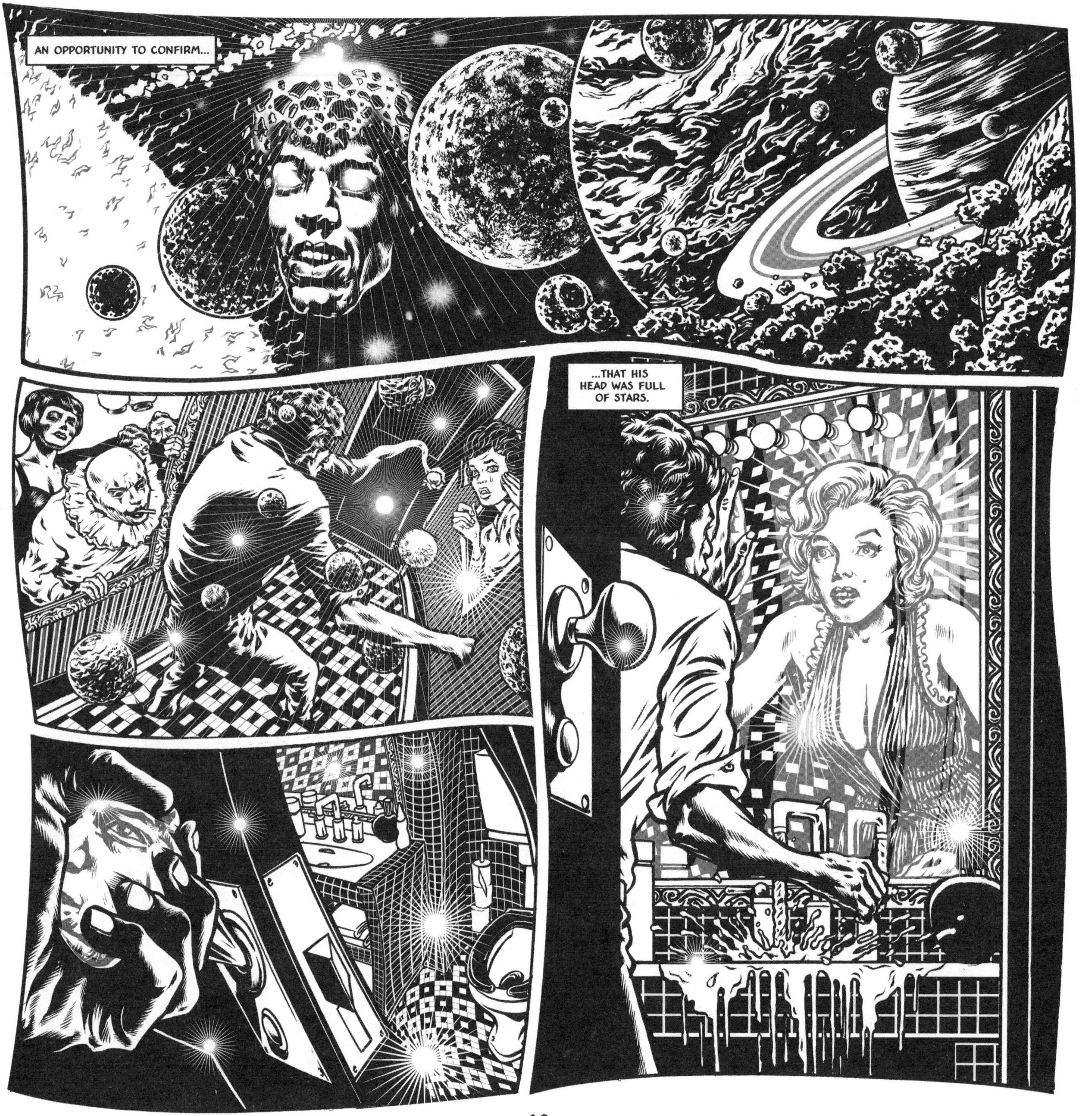
AN OPPORTUNITY TO CONFIRM...
...THAT HIS HEAD WAS FULL OF STARS.

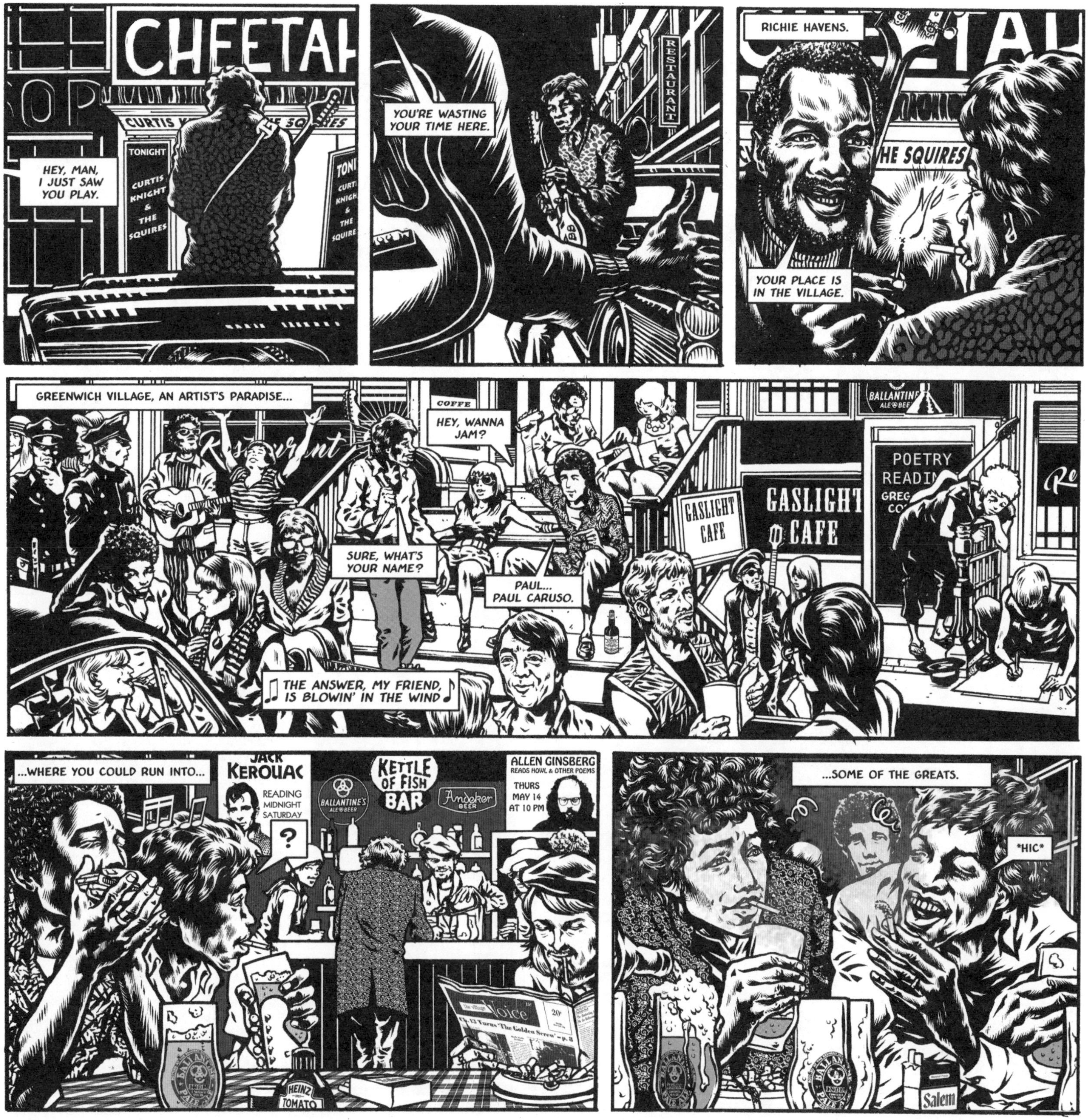
CHEETAH
TONIGHT CURTIS KNIGHT & THE SQUIRES
HEY, MAN, I JUST SAW YOU PLAY.
YOU'RE WASTING YOUR TIME HERE.
RESTAURANT
RICHIE HAVENS.
YOUR PLACE IS IN THE VILLAGE.
GREENWICH VILLAGE, AN ARTIST'S PARADISE...
HEY, WANNA JAM?
SURE, WHAT'S YOUR NAME?
PAUL... PAUL CARUSO.
♪ THE ANSWER, MY FRIEND, IS BLOWIN' IN THE WIND ♪
GASLIGHT CAFE
POETRY READING
...WHERE YOU COULD RUN INTO...
JACK KEROUAC READING MIDNIGHT SATURDAY
?
KETTLE OF FISH BAR
ALLEN GINSBERG READS HOWL & OTHER POEMS THURS MAY 14 AT 10 PM
...SOME OF THE GREATS.
HIC
Salem

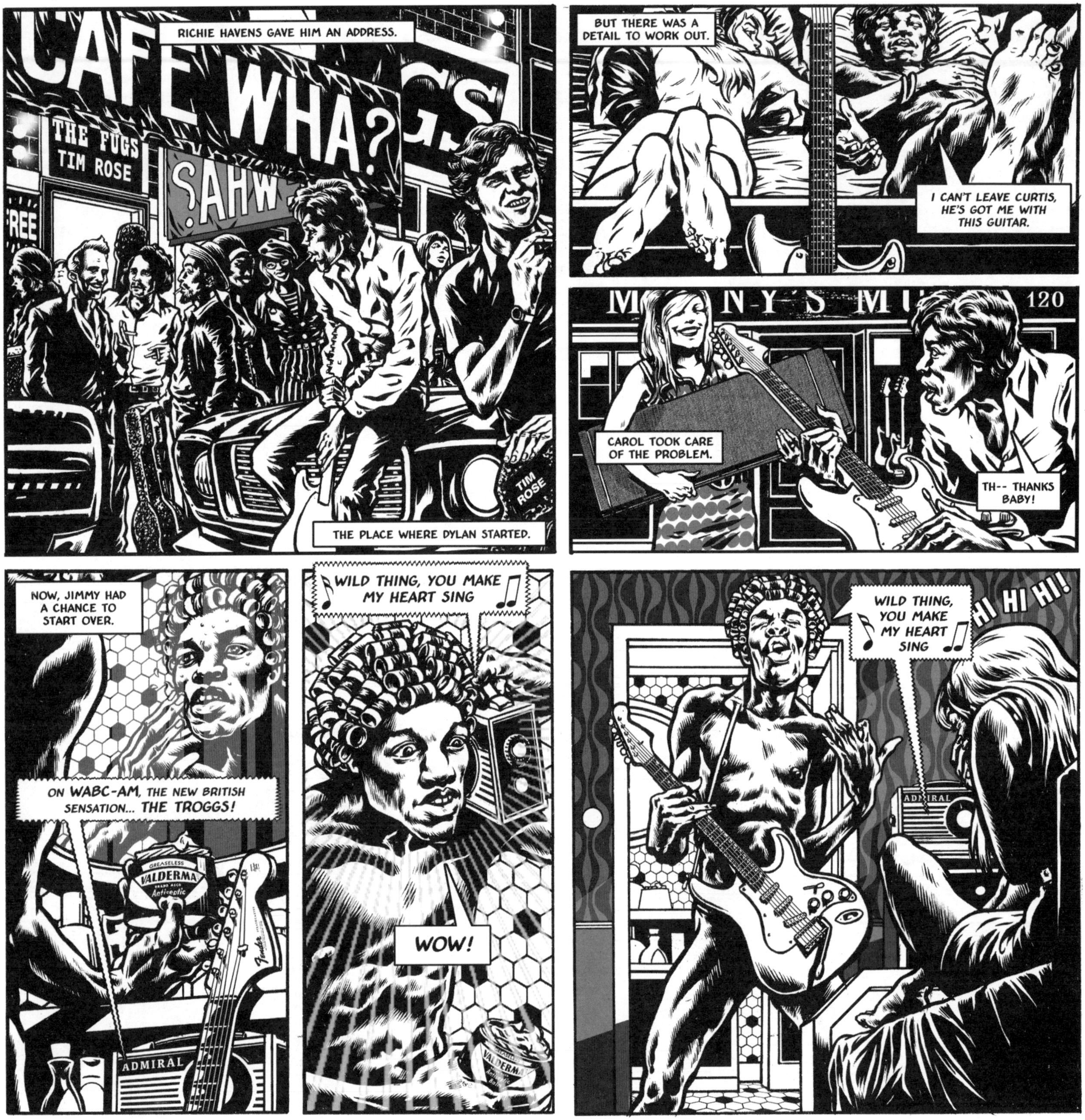
CAFE WHA?
THE FUGS
TIM ROSE
RICHIE HAVENS GAVE HIM AN ADDRESS.
THE PLACE WHERE DYLAN STARTED.
BUT THERE WAS A DETAIL TO WORK OUT.
I CAN'T LEAVE CURTIS, HE'S GOT ME WITH THIS GUITAR.
CAROL TOOK CARE OF THE PROBLEM.
TH-- THANKS BABY!
NOW, JIMMY HAD A CHANCE TO START OVER.
ON WABC-AM, THE NEW BRITISH SENSATION... THE TROGGS!
ADMIRAL
WILD THING, YOU MAKE MY HEART SING
WOW!
WILD THING, YOU MAKE MY HEART SING
HI HI HI!

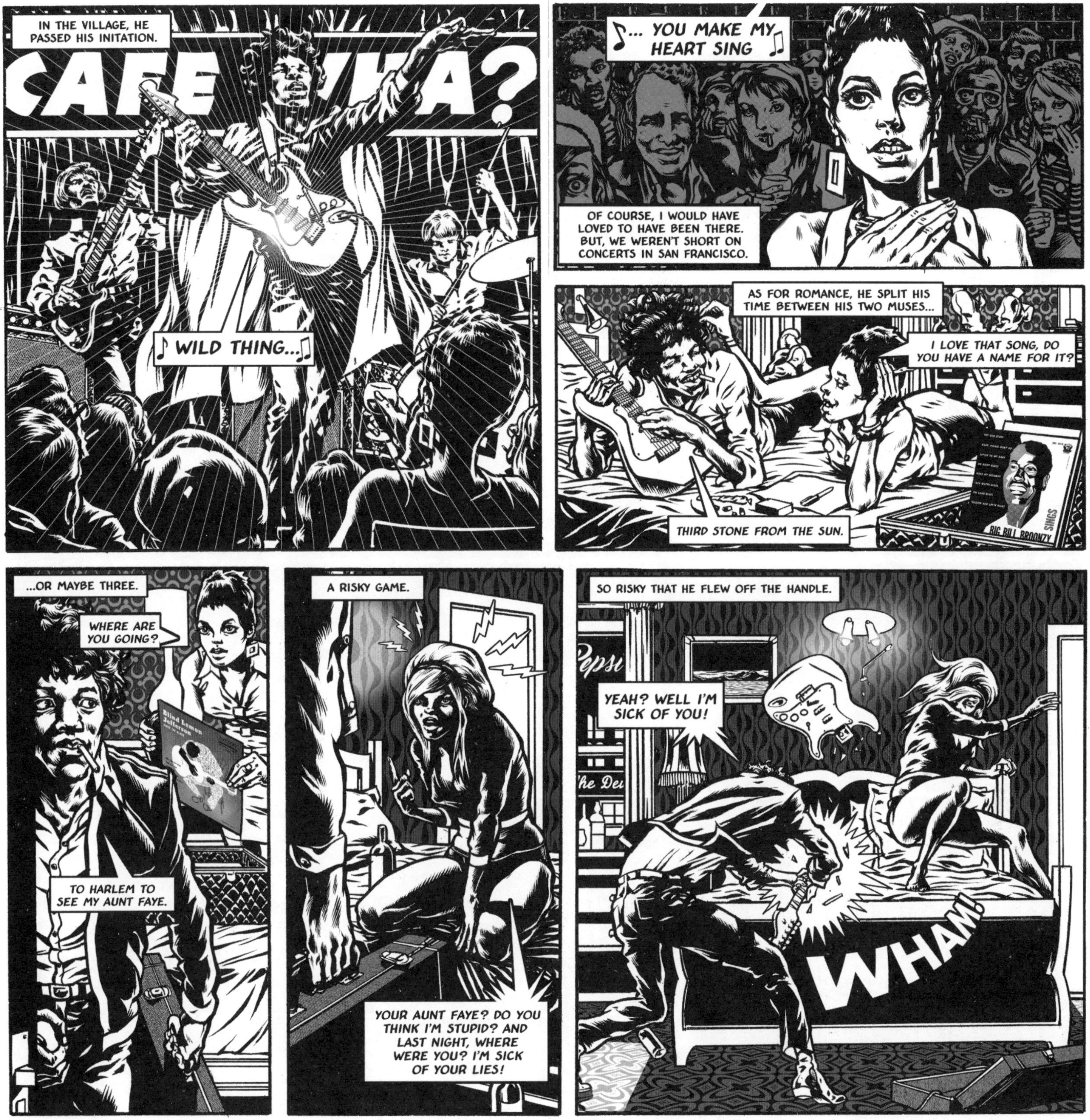
IN THE VILLAGE, HE PASSED HIS INITATION.
CAFE WHA?
WILD THING...
... YOU MAKE MY HEART SING
OF COURSE, I WOULD HAVE LOVED TO HAVE BEEN THERE. BUT, WE WEREN'T SHORT ON CONCERTS IN SAN FRANCISCO.
AS FOR ROMANCE, HE SPLIT HIS TIME BETWEEN HIS TWO MUSES...
I LOVE THAT SONG, DO YOU HAVE A NAME FOR IT?
THIRD STONE FROM THE SUN.
BIG BILL BROONZY SINGS
...OR MAYBE THREE.
WHERE ARE YOU GOING?
TO HARLEM TO SEE MY AUNT FAYE.
A RISKY GAME.
YOUR AUNT FAYE? DO YOU THINK I'M STUPID? AND LAST NIGHT, WHERE WERE YOU? I'M SICK OF YOUR LIES!
SO RISKY THAT HE FLEW OFF THE HANDLE.
YEAH? WELL I'M SICK OF YOU!
WHAM!

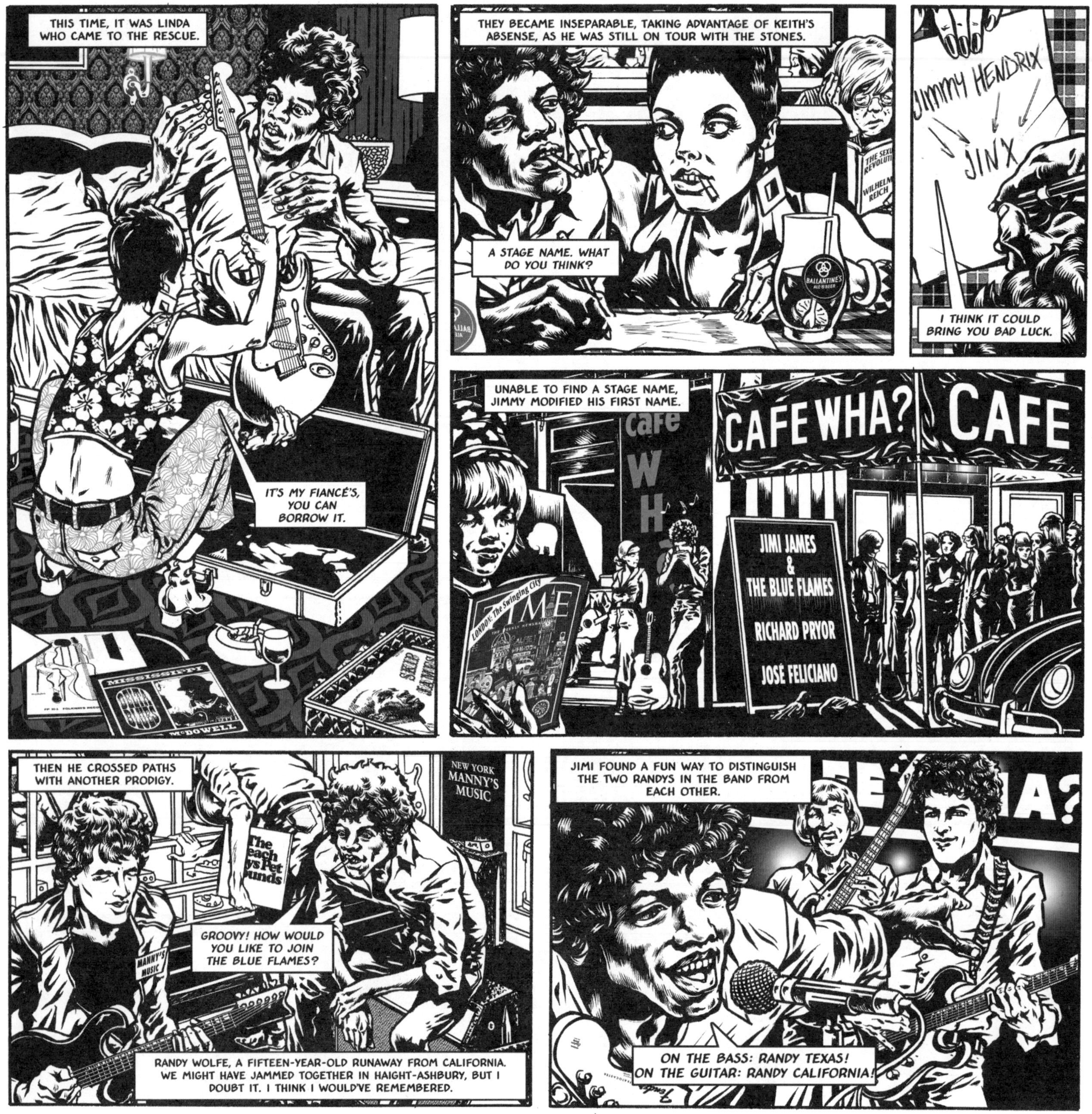
THIS TIME, IT WAS LINDA WHO CAME TO THE RESCUE.
IT'S MY FIANCÉ'S, YOU CAN BORROW IT.
MISSISSIPPI
McDOWELL
THEY BECAME INSEPARABLE, TAKING ADVANTAGE OF KEITH'S ABSENSE, AS HE WAS STILL ON TOUR WITH THE STONES.
A STAGE NAME. WHAT DO YOU THINK?
THE SEXUAL REVOLUTION
WILHELM REICH
BALLANTINE'S ALE & BEER
JIMMY HENDRIX
JINX
I THINK IT COULD BRING YOU BAD LUCK.
UNABLE TO FIND A STAGE NAME, JIMMY MODIFIED HIS FIRST NAME.
CAFE WHA?
CAFE
TIME
LONDON: The Swinging City
JIMI JAMES
&
THE BLUE FLAMES
RICHARD PRYOR
JOSÉ FELICIANO
THEN HE CROSSED PATHS WITH ANOTHER PRODIGY.
NEW YORK
MANNY'S
MUSIC
GROOVY! HOW WOULD YOU LIKE TO JOIN THE BLUE FLAMES?
MANNY'S MUSIC
RANDY WOLFE, A FIFTEEN-YEAR-OLD RUNAWAY FROM CALIFORNIA. WE MIGHT HAVE JAMMED TOGETHER IN HAIGHT-ASHBURY, BUT I DOUBT IT. I THINK I WOULD'VE REMEMBERED.
JIMI FOUND A FUN WAY TO DISTINGUISH THE TWO RANDYS IN THE BAND FROM EACH OTHER.
ON THE BASS: RANDY TEXAS!
ON THE GUITAR: RANDY CALIFORNIA!

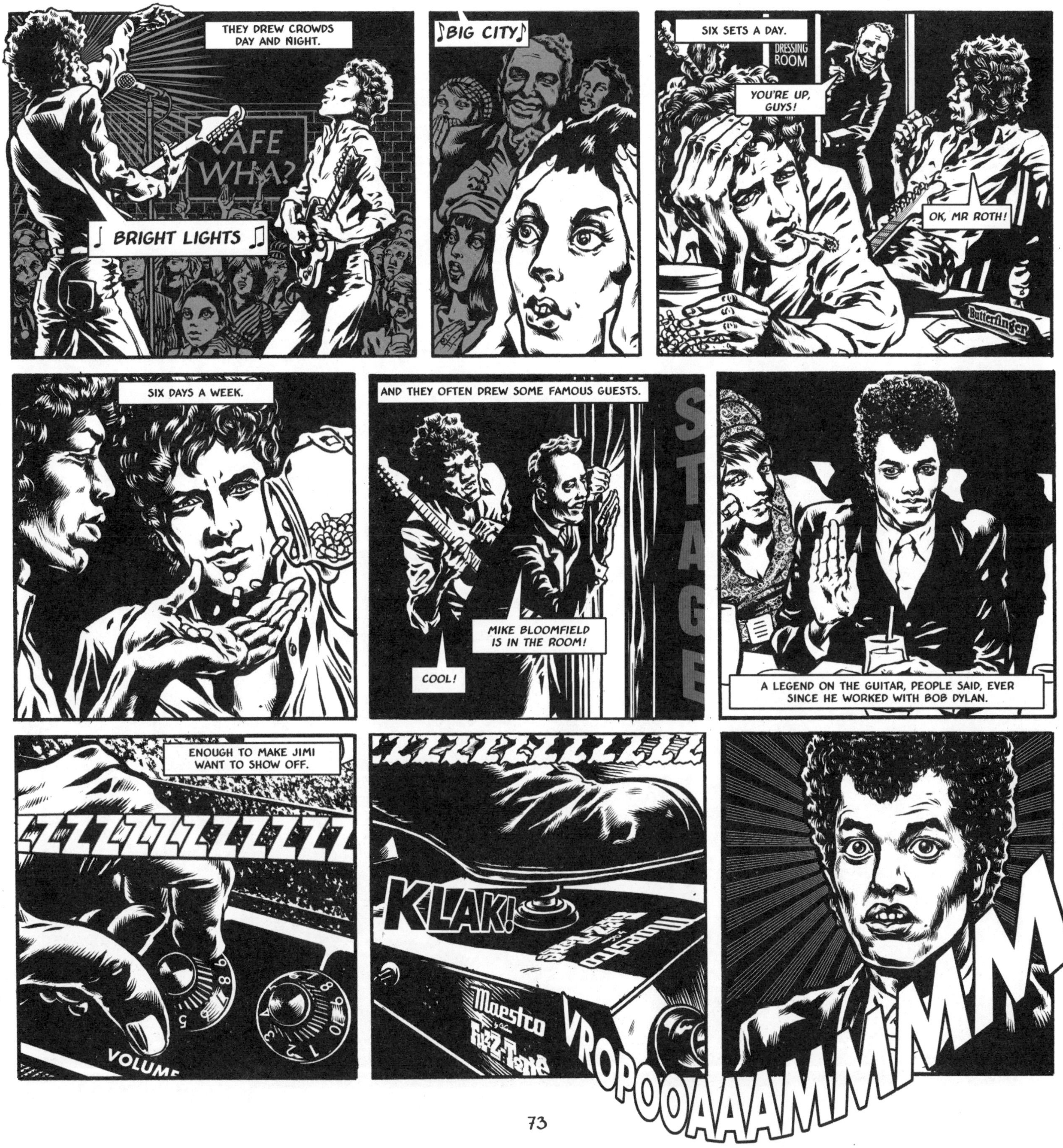
THEY DREW CROWDS DAY AND NIGHT.
AFE WHA?
BRIGHT LIGHTS
BIG CITY
SIX SETS A DAY.
DRESSING ROOM
YOU'RE UP, GUYS!
OK, MR ROTH!
Butterfinger
SIX DAYS A WEEK.
AND THEY OFTEN DREW SOME FAMOUS GUESTS.
STAGE
MIKE BLOOMFIELD IS IN THE ROOM!
COOL!
A LEGEND ON THE GUITAR, PEOPLE SAID, EVER SINCE HE WORKED WITH BOB DYLAN.
ENOUGH TO MAKE JIMI WANT TO SHOW OFF.
ZZZZZZZZZZZZ
VOLUME
ZZZZZZZZZZZZZZZ
KLAK!
Maestro Fuzz-Tone
VROPOOAAAMMMMMM!

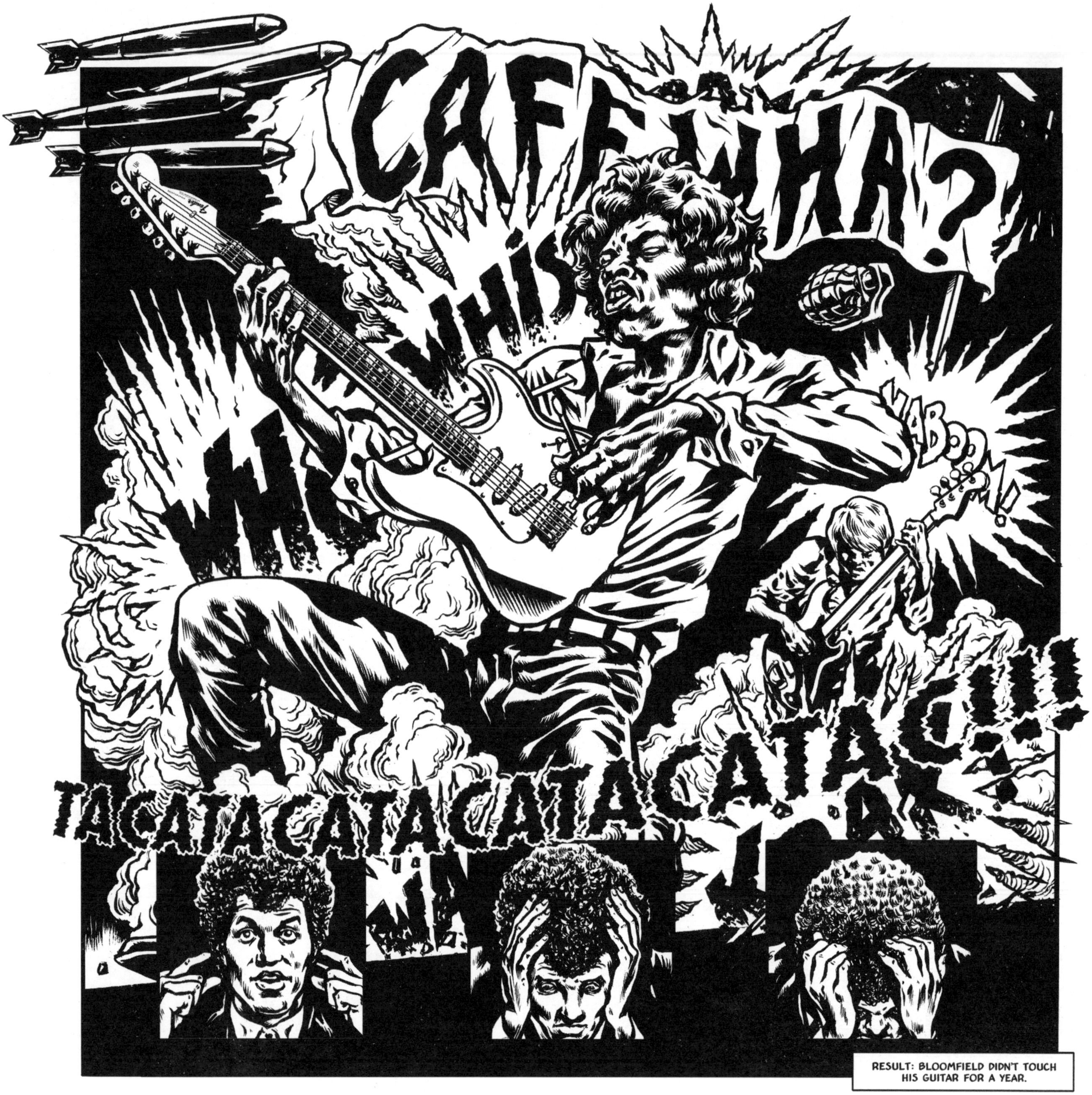
CAFE WHA?
TACATACATACATACATAC!!!
RESULT: BLOOMFIELD DIDN'T TOUCH HIS GUITAR FOR A YEAR.

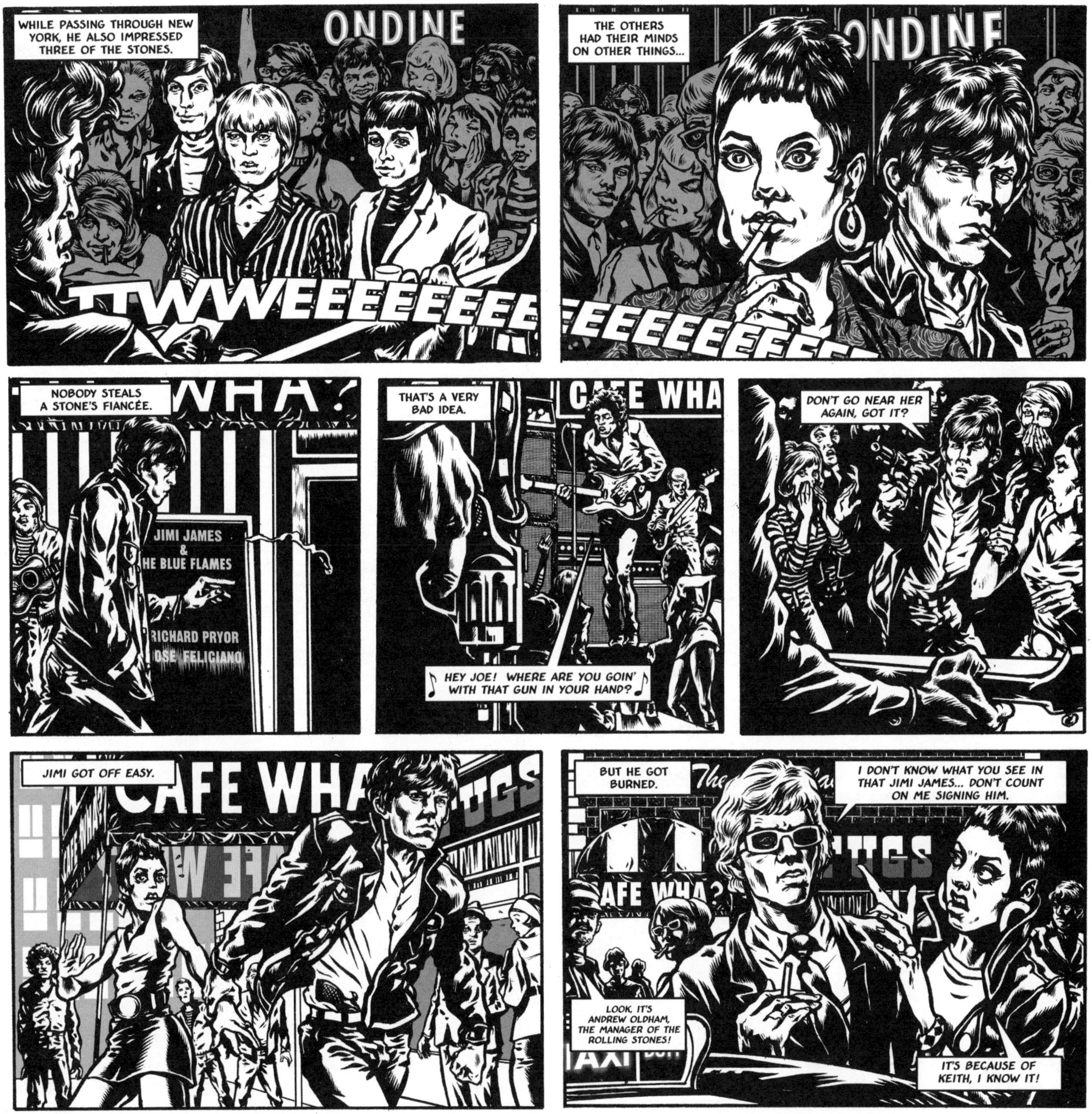
WHILE PASSING THROUGH NEW YORK, HE ALSO IMPRESSED THREE OF THE STONES.
ONDINE
TTWWEEEEEEEE
THE OTHERS HAD THEIR MINDS ON OTHER THINGS...
ONDINE
EEEEEEEEEE
NOBODY STEALS A STONE'S FIANCÉE.
JIMI JAMES & THE BLUE FLAMES
RICHARD PRYOR
JOSE FELICIANO
THAT'S A VERY BAD IDEA.
CAFE WHA
HEY JOE! WHERE ARE YOU GOIN' WITH THAT GUN IN YOUR HAND?
DON'T GO NEAR HER AGAIN, GOT IT?
JIMI GOT OFF EASY.
CAFE WHA
BUT HE GOT BURNED.
I DON'T KNOW WHAT YOU SEE IN THAT JIMI JAMES... DON'T COUNT ON ME SIGNING HIM.
LOOK, IT'S ANDREW OLDHAM, THE MANAGER OF THE ROLLING STONES!
IT'S BECAUSE OF KEITH, I KNOW IT!
TAXI

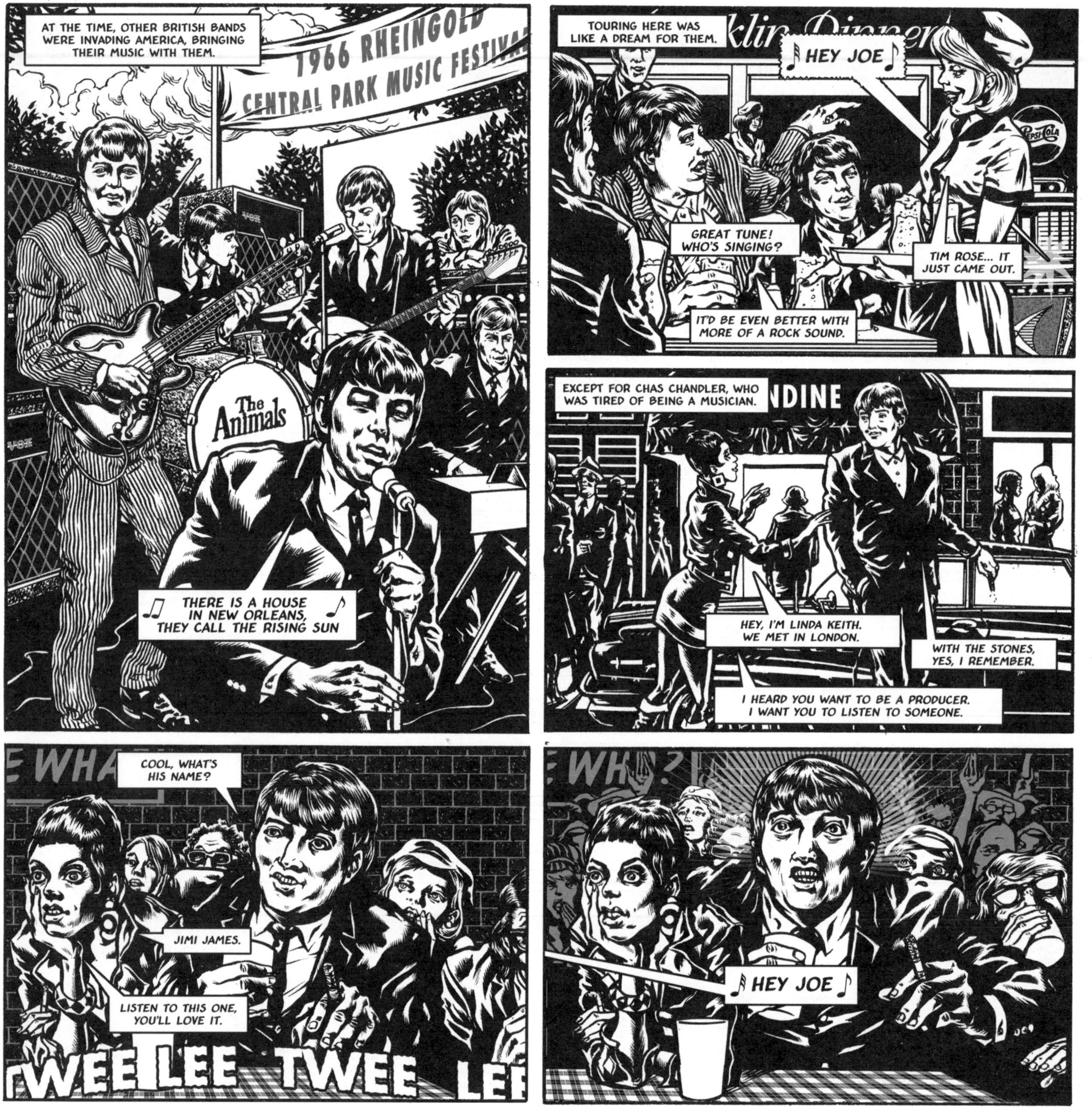
AT THE TIME, OTHER BRITISH BANDS WERE INVADING AMERICA, BRINGING THEIR MUSIC WITH THEM.
1966 RHEINGOLD
CENTRAL PARK MUSIC FESTIVA
The Animals
♫ THERE IS A HOUSE IN NEW ORLEANS, THEY CALL THE RISING SUN ♪
TOURING HERE WAS LIKE A DREAM FOR THEM.
♪ HEY JOE ♪
GREAT TUNE! WHO'S SINGING?
TIM ROSE... IT JUST CAME OUT.
IT'D BE EVEN BETTER WITH MORE OF A ROCK SOUND.
EXCEPT FOR CHAS CHANDLER, WHO WAS TIRED OF BEING A MUSICIAN.
HEY, I'M LINDA KEITH. WE MET IN LONDON.
WITH THE STONES, YES, I REMEMBER.
I HEARD YOU WANT TO BE A PRODUCER. I WANT YOU TO LISTEN TO SOMEONE.
COOL, WHAT'S HIS NAME?
JIMI JAMES.
LISTEN TO THIS ONE, YOU'LL LOVE IT.
TWEE LEE TWEE
♪ HEY JOE ♪

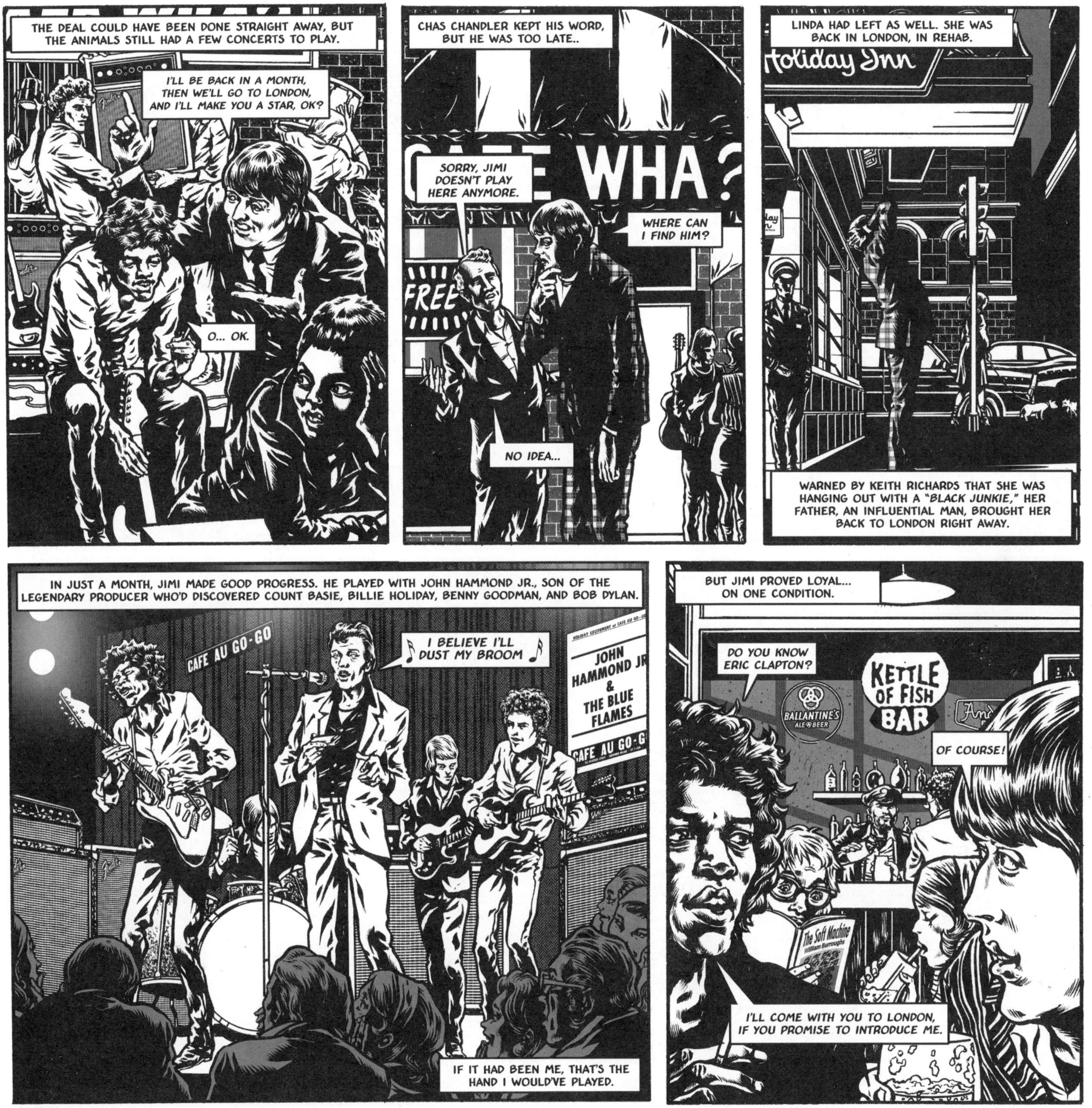
THE DEAL COULD HAVE BEEN DONE STRAIGHT AWAY, BUT THE ANIMALS STILL HAD A FEW CONCERTS TO PLAY.
I'LL BE BACK IN A MONTH, THEN WE'LL GO TO LONDON, AND I'LL MAKE YOU A STAR, OK?
O... OK.
CHAS CHANDLER KEPT HIS WORD, BUT HE WAS TOO LATE..
E WHA?
SORRY, JIMI DOESN'T PLAY HERE ANYMORE.
WHERE CAN I FIND HIM?
FREE
NO IDEA...
LINDA HAD LEFT AS WELL. SHE WAS BACK IN LONDON, IN REHAB.
Holiday Inn
WARNED BY KEITH RICHARDS THAT SHE WAS HANGING OUT WITH A "*BLACK JUNKIE*," HER FATHER, AN INFLUENTIAL MAN, BROUGHT HER BACK TO LONDON RIGHT AWAY.
IN JUST A MONTH, JIMI MADE GOOD PROGRESS. HE PLAYED WITH JOHN HAMMOND JR., SON OF THE LEGENDARY PRODUCER WHO'D DISCOVERED COUNT BASIE, BILLIE HOLIDAY, BENNY GOODMAN, AND BOB DYLAN.
CAFE AU GO-GO
♪ I BELIEVE I'LL DUST MY BROOM ♪
JOHN HAMMOND JR & THE BLUE FLAMES
CAFE AU GO-GO
IF IT HAD BEEN ME, THAT'S THE HAND I WOULD'VE PLAYED.
BUT JIMI PROVED LOYAL... ON ONE CONDITION.
DO YOU KNOW ERIC CLAPTON?
KETTLE OF FISH BAR
BALLANTINE'S ALE BEER
OF COURSE!
The Soft Machine
William Burroughs
I'LL COME WITH YOU TO LONDON, IF YOU PROMISE TO INTRODUCE ME.

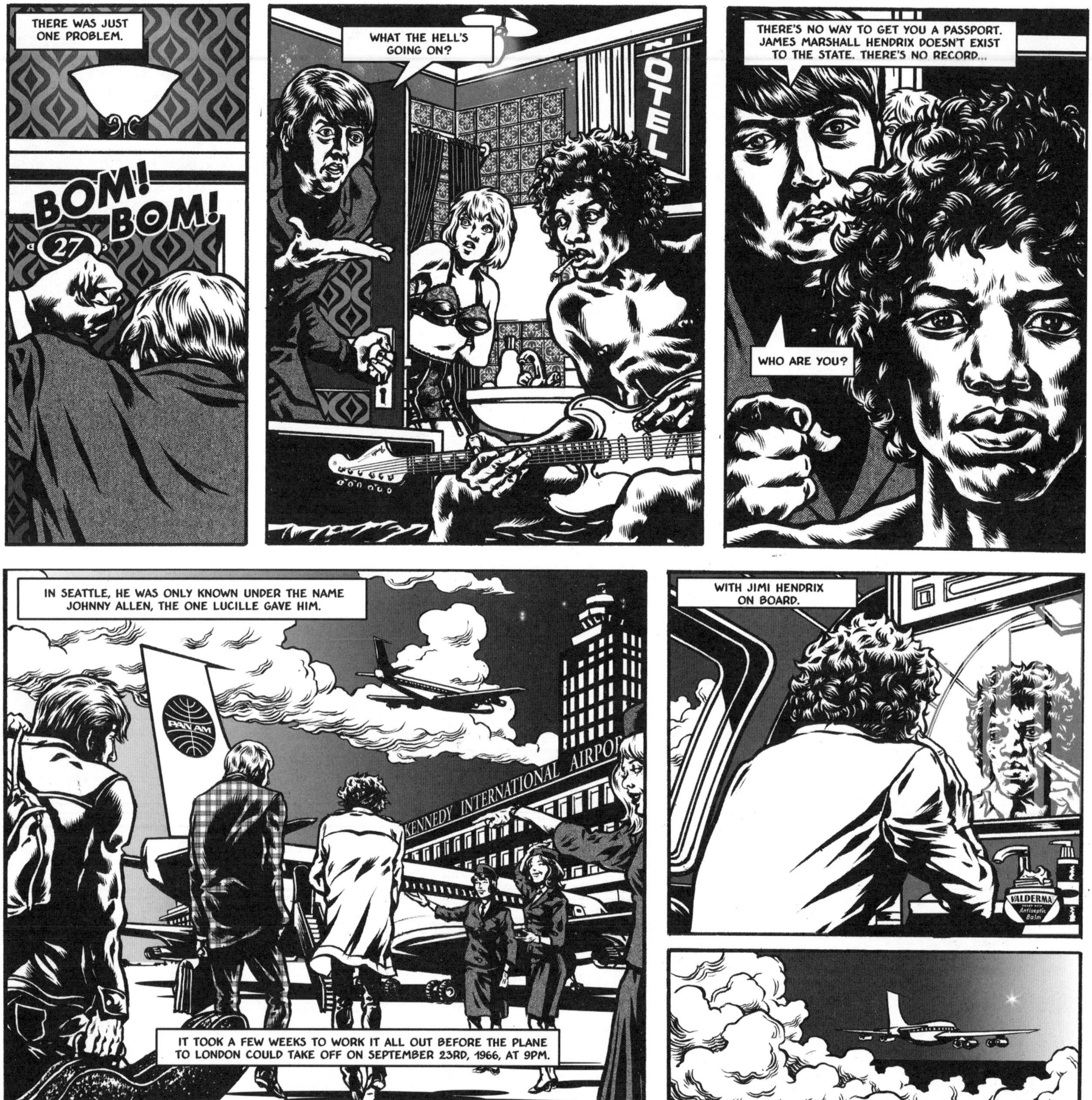
THERE WAS JUST ONE PROBLEM.
BOM! BOM!
27
WHAT THE HELL'S GOING ON?
THERE'S NO WAY TO GET YOU A PASSPORT. JAMES MARSHALL HENDRIX DOESN'T EXIST TO THE STATE. THERE'S NO RECORD...
WHO ARE YOU?
IN SEATTLE, HE WAS ONLY KNOWN UNDER THE NAME JOHNNY ALLEN, THE ONE LUCILLE GAVE HIM.
KENNEDY INTERNATIONAL
IT TOOK A FEW WEEKS TO WORK IT ALL OUT BEFORE THE PLANE TO LONDON COULD TAKE OFF ON SEPTEMBER 23RD, 1966, AT 9PM.
WITH JIMI HENDRIX ON BOARD.
VALDERMA
Antiseptic Balm

EVEN TODAY, AFTER ALL THESE DECADES, I WONDER WHAT HE FELT AS HE SOARED TOWARDS THE LIGHT, LEAVING BEHIND TWENTY-FOUR YEARS OF MISERY AND STRUGGLE. PERHAPS IT FELT LIKE A SECOND BIRTH, WHERE THIS TIME HE WOULD BE WANTED.

END OF PART ONE.

Well, I'm up here in this womb (...)
Well, I'm looking out my belly button window (...)
And I'm wondering if they don't want me around.

Jimi Hendrix - *Belly Button Window*

SOUNDTRACK

Page 8/panels 3 & 9
Chi-Baba Chi-Baba (My Bambino Go to Sleep),
Perry Como (1947)
Songwriters: Mack David, Jerry Livingston, Al Hoffman

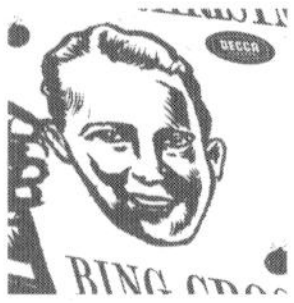

Page 12/panel 2
White Christmas,
Bing Crosby (1942)
Songwriter: Irving Berlin

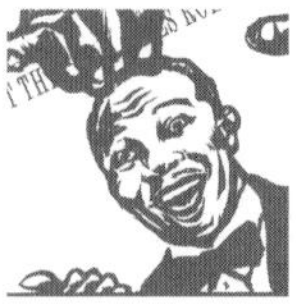

Page 12/panels 6 & 8
Let the Good Times Roll,
Louis Jordan and his Tympany Five (1946)
Songwriters: Sam Theard, Fleecie Moore

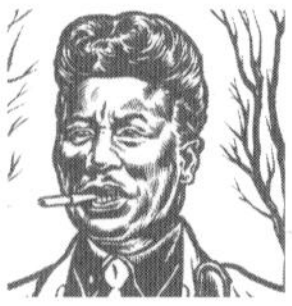

Page 20/panel 9
Mannish Boy,
Muddy Waters (1955)
Songwriters: Muddy Waters, Mel London, Bo Diddley

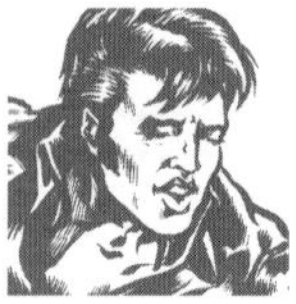

Page 21/panel 1
Hound Dog,
Elvis Presley (1955)
Songwriters: Jerry Leiber, Mike Stoller

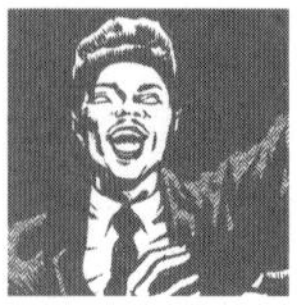

Page 21/panel 7
Tutti Frutti,
Little Richard (1955)
Songwriters: Little Richard, Dorothy LaBostrie, Joe Lubin

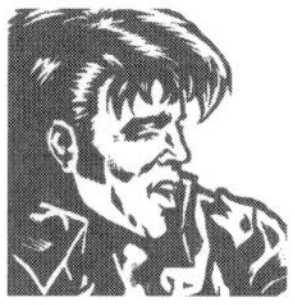

Page 23/panels 6 & 7
Blue Suede Shoes,
Elvis Presley (1956)
Songwriter: Carl Perkins

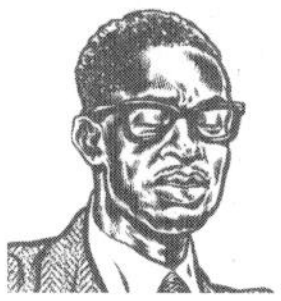

Page 26/panel 6
Dust My Broom,
Elmore James (1951)
Songwriter: Robert Johnson

Page 28/panel 2
Honky Tonk,
Bill Doggett (1956)
Songwriters: Billy Butler, Bill Doggett, Shep Shepherd, Clifford Scott

Page 28/panel 4
CC Rider,
Chuck Willis (1957)
Songwriters: Lena Arent, Ma Rainey

Page 29/panels 4 & 5
Blueberry Hill,
Fats Domino (1956)
Songwriters: Al Lewis, Larry Stock, Vincent Rose

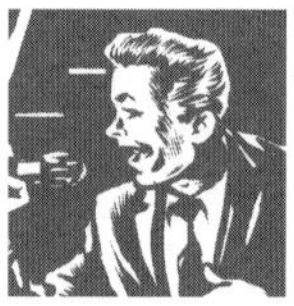

Page 29/panel 7
Louie Louie,
The Fabulous Wailers (1961)
Songwriter: Richard Berry

Page 30/panel 3
Come on,
Earl King (1960)
Songwriter: Earl King

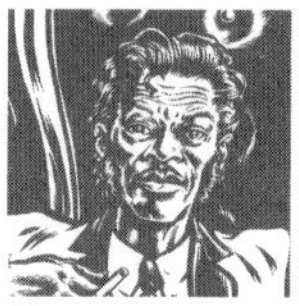

Page 33/panel 6
The Twist,
Chubby Checker (1960)
Songwriter: Hank Ballard

Page 36/panel 2
Stand by Me,
Ben E. King (1961)
Songwriter: Ben E. King, Jerry Leiber, Mike Stoller

Page 36/panel 4
Bright Lights, Big City,
Jimmy Reed (1961)
Songwriter: Jimmy Reed

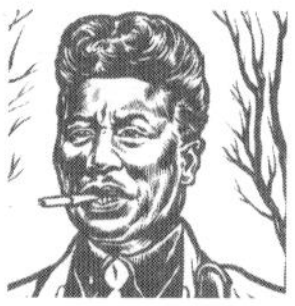

Page 38/panel 2
Got My Mojo Working,
Muddy Waters (1957)
Songwriter: Preston Foster

Page 38/panel 5
Poison Ivy,
The Coasters (1959)
Songwriters: Jerry Leiber, Mike Stoller

*When the song was covered by Jimi Hendrix with one of his bands, the credited performer is the one who recorded the most famous version.

**Page 42/panel 1,
page 43/panel 5**
What'd I Say,
Ray Charles (1959)
Songwriter: Ray Charles

Page 48/panel 4
Twist and Shout,
The Isley Brothers (1962)
Songwriters: Phil Medley,
Bert Berns

Page 54/panel 2
It's All over Now,
The Valentinos (1964)
Songwriters: Bobby Womack,
Shirley Womack

Page 43/panel 2
The Twist,
Hank Ballard
and The Midnighters (1959)
Songwriter: Hank Ballard

**Page 49/panel 6,
page 50/panel 2**
Testify,
The Isley Brothers (1964)
Songwriters: Ronald Isley,
O'Kelly Isley Jr, Rudolph Isley

Page 55/panel 4
Lucille,
Little Richard (1957)
Songwriters: Albert Collins,
Little Richard

Page 44/panel 1
It's All Right,
The Impressions (1963)
Songwriter: Curtis Mayfield

Page 49/panel 7
Mercy Mercy,
Don Covay
& The Goodtimers (1964)
Songwriters: Don Covay,
Ronald Alonzo Miller

Page 56/panel 2
Tutti Frutti,
Little Richard (1955)
Songwriters: Little Richard,
Dorothy LaBostrie, Joe Lubin

Page 46/panel 2
Do You Love Me,
The Contours (1962)
Songwriter: Berry Gordy Jr

Page 51/panel 2
*Everybody Needs
Somebody to Love*,
Solomon Burke (1964)
Songwriters: Bert Berns,
Solomon Burke, Jerry Wexler

Page 57/panel 1
I'm Jealous,
Ike & Tina Turner (1961)
Songwriters: Ike Turner,
Jane Bossung

Page 47/panel 5
The Things That I Used to Do,
Guitar Slim (1954)
Songwriter: Guitar Slim

Page 51/panel 4
*What Kind of Fool
(Do You Think I Am)*,
The Tams (1964)
Songwriter: Ray Whitley

Page 58/panel 1
My Diary,
Rosa Lee Brooks (1965)
Songwriters: Rosa Lee Brooks,
Jimi Hendrix, Arthur Lee

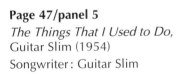
Page 48/panels 2 & 3
Twist and Shout,
The Beatles (1963)
Songwriter: Phil Medley,
Bert Russell

Page 53/panel 4
A Change Is Gonna Come,
Sam Cooke (1964)
Songwriter: Sam Cooke

Page 58/panel 2
Bama Lama Bama Loo,
Little Richard (1964)
Songwriter: Little Richard

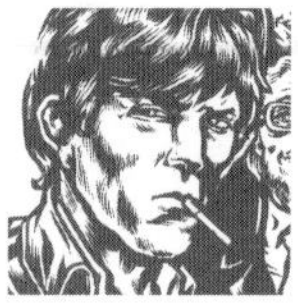

Page 59/panel 4
Mercy, Mercy,
The Rolling Stones (1965)
Songwriters: Don Covay,
Ronald Alonzo Miller

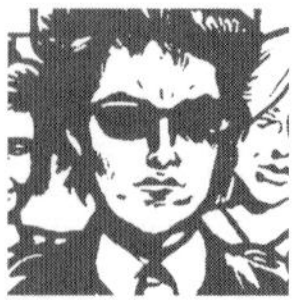

Page 59/panel 6
Like a Rolling Stone,
Bob Dylan (1965)
Songwriter: Bob Dylan

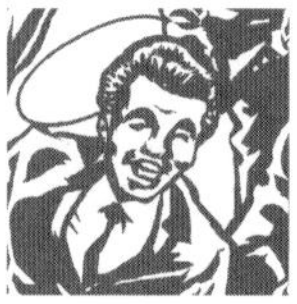

Page 61/panel 1
Peppermint Twist,
Joey Dee and the Starliters (1961)
Songwriters: Joey Dee,
Henry Glover

Page 61/panel 4
I Ain't Got You,
The Yardbirds (1965)
Songwriter: Calvin Carter

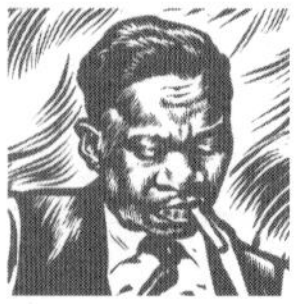

Page 62/panels 1 & 2
Sweet Little Angel,
BB King (1956)
Songwriters: Lucie Bogan,
Jules Taub, BB King

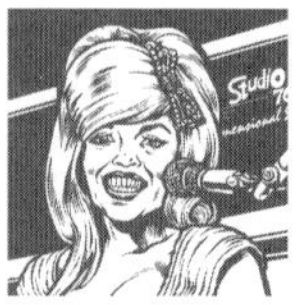

Page 64/panel 1
Suey,
Jayne Mansfield (1966)
Songwriters: Ed Chalpin,
Jocko Henderson

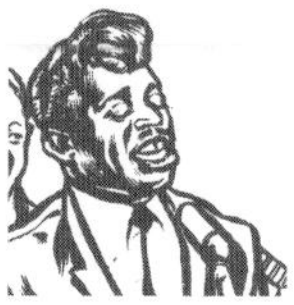

Page 64/panel 3
When a Man Loves a Woman,
Percy Sledge (1966)
Songwriters: Calvin Lewis,
Andrew Wright

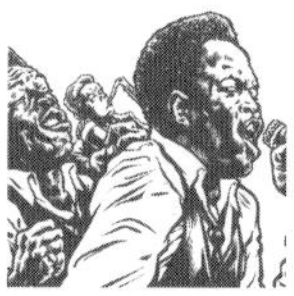

Page 65/panel 1
Hold on, I'm Comin',
Sam & Dave (1966)
Songwriters: Isaac Hayes,
David Porter

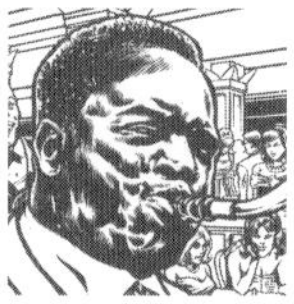

Page 65/panel 3
How Would You Feel,
Curtis Knight
& The Squires (1965)
Songwriter: Curtis Knight

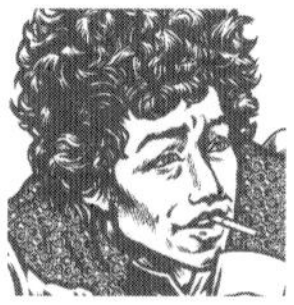

Page 67/panel 4
Leopard-Skin Pill-Box Hat,
Bob Dylan (1966)
Page 71/panel 5
Rainy Day Women #12 & 35,
Bob Dylan (1966)
Songwriter: Bob Dylan

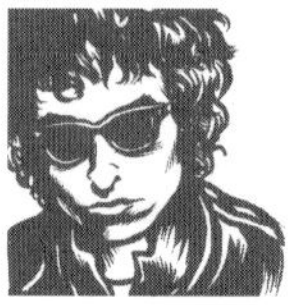

Page 69/panel 4
Blowin' in the Wind,
Bob Dylan (1963)
Songwriter: Bob Dylan

Page 70/panels 5 & 6,
page 71/panels 1 & 2
Wild Thing,
The Troggs (1966)
Songwriter: Chip Taylor

Page 73/panels 1 & 2
Bright Lights, Big City,
Jimmy Reed (1961)
Songwriter: Jimmy Reed

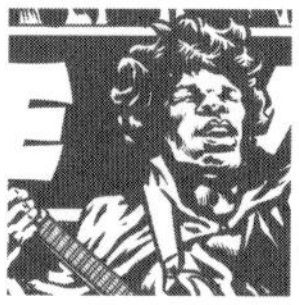

Page 75/panel 4
Hey Joe,
Jimi Hendrix (1966)
Songwriter: Billy Roberts

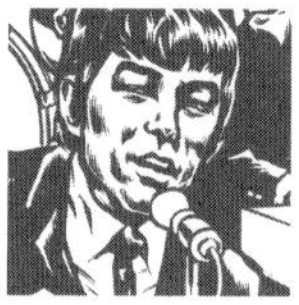

Page 76/panel 1
House of the Rising Sun,
The Animals (1964)
Songwriter: Traditionnel
(arrangement Alan Price)

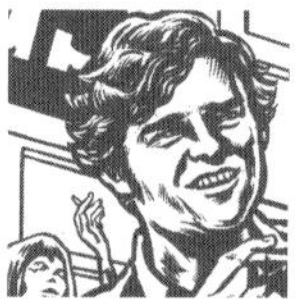

Page 76/panel 2
Hey Joe,
Tim Rose (1966)
Songwriter: Billy Roberts

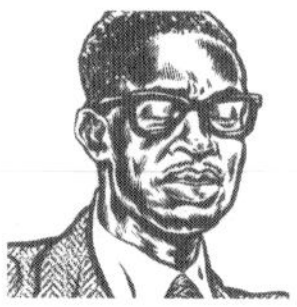

Page 77/panel 4
Dust My Broom,
Elmore James (1951)
Songwriter: Robert Johnson

SOURCES

BOOKS

My Son Jimi,
James A. Hendrix (AlJas Enterprises), 1999.

Jimi Hendrix. A Brother's Story,
Leon Hendrix (Thomas Dunne Books), 2012.

Jimi Hendrix. Voices From Home,
Mary Willix (Creative Forces Publishing), 1995.

Becoming Jimi Hendrix,
Steven Roby & Brad Schreiber (Da Capo Press), 2010.

Jimi Hendrix. L'Expérience des limites,
Charles R. Cross (Camion blanc), 2006.

Jimi Hendrix. Electric Gypsy,
Harry Shapiro & Caesar Glebeek (St. Martin's Press), 1995.

Jimi Hendrix. Vie & légende,
Charles Shaar Murray (Points), 1989.

Jimi Hendrix Musician,
Keith Shadwick (Backbeat Books), 2012.

Hendrix: Setting the Record Straight,
John McDermott & Eddie Kramer (Warner Books), 1992.

Hendrix on Hendrix,
Steven Roby (Chicago Review Press), 2012.

Black Gold. The Lost Archives of Jimi Hendrix,
Steven Roby (Billboard Books), 2002.

Univibes. International Hendrix Magazine,
Jimpress (Steve Rodham).

Jimi Hendrix. The Ultimate Experience,
Johnny Black (Thunder's Mouth Press), 1999.

Jimi Hendrix. Photos, manuscrits & chansons,
Janie L. Hendrix (White Star), 2013.

The Rough Guide to Jimi Hendrix,
Richie Unterberger (Rough Guides), 2009.

Jimi Hendrix. La Totale,
Jean-Michel Guesdon & Philippe Margotin (E, P, A), 2019.

Mémoire d'Outre-Monde,
Jimi Hendrix (JC Lattès), 2013.

Jimi Hendrix. Soundscapes,
Marie-Paule McDonald (Reaktion Books), 2016.

'Scuse Me While I Kiss the Sky,
David Henderson (Atria Paperback), 2008.

Midnight Lightning. Jimi Hendrix and The Black Experience,
Jean-Marie Rous (Éditions du Rocher), 1995.

Jimi Hendrix Gear. The Guitars, Amps & Effects that Revolutionized Rock 'n' Roll,
Michael Heatley (Voyageur Press), 1999.

Hendrix. Electric Life,
Vincent Brunner (City), 2010.

Jimi Hendrix,
Olivier Nuc (Librio), 2000.

Jimi Hendrix,
Franck Médioni (Gallimard), 2012.

Jimi Hendrix,
Benoot Feller (Albin Michel), 1976.

Jimi Hendrix,
Jean-Marie Rous (Éditions du Rocher), 1995.

Jimi Hendrix,
Frédéric Martinez (Tallandier), 2010.

Jimi Hendrix, le gaucher magnifique,
Jean-Pierre Filiu (Mille & Une Nuits), 2008.

La Rockambolesque histoire de Little Richard,
Charles White (Éditions N° 1), 1990.

Sweet Soul Music,
Peter Guralnick (Allia), 2008.

Encyclopédie du Rhythm & Blues & de la Soul,
Sébastian Danchin (Fayard), 2002

Move on Up. La soul en 100 disques,
Nicolas Rogès (Le Mot & le reste), 2018.

Rock my Soul,
Patrice Blanc-Francard (Calmann-Levy), 2022.

FILMS

Jimi Hendrix,
Joe Boyd (Warner Bros Entertainment), 2000.

Jimi Hendrix. Hear My Train a Comin',
Bob Smeaton (Sony Music Entertainment), 2013.

Jimi Hendrix. The Uncut Story
Steven Vosburgh (Music Sales), 2004.

WEB

Ken Voss/Jimi Hendrix Information Management Institute (Facebook).

Brume Pourpre,
http://brumepourpre.hendrix.free.fr/Brumepourpre.htm

ACKNOWLEDGMENTS

Yazid Manou, Hendrix expert,

for his enthusiastic support and insightful comments.

Charles R. Cross, Steven Roby, Brad Schreiber, Harry Shapiro,

Caesar Glebbeek, Charles Shaar Murray, John McDermott

and Keith Shadwick whose works have been infinitely valuable to us.

Al Hendrix and Leon Hendrix for their equally precious memories.

Don Hogan Charles for his powerful and committed vision.

Panel 4 on page 63 is inspired by one of his photographs.

Leo Fender, without whom Jimi would be less Jimi.

And also:

Nicole «Gypsy Eyes» Berthoux,

Véronique «Foxy Lady» Dupont-Moreau.

John Allouise, Scott Barretta, Joël Bernardis

and Sylvie Lecurieux-Clerville, Larry Cohn, Saddri Derradji,

Nicolas Duthuillé, Lionel Eskenazi, José Ferré, Terence Jones,

Gilles Poussin, Stéphane Redon, Michel Seban, Roger Stolle.

Benoit Cousin, Cécile Dumas, Caroline Longuet.

An immensely sad thought for Éric «Dada» Damoisy,

the most rock 'n' roll of notaries.

Hélène and Claude, my parents, in 1959.
She was 17 and he was 18. They danced to 'Only You' by the Platters. It was their song, my mother remembers.
Thank you for your unwavering kindness.
Mezzo

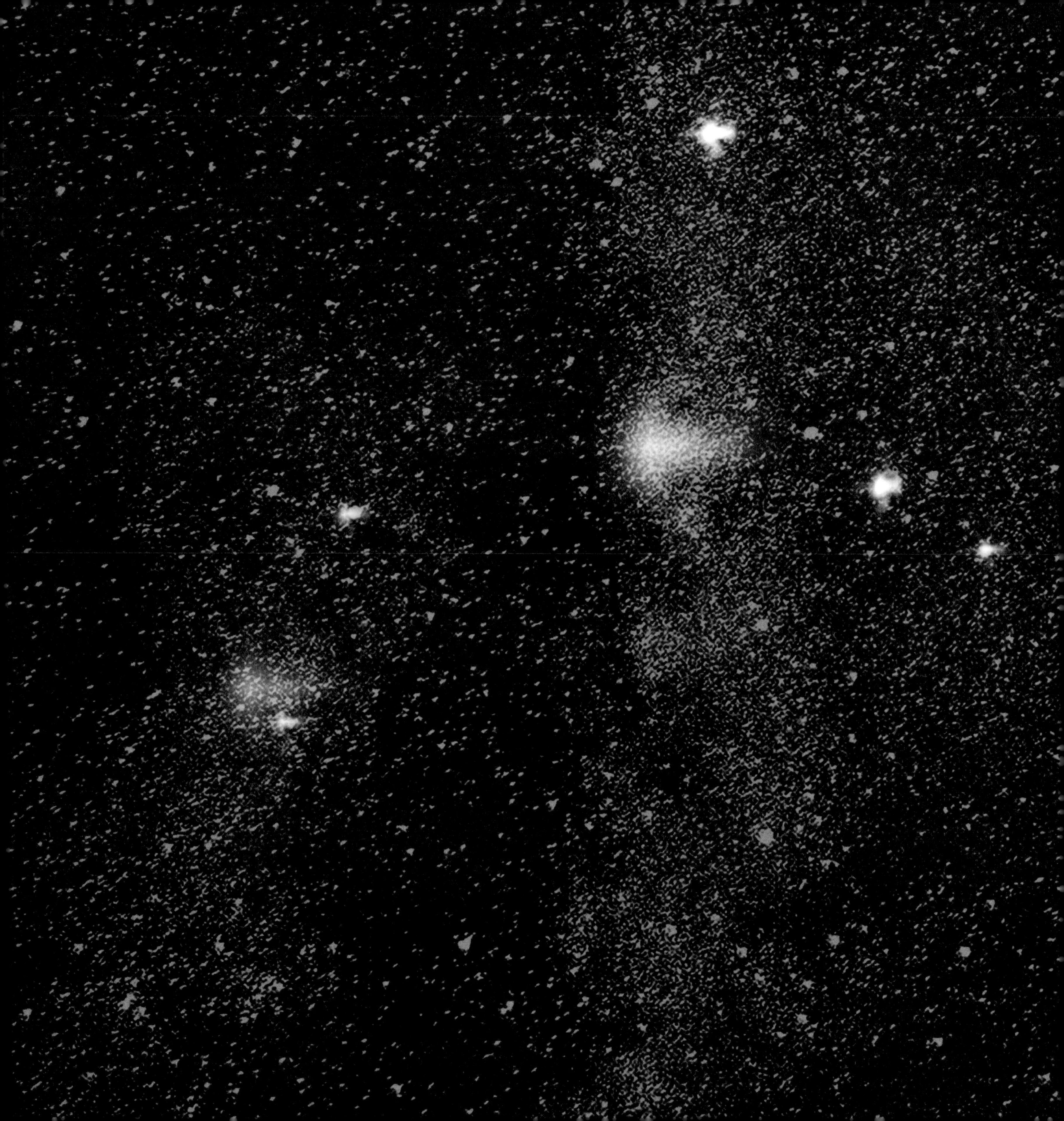

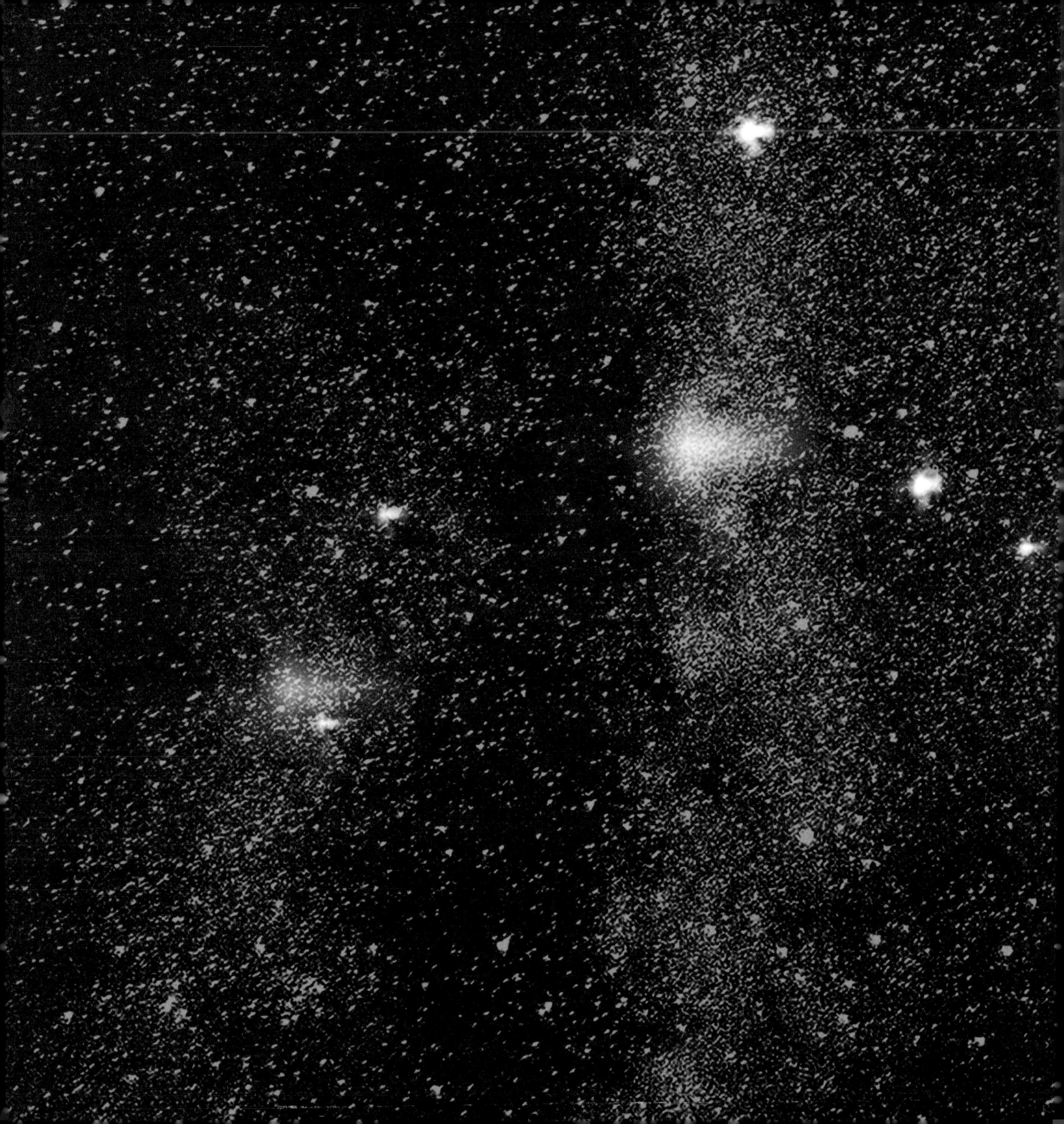